COLLABORATIVE APPROACHES TO RESOLVING CONFLICT

COLLABORATIVE APPROACHES TO RESOLVING CONFLICT

MYRA WARREN ISENHART / MICHAEL SPANGLE

Sage Publications, Inc.
International Educational and Professional Publisher
Thousand Oaks ■ London ■ New Delhi

For information:

Sage Publications, Inc.
2455 Teller Road
Thousand Oaks, California 91320
E-mail: order@sagepub.com

Sage Publications Ltd.
6 Bonhill Street
London EC2A 4PU
United Kingdom

Sage Publications India Pvt. Ltd.
M-32 Market
Greater Kailash I
New Delhi 110 048 India

Printed in the United States of America

Library of Congress Cataloging-in-Publication Data

Isenhart, Myra Warren.
  Collaborative approaches to resolving conflict / by Myra Warren
Isenhart, Michael Spangle.
      p. cm.
Includes bibliographical references and index.
  ISBN 0-7619-1929-5 (cloth: acid-free paper)
  ISBN 0-7619-1930-9 (pbk.: acid-free paper)
  1. Conflict management. 2. Dispute resolution (Law) I. Spangle,
Michael. II. Title.
  HM1126 .I74 2000
  303.6′9—dc21
                                          99-050649
This book is printed on acid-free paper.

    01   02   03   04   05   06   7   6   5   4   3   2

Acquisition Editor:	Margaret Seawell
Editorial Assistant:	Sandra Krumholz
Production Editor:	Sanford Robinson
Editorial Assistant:	Victoria Cheng
Typesetter/Designer:	Marion Warren
Cover Designer:	Candice Harman

Contents

Preface

Collaborative Approaches to Resolving Conflict was written in response to the growing number of students and practitioners in the conflict management field. Our goal is to provide a conflict management survey book, blending both theory and practice, as well as introduce readers to the wide variety of methods available for managing or resolving conflict.

The subject matter of this book addresses the needs of several audiences. One group of readers is college and university students engaged in the study of conflict. There is an explosion of courses and programs focusing on conflict management in higher education. The movement toward more collaborative approaches for dealing with conflict is a global trend. In addition, courses in conflict management are beginning to appear in schools of social work, international studies, business schools, and even in liberal arts.

A second major audience is composed of professionals in departments of human resources who want to know how to avoid the high costs of employee conflicts. Many human resource specialists and corporate counsels are adopting procedures that are more collaborative, less formal, and less costly. Outcomes are encouraging, but selecting the most appropriate method for a specific conflict requires knowledge about the various methods available.

Organizations that include conflict management skills training in leadership development packages will find this book useful. The book provides alternatives for managing conflict and describes the skills necessary to resolve it.

Divisions of the chapters, such as "definitions," "values," "typologies," or "strengths and weaknesses," enable the reader to both clarify the central factors of an approach and make comparisons with other approaches. Because the ability to manage conflict involves more than just information about conflict, each of the chapters includes profiles of professionals where the reader is able to see what experienced and respected practitioners regard as most important. We believe that these profiles will bring the reader closer to current practice in the field.

So that readers could make comparisons between the challenges and opportunities in conflict management, the same set of questions was asked of practitioners in 30- to 90-minute interviews. The variety of responses to the questions demonstrates the wide range of opinions about how conflict is best managed. Chapter 10 summarizes the commonalities and differences found in interview responses. Readers who are interested in current debates in the field will find this discussion insightful.

Based on a review of the conflict management literature and feedback from colleagues in the field, the following interview questions were asked:

1. How did you become involved in the practice of negotiation, mediation, etc.?
2. What kind of work do you currently do?
3. What skills or training would you recommend for a beginner?
4. What makes you good at what you do?
5. How do you prepare for a session?
6. Describe a typical session.
7. What is essential for success?
8. What are challenges in your work?
9. Have you made mistakes, and, if so, what have you learned from them?
10. What changes do you see occurring in the conflict management field?

The authors are both university-based teachers and practitioners in the field, and we bring a broad experience to the task of understanding and managing conflict. Our backgrounds include conflict management consulting in health care, engineering, government, education, churches, and industry. Mike Spangle serves as director of the Applied Communications and Alternate Dispute Resolution department at the University of Denver; Myra Isenhart is a full-time consultant and trainer for industry and community groups. Both of the authors teach university courses in the areas of conflict management, negotiation, and facilitation.

We believe that our students, our community, and the field of conflict studies will benefit from this overview of both traditional and contemporary methods for managing and resolving conflict. The book was designed to be practical; its content is supported by current examples and grounded in the work of many scholars.

Acknowledgments

Many people have contributed to the completion of this work. We wish to thank our editors, particularly Marquita Flemming, who grasped the concept of blending theory and practice in addressing a growing national need for more constructive approaches to dealing with conflict. We wish to express our gratitude to our families, who assisted, encouraged, and waited patiently during the prolonged production of this book. We want to express our thanks to Laura Buseman, PhD, who provided encouragement during editing of some rough first drafts. Special appreciation goes to graduate students who assisted in various ways: Tina Martilan wrote verbatims of the interviews; Barbara Cashman Hahn and Marie Hays were tireless in their editing contributions; and many graduate students and faculty from the University of Denver who provided feedback along the way.

Introduction

Collaborative Approaches to Resolving Conflict challenges traditional assumptions about how to resolve conflict. Since the dawn of recorded history, humans have resorted to making demands and using force to get their way, often at high costs. Wars destroy nations. Going to court often costs tens of thousands of dollars and years of delay in getting court dates. Workplace disputes often become violent. How we manage our conflicts powerfully affects our relationships, business success, and quality of life.

The movement toward constructive methods for solving problems parallels the national trend toward greater use of teams and collaborative approaches. Organizational specialist Peter Drucker (1995) argues that the single most important shift in the way Americans do business involves a shift from *ownership* to *partnership,* and from *commanding* to *consensus.* Symbolic of the movement toward partnerships, a cooperative alliance of 15 nations, including the United States, recently celebrated the first stage of construction of Unity, the $50 billion orbiting space station. Hargrove (1998) points out that during 1996 alone, 10,000 strategic alliances, joint ventures, or mergers took place.

This book notes that a similar shift is occurring in our approaches to conflict. Communities and businesses are moving from discussions of *rights* to *interests,* and from *forcing* to *negotiation.* The significance of the shift grows as blended families look for ways to build cohesion, highly diverse communities seek ways to reduce violence, and companies attempt to deal with change.

Hamlet said, "There is nothing either good or bad but thinking makes it so" (*Hamlet* II.2). So also with conflict. We can approach conflict expecting a fight and a host of negative consequences, or we can approach it as an opportunity to create alliances. We can view others as adversaries and remain forever entrenched, or we can build bridges with strategic partnerships that advance our objectives further than we could do alone.

The movement toward nonjudicial processes for conflict resolution is fast becoming the norm, both nationally and internationally. Forty-eight states have mediation centers, and at least five require mediation before a case is allowed to go to court. Supreme Court Justice Sandra Day O'Connor stresses the importance of looking for solutions outside the courtroom. In her assessment, "The courts of this country should not be the place where the resolution of disputes begins. They should be the place where disputes end, after alternative methods of resolving disputes have been considered and tried" (Wolff & Ostermeyer, 1998, p. 51).

The first two chapters lay a conceptual foundation for understanding the dynamics and challenges of conflict. Chapters 3-9 provide an in-depth look at a variety of methods for managing or resolving conflict. Each chapter includes templates for how to use the method efficiently, plus its advantages and disadvantages. The examples used in the chapters involve actual conflicts, although the names have been fictionalized. We follow each chapter with interviews of conflict management professionals who are respected by their peers for their expertise. Chapter 10 summarizes the themes, approaches, and commonalities contained in the interviews. Our overall strategy involves matching theoretical principles (why) with current practice (how).

The Navajo Indians believe that if one ends a dispute by having a winner and a loser, one dispute may have ended but another dispute surely will have started, because harmony will not have been restored. This book looks at the methods that many have used to achieve harmony. When we use a collaborative approach to resolve conflict, we attempt to create conditions that prevent the escalation of conflict, reduce the destructive aspects of conflict, and create a working climate that preserves relationships.

Chapter 1

Theoretical Perspectives

The place we need really imaginative new ideas is in conflict theory. That's true with respect to war and peace, but also it's true domestically. The real weakness throughout the country is lack of conflict resolution methods other than litigation and guns. (Toffler, 1991, p. 13)

Conflict consumes an enormous amount of time, energy, and money in modern American life. Community Boards in New York City see more than 14,000 neighborhood disputes per year. Currently, there are more than 400 community justice centers and 100 victim-offender programs in the United States. The U.S. Postal Service reports 150,000 grievance proceedings and 69,000 disciplinary actions per year. During 1994, Americans filed 18 million cases in courts at a cost of $300 billion (Hoffman, 1996). Some estimate that litigation activities consume as much as 20% of Fortune 500 executives' work time. In the United States, 95% of the law schools and most colleges and universities offer courses in conflict management or alternate dispute resolution as part of their curricula.

Weeks (1992) states, "Conflict is an inescapable part of our daily lives, an inevitable result of our highly complex, competitive and often litigious society" (p. ix). Conflict is intrinsic to organizations, families, and modern city life. Headlines in a recent newspaper reflect recurring themes in the United States:

- Boy Arrested After Threat to School Official
- Agency Offers Battered Women Some Security
- Union Chief Rouses Strikers
- Employee Endures Racially Hostile Environment
- Road Rage Campaign Fields 3500 Complaints

The increase in community violence, family breakups, work grievances, and court cases suggests that we are not doing very well with managing our conflict. Fisher, Kopelman, and Schneider (1994) call conflict a "growth industry" (p. 1).

In most settings, when humans live and work together, conflict erupts, sometimes in very unexpected ways (Box 1.1).

Levine (1998) proposes that the growth of conflict in American culture results from many forces, which include the following:

- Breakdown in the covenant of trust among people who are members of the same community
- Lack of communication
- People focusing on themselves
- Concerns about rights and entitlements without thinking about the responsibilities toward others. (p. 15)

The growth of conflict may also be related to urbanization, that is, more people in a smaller area. It may be the long-term result of the alienation that occurs when people lose a sense of community. In every presidential election campaign, politicians cite the breakdown of moral values and dissolution of families as the fueling factors for cultural problems.

Conflict Is. . .

Because of its many overlapping dynamics and processes, conflict is complex. If conflict involved only a decision between two choices, most of us would compromise or negotiate. But often, conflict involves a struggle for power, the way decisions are made, the way we talk to each other, or unresolved problems from past interactions. Several of these factors may be occurring at the same time, so that we are not sure what the real problem is. Thus, defining conflict in a specific situation can be a difficult task.

Because conflict is complex, definitions tend to focus on a combination of many factors, such as the circumstances that lead up to a conflict or the behaviors of disputants that produce perceptions of disagreement. Some who view conflict look from the perspective of episodes, where discussion focuses on specific beginnings and endings of disputes (Cupach & Canary, 1997). Box 1.2 provides examples from the many definitions of conflict.

Theoretical Perspectives

A variety of theoretical perspectives attempt to explain the dynamics of conflict. Theories help us to get to the underlying factors, the "whys" and "whats" that fuel and sustain disputes. They provide insight about the issues that need attention if we are to be able to achieve resolution. Each approach reveals assumptions about the importance of internal or external forces, behaviors that trigger or sustain interactions, or the impact of competing goals or interests.

BOX 1.1
Food Fight

A dispute between two co-workers last week resulted in an assault complaint and a Denver police investigation. The weapon? A carrot, according to the police report.

The victim alleges that her assailant at the Fresh Vegetable Package Company in northwest Denver hurled a barrage of fruit at her for "laughing at her." The conflict escalated to vegetables, and her attacker, "for no reason," hurled a 4-inch-diameter carrot at her. The victim, who is 5 months pregnant, complained of stomach pains and was taken to Denver General Hospital. The detective reported, "All she wants is that the suspect leave her alone. I'm going to call up and talk to the supervisor and have the assailant moved from the dangerous weapon section, back from vegetables to fruits." The Denver district attorney's office refused to file charges. Assault with a deadly vegetable apparently would not sit well with a jury.

BOX 1.2
Definitions of Conflict

A conflict exists because of a real or apparent incompatibility of parties' needs or interests. (Bush & Folger, 1994, p. 56)

Conflict occurs when two people cannot agree on the actions that one person takes or that he or she doesn't want the other to take. (Edelman & Crain, 1993, p. 18)

Conflict means perceived divergence of interests, or a belief that the parties' current aspirations cannot be achieved simultaneously. (Rubin, Pruitt, & Kim, 1994, p. 5)

Conflict involves a struggle over values and claims to scarce status, power and resources in which the aim of opponents is to neutralize, injure, or eliminate rivals. (Coser, 1967, p. 8)

Conflict is an intermediate stage of a spectrum of struggle that escalates and becomes more destructive: differences, disagreement, dispute (conflict), campaign, litigation, and fight or war. (Keltner, 1987, pp. 1-2)

Conflict is an expressed struggle between at least two interdependent parties who perceive incompatible goals, scarce resources and interference from the other party in achieving their goals. (Hocker & Wilmot, 1991, p. 23)

The perspective we choose will affect the claims and conclusions we make about conflict. In addition, the theoretical perspective we use will influence our choice of strategy. For example, a consultant may recommend psychotherapy for a troubled employee if the consultant believes that the conflict is generated by personal problems. But if the employee's problem seems to be created by lack of support in the department, the focus may be on the interactional dynamics of staff. The following section describes a few of the theories valued most by practitioners to explain the dynamics of conflict.

Attribution Theory

Grounded in the work of scholars such as Heider (1958), Jones and Nesbitt (1971), Ross (1977), and Sillars (1980), the attribution perspective proposes that people make sense of their world by assigning qualities and causes to people and situations based on what is most relevant to them. Attributions are explanations that people have for the cause of events. For example, based on experiences in childhood with his mother, a husband may conclude that his wife is too possessive. So, he interprets requests from his wife as attempts to further limit his freedom.

Fincham, Bradbury, and Scott (1990) describe six dimensions of attributions that people make:

- ❏ *Blameworthiness*—assigns responsibility for failure
- ❏ *Globality*—cause of problem seen as narrow and specific to situation or wide and explains many situations
- ❏ *Intent*—belief that conscious decision or planning was involved
- ❏ *Locus*—assumptions about where the problem lies
- ❏ *Selfishness*—belief that motives are self-serving
- ❏ *Stability*—belief that this is a one-time occurrence or will occur many times

Research from this perspective has produced a wealth of information about attributional bias, which explains many of the behaviors that occur in conflict situations. For example, Bradley (1978) found that people frequently attribute positive consequences to their own actions and negative consequences to the actions of others. Sillars and Scott (1983) looked at intimate relationships (friends, family) and found that partners develop overgeneralized labels to explain the behaviors of others and assign blame based on negative personality traits that they perceive in others. In addition, they found that attributional bias occurred most widely during emotionally expressive conflicts, during highly stressful interactions, and where attitudes are dissimilar. Finally, Thomas and Pondy (1977) found that when people engage in conflict, they frequently characterize their own tactics as cooperative and the tactics of others as uncooperative.

To deescalate conflict, disputants need to expose misperceptions created by inaccurate attributions. They need to uncover the "I just assumed" judgments that create barriers to resolution of problems. And to reduce polarization, they need to reduce blaming, see how each party has contributed to escalation of the problem, and accept responsibility for resolution.

Equity Theory

Scholars such as Homans (1958), Blau (1964), and Walster, Walster, and Berscheid (1978) view conflict from the perspective of distributive justice. People become distressed, frustrated, and angry when they perceive that they are not receiving fair distribution of something they value. Muldoon (1996) explains, "Each of us has an internal moral gyroscope that keeps us in balance with the outside world. It becomes distorted when we feel that others are benefiting at our expense or when we are unfairly benefiting at someone else's expense" (p. 83).

Roloff (1981) defines an equitable relationship "as one in which some person (a participant in the exchange or outside observer) perceives that the relative gains of two people in an exchange are equal" (p. 57). Societal or organizational norms define our understanding of what relative gain may mean. What might have been perceived as fair or equitable a century ago might be perceived as exploitation today. Roloff points out that perceptions of equity change as we learn more about people or situations, as events alter roles or responsibilities, as people developmentally change, or as we value the benefits of a relationship with new criteria. So, perceptions of inequity or imbalance change as people and situations change.

Restoring equity may involve one of many tactics: (a) raising awareness of harm so that parties may correct the injustice, (b) restoring a psychological balance by getting the person doing the harm to apologize, (c) creating a sense of fairness by finding ways to compensate the person harmed, or (d) discussing the rules or norms that guide how resources are divided.

Field Theory

Based on the work of Kurt Lewin (1951), this perspective views people's actions as a product of contextual forces. Lewin stressed that these forces are seen in impulses to do something and impulses not to do other things. There is a push and a pull based on expectations, commitments, and loyalties. Each context, such as family, community group, or work setting, serves as a psychological field where antagonistic interests or competing attitudes create safe or hostile climates. From this perspective, Heitler (1990) defines conflict as "a situation in which seemingly incompatible elements exert force in opposing or divergent directions. These divergent forces evoke tension" (p. 5).

This approach explains why a person may be passive in the presence of family and yet highly aggressive in a work setting. Different forces motivate or inhibit behaviors. Field theory explains why someone, regarded as cooperative by friends, becomes competitive in an unsafe work climate. Competitiveness serves as a tactic to combat the perceived threats at work.

Conflict management from this perspective may begin by identifying systemic forces that affect organizations. Disputants may be helped to see that their co-workers are not the enemy; the enemies are the forces creating the conditions for conflict. For example, in one school, the staff blamed each other for a breakdown of school discipline. A consultant identified changes in school district policies that made enforcement of rules more difficult. The staff discussed how they could strategically meet the expectations of the district instead of engaging in conflict with each other over the changes.

Interactional Theory

Many writers have suggested that "all life is a drama." This orientation parallels the interactional perspective. The meaning we use to guide our behavior arises out of our interaction with others. Influenced by the writings of William James, John Dewey, George Mead, and Anselm Strauss, interactionalists view conflict as a process of ongoing negotiation about what is valued, how behaviors are to be interpreted, and the meaning of events. Folger, Poole, and Stutman (1993) explain, "People create the situations they perceive, [and] what they perceive is also influenced by what they do" (p. 47). Strauss (1978) views each negotiation as larger than the specific context in which it occurs. It is a fundamental process where culture is formed, refined, and remade.

Application of this perspective is not difficult to apply in many kinds of conflict. For example, in families, negotiation over a specific problem influences a series of continual changes in role, expectations, and authority. In an organization, each staff negotiation over how work should be done creates additional understandings about roles and expectations. In negotiation, a small concession may serve as a trust-building measure, reflecting the interactionalist's view that behavior can influence perceptions. Similarly, looking for "agreements in principle" shapes a perception of progress that may influence future behaviors. Interactions influence perceptions.

Phase Theory

Cupach and Canary (1997) define the phase model of conflict as describing "the sequences of behaviors that interactants display as conflict unfolds over time" (p. 152). For example, Rummel (1976) describes the development of conflict as passing through predictable phases: attitudes and objectives (*latent phase*) become triggered (*initiation*) by an event; force and threats are used (*attempt to balance power*) as parties confront the issue; parties may reach a level of resolution (*balance of power*) until another event triggers further confrontation (*disruption*).

Walton (1969) characterizes conflict in just two phases: differentiation, where parties raise the conflict issue, clarify positions, and discuss reasons behind the position; and integration, where parties engage in problem solving. Cupach and Canary (1997) point out that in order to manage conflict in two phases, the parties must be able to define the problem in mutually understood terms during the differentiation phase, and they must display cooperative tactics during the integration phase.

Although scholars may differ on the names and numbers of phases of conflict, they agree on many aspects of the phases:

- ❑ Conflict proceeds through a predictable sequence of behaviors.
- ❑ Behaviors that ignite confrontation can be identified.
- ❑ Specific behaviors tend to perpetuate the continuation or escalation of conflict.

Organizational consultants use this perspective when they ask about the series of events that led up to the conflict or ask about the behaviors that escalated the conflict. Managing or resolving the conflict may involve helping parties identify the behaviors that trigger the conflict, establishing a monitoring system to warn parties when the current course of action is unproductive, or creating new discussion procedures to prevent conflict escalation.

Psychodynamic Theory

Psychologists such as Freud (1925), Adler (1927), Erickson (1950), and Hall (1979) explain that people approach problems from one of many internal unconscious states, such as anxiety, ego, fear, aggressiveness, or guilt. These states influence people's perception of choices available to them. In addition, unconscious states shape judgments about their own behavior and assumptions about the motivations of others. Internal tensions and pressures build up to a point where they demand release, often in destructive ways.

A phenomenon called *displacement* occurs when parties who are unable to direct their anger toward the source of their frustration (the boss), direct it instead toward a more accessible target (coworker or family member). For example, a husband, frustrated with the direction of his career, may displace the frustration by complaining about his wife.

Based on a psychodynamic perspective, Hilgard and Bower (1966) explain how disputants will engage in compulsive or repetitive destructive conflict behaviors despite their awareness about how counterproductive their actions are. Unconscious internal drives cause people to do what they know might harm them. Despite the fact that workers may lose their jobs if they argue with their manager, they see no other choice for course of action. Despite loss of reputation, a community member may explode in anger at a public meeting because "they had it coming."

Practitioners who view conflict from this perspective will often try to redirect destructive energies (aggression) into constructive outlets. Conflict managers may attempt to help parties gain insight about how their behaviors contribute to the problem or about how their feelings may not accurately reflect events. They may recommend therapy for workers with personal problems who displace the target of the problems.

Social Exchange Theory

Homans (1958), Thibaut and Kelley (1959), and Blau (1964) proposed that we view conflict from the perspective of market analysis. They argue that people make choices based on self-interest; during interactions, they weigh the rewards and costs of specific courses of action. Roloff (1981) points out that conflict emerges when people perceive that their rewards are too low, their costs are too high, or they anticipate resistance if they attempt to reach their goals. For example, a spouse may tolerate verbal abuse until the children are grown. The emotional cost is worth preservation of the family. But once the children leave home, the costs are deemed too high, and a separation or divorce follows.

Conflict from this perspective involves identifying the needs and values of each party to create a satisfying set of trade-offs. In the above example, the abusing spouse will need to reduce the verbal aggression to make the relationship an emotionally cost-effective investment for the other spouse. Scholars such as Marwell and Schmitt (1967), Miller, Boster, Roloff, and Seibold (1977), and Roloff (1976) identify many tactics designed to influence the exchange of resources: promises, threats, revenge, arguing, physical aggression, forgiveness, pleading, insulting, pouting, and crying. Managers of conflict might attempt to reduce the frequency of destructive tactics while creating a set of trade-offs where all parties achieve their goals.

Systems Theory

Based on elements from interactional and field theories, the systems perspective views families, groups, and organizations as units of interrelated parts who influence each other and function within a larger environment. Systems pioneer Ludwig von Bertalanffy (1955) pointed out that groups possess organization much like biological organisms. Groups demonstrate qualities of wholeness, directiveness, and differentiation. Like biological organisms, systems can be characterized as *open or closed* based on responsiveness to information external to the system. They are *homeostatic* in that parties will adjust their communication to achieve or maintain equilibrium. Members of systems are interdependent, so much so that they may influence each other simultaneously. And systems can be characterized by *nonsummativity*, that is, the whole is greater than the sum of its parts.

Cupach and Canary (1997) describe three categories of system breakdown. The first is transactional redundancy, where people perpetuate conflict by engaging in the same, unchanging patterns of interaction. People within the system are either unable to see the ineffectiveness of the patterns or unwilling to change the patterns. A second cause of system breakdown is when one part of the system, a subsystem, becomes ineffective. The lack of cooperation or failure of a subsystem makes it more difficult for the system to achieve its goals. A third cause involves members exceeding their roles. When someone exceeds expectations or power in his or her role, imbalances occur elsewhere.

Sociologists Talcott Parsons, Robert Merton, and Emile Durkheim use systems concepts to describe the impact of conflict on the health or effectiveness of a group. They describe a stable, functional system as one where each of the members fits harmoniously into the larger whole. Dysfunction occurs when people disrupt the otherwise stable system. For example, a family may not experience a great deal of significant conflict as the children grow during the first 10 or 12 years. But as the children enter their teen years, they may demand more autonomy, a greater share of the resources, or more say in decision making. The stable system becomes disrupted by changes in expectations.

The professional who approaches conflict from a systems perspective looks for the behaviors that disrupt the group's normal harmony. Questions might be asked, such as "What is different now from 6 months or a year ago?" Second, although one member may be singled out as the cause of problems, the professional looks for issues that might be causing the member's deviance, such as leadership, roles, and rewards. The problem person may be only a symptom of deeper, systemic issues. Third, an outsider will find it difficult to understand what is functional or nonfunctional for a group unless he or she is able to see the group working together.

Transformational Theory

Transformational scholars focus more on change and process than on explanations about why conflict occurs. Their perspective attempts to account for the dynamic, changing quality of roles, relationships, and expectations and the shifting environment in which they exist. The emphasis is on process.

For example, Northrup (1989) points out that conflict goes through stages, and each of the stages may require different strategies. Wallenstein (1991) argues that solutions may not actually represent resolution. Resolution of conflict in many settings may actually perpetuate the inequality or injustices that exist.

Thus, whereas other theories view conflict as dysfunctional and unhealthy, this perspective views conflict as a vital social function where tensions are released and new communal norms are established or refined. As Coser (1957) explains, "Conflict not only generates new norms, new institutions . . . it may be said to be stimulating directly in the economic and technology realm" (p. 198). From the transformational perspective, conflict is the tension between what is and what people believe ought to be. Conflict forces parties to deal with deeper issues and thus serve as a constructive social process. For example, tensions between labor unions and management frequently facilitate higher wages or better working conditions for workers. Political debate between Republicans and Democrats may generate new policies or values that influence policy choices.

This perspective serves as the foundation for transformational mediation, where the goal is to move beyond solutions to transforming relationships. The transformational mediator attempts to influence interaction patterns, change how the partners talk about themselves and each other, and provide opportunities "to strengthen both their sense of how to work on life's problems and their ability to relate to others" (Bush & Folger, 1994, p. 135). Transformation occurs when people alter perceptions about themselves and others or change the way they relate. Bush and Folger (1994) summarize the value of this approach:

> The strongest reason for believing that the Transformational Story should guide mediation is the story's underlying premise: that the goal of transformation—that is, engendering moral growth toward both strength and compassion—should take precedence over the other goals mediation can be used to obtain, even though these other goals are themselves important. (pp. 28-29)

Box 1.3 provides a case study in which attribution and interaction theories might be useful for explaining the dynamics of a conflict. Although Harriet had been gone for 20 years, Willard and Emma were ready to resume a longtime move-countermove feud with Harriet's family. All parties attributed negative intentions to the actions of the others. Resolution, although difficult, would involve breaking 30 years of patterned interactions between the families and creating a more productive set of attributions.

Based on the theoretical perspectives provided earlier, Harriet's conflict could be described in other ways as well. Perhaps both Harriet and Emma used the assisted-living facility as an opportunity to express their need for power, or escalation of the problems may be a function of ineffective conflict styles. How we define conflict becomes an extension of these theoretical perspectives.

Summary of Theoretical Perspectives

Conflict can be viewed from a variety of perspectives, as evidenced in the previous discussion. Focus can be placed on the individual's contributions to conflict, as we find in the attribution and psychodynamic perspectives. We can explore the escalation of conflict through the interaction of parties or through its development through phases. We can explain behaviors based on how parties address their self-interests in trade-offs or how they perceive the fairness of their treatment during discussions. Or, we can step back and view conflict in terms of the functioning of the group or organization. The last of the theories, the transformational perspective, focuses more on managing conflict than it does on explanations of cause. Its role will be seen more clearly later when we discuss the goals for negotiation, mediation, or facilitation. Although there are many differences in the theoretical perspectives, there are principles they share in common:

BOX 1.3
Example of a Conflict That Enveloped a Whole Community

Harriet Cropwhiler grew up in Lone Pine, Nebraska, a town of 1,500 residents. For most of her growing-up years, her family had subtle but very real conflict with the neighbors, Emma and Willard Gerbels.

Harriet went to nursing school in Lincoln, followed by a successful career as a registered nurse at Lincoln hospitals. But she missed her small town. She decided to move back to Lone Pine and open up an assisted-living facility for elderly residents.

She bought a home, built in 1990, that occupies a lot that was formerly an alfalfa field. When the home was built, several of the neighbors, including Emma and Willard, expressed a great deal of anger about the home's location. It obstructed their view of the corn and bean fields.

Harriet called her 50-bed assisted-living facility Harriet's Hideaway. Several months ago, 92-year-old George Schmidt, who was in the early stages of Alzheimer's disease, wandered out of Harriet's Hideaway and into an adjacent cornfield. Seeing George in the field, Harriet went out to retrieve him. He did not want to come back and resisted. He fought her with his cane, but Harriet forcibly grabbed him by his wrists and brought him back.

Emma and Willard had been peering through the window during the time of this conflict. In "horror at the mistreatment of this fine gentleman," they called the police and reported Harriet. When the police arrived, they found George asleep in his chair, but with bruises on his wrists. Harriet was arrested for abuse of a patient. The offense carries maximum penalties of a $10,000 fine, loss of her nursing license, a 1-year jail term, and the potential closing of the facility.

Most residents of the town were upset because they liked Harriet and wanted the assisted-living facility in town. They held a town meeting to discuss the issue. Emma and Willard rallied several neighbors and former Hideaway workers against Harriet. Emma characterized the new room intercom system as "a listening device whose purpose was to hold residents captive." One newspaper editorial depicted Harriet as a person who committed "a reckless assault upon a helpless citizen." Another advocated community support for a "professional with compassion and 20 years of an unblemished healthcare record." The battle escalated with letters to the state senators and an appeal to the governor.

- Conflict is an inevitable consequence of social life.
- Patterns of conflict behavior tend to perpetuate themselves.
- Although conflict may appear chaotic, many elements can be understood.
- Conflict is maintained by a series of moves and countermoves.

- Conflict is an inevitable consequence of social life.
- Patterns of conflict behavior tend to perpetuate themselves.
- Although conflict may appear chaotic, many elements can be understood.
- Conflict is maintained by a series of moves and countermoves.
- Conflict affects the relationships of parties involved.
- Communication plays a central role in the management of conflict.

Understanding how and why conflict occurs improves the likelihood that managers of conflict will choose the most efficient method for creating collaborative conditions. For example,

- If the parties are making inaccurate assumptions or attributions of others, the attributions need to be corrected in order to facilitate collaboration.
- If a staff believes that current department processes create barriers for working together, they will need to negotiate more effective procedures.
- If there are perceptions of inequity or unfairness, parties need to talk about what might be needed to make the agreement fair for all parties.
- If parties perceive their goals to be incompatible, a third party may need to help them identify a superordinate goal toward which they can work together.

Discussion of ways of dealing with conflict without going to court is dependent on an understanding of the issues and processes driving the conflict. Often, conflicts are sustained by intangible resources, such as respect and listening, that can be provided at low cost. Many court cases can be prevented if disputants are willing to ask more questions and address underlying issues.

Chapter 2

Conflict in Action

Instead of struggling to erase negative emotions, we can learn to use them in positive ways. . . . Rather than work against ourselves all we need to do in many cases is to point our weaknesses or unpleasant tendencies in a different direction than we have been. (Hoff, 1982, p. 59)

Conflict can be expensive. Organizationally, costs include low morale, high employee turnover, and loss of productive work time. Personally, costs often involve loss of sleep, loss of motivation, and damage to relationships. Too often, damage occurs when people are out of control. Later, it is common to hear someone lament, "I wish I hadn't said that. I don't know what came over me."

At times, the damage that conflict causes is unrepairable. Recently, a company vice president exploded in anger at members of his staff and at a fellow vice president. He spent months trying to smooth over the damage. The human resource director said, "Despite all of his efforts, the damage is not repairable. He can't fix the loss of confidence and trust from his staff."

Conflict in American culture is seen in a variety of new settings:

Computer chat room—People can now argue on-line with other people whom they have never met.

Voice mail—Customers become frustrated as they navigate their way through a series of menu directions.

Public schools—Students engage in violence as an answer to their problems.

Freeways—Drivers engage in road rage as a way to manage crowded freeways.

Public buildings—Public servants become the target for unhappy community members.

Office settings—Frustrated employees express their anger in outbursts against coworkers.

A good beginning for preventing or managing conflict involves understanding the many sources of conflict and the kinds of events that escalate conflict. In addition, it is useful to identify and understand the conditions that lead up to unresolvable conflict. The options become more limited as disputants move from disagreement to polarization of positions and the use of destructive tactics.

Sources of Conflict

Identifying underlying issues that fuel bad feelings and damage relationships is one of the central tasks for resolving conflict. Conflict resists resolution when one party fails to address the issues of most significance for other parties. When we are not addressing the agenda most relevant to other parties, we will hear statements such as, "You're not hearing me," or "You don't care about my concerns." Scott (1990) explains, "Unless these basic [underlying] needs and wants are identified and dealt with, the conflict will probably continue along with growing frustrations. . . . These needs and wants dictate a person's reaction (or lack thereof) to a situation" (p. 70). For example, when a housewife who wants respect from her husband hears that bringing home a paycheck demonstrates love for his family, she does not feel heard and will resist cooperation. She wants equal value placed on her contributions to the home. By focusing our efforts on the issues of immediate concern first, we can best use our energy for resolving conflict.

The many sources for conflict suggest why it is so difficult for parties to be focused on the same issue. Figure 2.1 lists the most common sources of conflict. Each of the sources may affect the others. For example, a poor relationship may influence respect that one party has for the other's role. A power imbalance may create a need for procedures that weaker parties believe are fair.

Data—People often have differences of opinion about the best source, reliability, or interpretation of data. Do the facts suggest that the earth's ozone layer is being depleted, or are we in a temporary cycle? Disputes about contractual, environmental, or physical loss or reimbursement for damages often require objective standards or interpretation by neutral third parties to resolve disagreement.

Interests—Specific, tangible wants or perceived needs are the most common source of disagreement. Disputes such as divorce settlements, work agreements, or organizational policies frequently involve stipulations about how specific interests of all parties will be met.

Procedures—Parties may not engage in discussion if they do not agree with a way to solve a problem, make a decision, or resolve conflict. People abide by election results because they believe that election procedures are fair. People abide by a court's decision because the trial followed a predictable process.

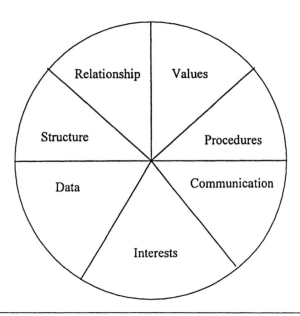

Figure 2.1. Sources of Conflict

Values—Frequently, the hardest conflicts to resolve involve differences of opinion about the importance or priority of interests, options, or choices of direction. Do the children belong with the father or the mother? Should industry be allowed to clear timberland to do mining? Problems such as these begin with a value about the way things should be.

Relationships—People may resist cooperating if they do not trust others, do not feel respected by others, do not believe that the other person is honest, or do not feel listened to. Collaboration often begins by establishing a relationship with a high comfort level.

Roles—Professional, community, or family roles often create conflict because of expectations for the role or power imbalances created by the role. For example, negotiation between a supervisor and an employee can be difficult if the employee believes that his or her lack of power prevents any worthwhile discussions.

Communication—Conflict frequently results from how something is said. It is common to hear, "I know you said that. I wish I had a tape recording of it." In addition, people's emotions become triggered by words that another takes personally or interprets as threatening. Or, parties in a dispute may become angry because some information that they believe is relevant is not shared.

Box 2.1 reviews a conflict between the owner of a small pet store, Gary, and the management group of a small shopping center. The conflict illustrates differences in perceptions about appropriate procedures for decision making, values

---

BOX 2.1
A Decision That Created Many Sources of Conflict

Gary owns Just for Pets, a small pet store in a 14-store strip mall shopping center. For 23 years, Gary has leased the space from American Management Corporation (AMC). Currently, the rent is $3,000 per month. Just for Pets provides personalized service to pet owners of the local neighborhood.

Two weeks ago, AMC announced in a memo that the Walgreens store that anchored the shopping center will be replaced by Pets America, a large chain pet store that provides full services for all varieties of pet owners. They explained that the store will heighten visibility for the shopping center and provide $13,000 per month in rent.

Gary was devastated. He believes that Pets America will put him out of business. Costs are prohibitive for him to move his store. Owners of the other small businesses were equally disappointed. Gary points out that neither he nor the other business owners were consulted about the decision. Values of profit and marketing were given priority over relationships. Gary lamented, "There's no loyalty to a 23-year business and to their customers." AMC must wait and see if there will be a backlash from the other business owners.

---

about doing business, and incompatible interests. In addition, in the short term, there will be conflict in the relationship between Gary and the management group, and in the long term, the potential for conflict in relationships between AMC and the other store owners.

It is important to distinguish between actual and perceived conflict (Deutsch, 1973). Both actual and perceived conflict create conditions for disagreement. Perceived conflicts may be just as important to parties as anything that might be described as real. In fact, determining what is real and what is perceived may be a difficult task. Sillars, Weisberg, Burggraf, and Zeitlow (1990) found that married couples only recall 35% of what they talked about in the past hour. Stafford and Daly (1984) found that people recall only about 9% of what they actually talked about days earlier. Collaboration frequently becomes a negotiation of what is real and imagined. When parties are functioning with incomplete information, imagined problems can have a great influence over beliefs about real problems. Thus, resolving conflict must deal with what parties think the conflict is, as well as specific issues in dispute.

Box 2.2 illustrates how relationships can pose a problem that affects procedures, interests, and interpretation of data. Had a good relationship existed between the Forest Service and the managing engineer of the utility, the conflict might have been prevented or, if not prevented, at least handled quickly with lower stress.

BOX 2.2
Poor Relationship May Create Additional Conflicts

Bill Oakes worked for the U.S. Forest Service until he had a difference of opinion with Forest Service personnel. He went to work for Mountain Water, a privately owned utility that manages water resources for rural and mountain regions of a state. Within this region, responsibility for managing the Crested Ridge Dam also belongs to Mountain Water. Because the Forest Service has liability for all dams, once a decade, it requires utilities responsible for dams to inspect the dams for damage that might cause significant environmental impact. Impacts consider the risks to endangered species, humans, or loss due to floods if the dam should break.

Mountain Water complied with permit requirements. Its engineer found that the Crested Ridge Dam was at low risk for any potential damage to the environment. There were very few people in the region and no endangered species. About this same time, the Forest Service decided to conduct its own assessment. Its ranger reported, "Currently, the dam poses moderate risk. It requires upgrades to move it back to low risk." Oakes was appalled by the difference of assessment. Because there were no roads to the dam, all machinery, supplies, and housing to do repairs had to be flown in by helicopter. The improvements would cost millions of dollars. He said, "We complied with the permit. We are not liable. We'll fight them."

Because Oakes had a bad relationship with the Forest Service, he could not deal with it directly. He needed a third party to find out what the words "significant damage" mean, the kinds of risk the Forest Service believes are present, and whether there was the possibility of hiring a neutral third party to reassess potential risk. If the conflict escalates, the bad relationship could cost the utility millions of dollars.

Conflict Spirals

People will reciprocate in an intensified and negative manner to behaviors they perceive as threatening, devaluing, or insulting (Alberts & Driscoll, 1992; Carroll, 1987). Each threatening communication incites even more threatening responses in a move-countermove sequence. In addition, the number of issues proliferates as the parties become absorbed in the emotions of the situation. Blame, fear, and anger produce psychological states that fuel self-perpetuating sequences. "This model helps understand the perpetuation of high levels of escalation—that is, the fact that heavy tactics, once used, often continue to be employed" (Rubin et al., 1994, p. 75). For example, one party says, "You should have . . . ," and this facilitates a defensive response in the other party, "It wouldn't have happened if you hadn't . . ." Innuendo provokes defensiveness, which incites argument and anger.

As disputants struggle to establish control over others through attack and intimidation, there is the likelihood of greater rigidity, polarization, and defensiveness. For example, in one of the earliest studies that looked at spiraling conflicts, French (1941) identified 600 offensive remarks made in a group that met for 45 minutes. Collaborative approaches to conflict seek to recognize these patterns quickly and alter the sequence.

Carpenter and Kennedy (1988) identify the sequence of events common to conflict spirals that occur in group, organization, or public policy disputes:

1. Problem emerges.
2. Sides form as controversy grows.
3. Positions harden as parties become narrower and more rigid in their perspectives.
4. Communication stops and parties become adversarial.
5. Conflict goes outside of the immediate context as parties look for support and power.
6. Perceptions become distorted and parties lose objectivity.
7. Sense of crisis emerges as community divides into factions and coalitions.
8. Uncertainty arises about outcomes as options for parties become fewer.

Spirals become destructive as mistrust and suspicion grow. Each side raises the stakes and reduces constructive options as it turns to coalitions for support instead of talking directly to those with whom it is in conflict.

Frequently, the cost of these destructive spirals in organizations is a breakdown of relationships, disruption of work processes, loss of time and energy diverted to problems caused by the conflict, and even the loss of productive employees. Carpenter and Kennedy (1988) add, "The lesson of the conflict spiral is not that the progress is inevitable but that it is predictable when nothing is done to manage the conflict" (p. 17).

Occasionally, conflict spirals result from a special kind of alliance called *triangulation* (see Figure 2.2). Triangulation occurs when someone attempts to enhance his or her power over another by enlisting the support of another. Using tactics designed to manipulate, the alliance seeks to devalue or undercut the power of the third party. If this third party suspects the alliance, interactions will be characterized by chronic antagonism. For example, a teenage son may persuade his mother that the teacher is unfair and unreasonable and that she should not make him go to class or do the homework. An employee may enlist the aid of colleagues to jointly complain about an unreasonable supervisor. The third person in each case serves as a common enemy whom the parties blame for unfair distribution of resources or poor behavior.

Triangulation perpetuates blaming and rationale for negative behaviors toward a third person. This coalition, as a social entity, becomes stronger than the need to resolve the source of the conflict. Breaking the destructive cycle that occurs involves pointing out the behavior, depersonalizing the issues, and refocusing efforts on satisfying the underlying needs and interests of the involved parties. In particular, mediators of conflict need to be on guard against getting

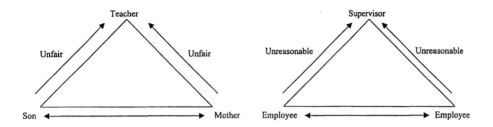

Figure 2.2. Triangulation

hooked by one of the parties into a triangulation against one of the other parties of a dispute. The person to whom the alliance is directed will become more resistant to cooperation.

Face Saving

Frequently, parties unknowingly fuel destructive spirals by inciting defensive, image-protecting behaviors called *face saving*. Face saving occurs when parties perceive threats to their social identities. Cupach and Canary (1997) point out, "Conflict creates circumstances that are inherently face threatening" (p. 110). For example, face threatening occurs when one party casts doubt on the competence, motivations, or truthfulness of another. It occurs when people believe that their perspective has been devalued or that they are being blamed for something for which they do not feel responsible. Threats to one's social identity will create barriers to any further constructive discussion. As Keltner (1987) explains,

> People in a dispute engage in many antagonistic behaviors in an attempt to protect or repair the image others have of them. Fear of losing, of being perceived as weak and vulnerable, and of being undervalued will often intensify and dominate the struggle. (p. 132)

Steps to end conflict get bogged down as parties devote energy to protecting their image instead of resolving issues. Helping others save face prevents escalation of conflict or becomes the key to promoting collaboration. A few of the ways to *give* face are to do the following:

1. Frame their motivations or intentions in a favorable manner, such as "I know you meant . . ." Give them a way out.
2. Acknowledge the value of the other's perspective.

BOX 2.3
Example of Multilevel Conflict and Face Saving

Gustaf, a citizen of Russia, served for many years as manager of emergency communication for a Caribbean nation. Gustaf's credentials included a medical degree and a PhD. Three months ago, he was hired by a state to serve as Director of Emergency Communication and Civil Defense. According to Human Resources, "He held the best academic and professional qualifications of the 30 candidates," and he was recommended by several prominent officials in the state government.

Conflict began almost immediately after Gustaf started his job. The federal Departments of Energy (DOE) and Defense (DOD) pointed out that Gustaf was a foreign national from a politically sensitive nation. Each time state or federal employees have contact with Gustaf, they must file a written report about the meeting's content. Because Gustaf's job required him to interface with 125-150 people regularly, most of whom have clearances, the workload for those who have to do security reports just went up exponentially.

The DOD threatened to pull the security clearances of all workers who had regular contact with Gustaf. The DOE, which funds 85% of the state's Civil Defense planning activities and a small part of Gustaf's salary, threatened to suspend funding because of his noncitizen status. One state official said, "We won't be threatened. He's qualified to do the job. We made the right decision."

Additionally, many of the state's rural residents resisted Gustaf's role as director of planning. They did not believe that a foreign national should be guiding civil defense or emergency operations in their areas. Thus, the governor's office requested that Gustaf have no further contact with rural communities nor serve as a spokesman for the agency. Gustaf gave these responsibilities to his staff. These kinds of extra tasks created conflict for Gustaf's staff. One said, "I'm not paid enough to do both a manager's job and my own."

The state's Human Resources department had no grounds to fire Gustaf and were worried about a lawsuit if they transferred him. The state officials who recommended Gustaf did not know that he was a foreign national and blamed Human Resources for not checking it out. Others said, "The federal government can't tell us who to hire." Communication broke down between all parties. Gustaf did what little he could in his job, while his staff did much of his work. Human Resources and state officials stood by their initial decision.

---

3. Apologize for creating the ill feeling.
4. Reframe your initial comments in a more favorable light, such as, "I said X, but that is not what I really meant. Let me say it again in a different way."

Box 2.3 provides an example of competitive parties who engage in a complex conflict. The conflict possesses elements of power, competing interests, interference, a conflict spiral, and face saving.

Intergroup Conflicts

Some studies suggest that there are more conflicts between groups than between individuals (Komorita & Lapworth, 1982; McCallum et al., 1985). There are many factors that promote these kinds of conflicts. One of these is a phenomenon called *ethnocentrism*. This factor explains a group's tendency to favor group perceptions, values, and aspirations, and to derogate these factors in other groups. For example, management will speak of employee unwillingness to consider corporate realities, and employees will complain that management lacks appreciation for their contributions. The stronger the group's identity and the lower the chance that members will go to the other group, the stronger the ethnocentrism.

A strong group identity strengthens the resolve of group members to achieve the group's aspirations. They will become positional as interest and goals become the agenda for a *common cause*. Group identity fosters a perception of fraternalistic deprivation, the sense that members have been treated unfairly by other groups. The group develops a common goal of defeating the enemy.

For example, employees in a contract negotiation may begin asking for changes in work rules. As discussion proceeds, they become more entrenched until they reach the level of *cause*. They develop a shared vision that might be labeled "fighting the injustice of worker conditions created by management." Causes reflect polarizations created by lack of listening and a perception that one side lacks respect for the other side's perspective.

A third factor, enhanced by group cohesiveness and shared identity, involves *runaway norms* (Raven & Rubin, 1983). The group conforms to patterns of behavior that seem normal to members but appear contentious and polarizing to others. The norms become justification for heightened distrust and insults directed at other groups. As the behaviors produce reciprocal behaviors in the other groups, a negative conflict spiral evolves.

Occasionally, negotiating settlements between groups in conflict begins by clarifying inaccurate assumptions that group members make about each other. It begins by identifying common ground and promoting behavioral norms that contribute to a collaborative climate. Rubin et al. (1994) suggest that breaking up cohesive groups for the purpose of problem solving can reduce collective dissent. For example, resolution of an environmental problem may involve breaking up a large, contentious group into subgroup task forces. A mediator may want to break up an employee group into two or three problem-solving subgroups to reduce the influence of divisive leaders.

Frozen Conflicts

On October 3, 1997, 1,000 steelworkers walked off their jobs at C F & I Steel Mill in Pueblo, Colorado. On this same date 1 year later, 800 of the workers still refused to return to work. Union president Ernest Hernandez said, "After 12 months, we're winning the financial battle. Sooner or later, the shareholders will have to bring an end to this and tell the company it has to bring its workers back" ("No end for steel strike," 1998, p. 4B). Michael Lowry, a stock analyst with Black & Company, disagreed with labor. In his estimation, the strike had little or no effect on the steel mill. University of Southern Colorado management professor James Browne agreed, pointing out that labor overestimated the damage they could do. As late as October 1999, the strike continued. The situation meets the criteria for a genuine impasse.

Keltner (1987) lists conditions that suggest intractable or frozen struggles. These are struggles in which resolution of differences is unlikely and deescalation is difficult:

- ❏ Rigid and unchanging perceptions of differing interests
- ❏ Incompatible values
- ❏ Communication that is poor or nonexistent
- ❏ Parties that perceive the situation as win-lose and move only to positions that give them advantage over the others
- ❏ Rigid and unchanging perceptions of self in relation to the rest of the world (p. 170)

Examples of intractable or frozen conflicts include the Cold War between the U.S. and former Soviet Union, the conflict between Irish Catholics and Protestant Unionists, or the long-term hostilities among nations of the Middle East.

When struggles become frozen, collaborative discussion and problem solving become increasingly more challenging. In the steel strike, all parties lose as the strike goes on. Rail customers complain of substandard bailing wire produced in the plant. Shipments from the plant are down 23% for the quarter. For 6 months, the steel mill was unable to get more credit through refinancing its loans. Striking employees live at a poverty level. Many lack health insurance. Each side appears solidly frozen in its position.

Northrup (1989) formulated a theory about stages through which disputants go before they reach the frozen position described by Keltner:

1. A strong sense of threat to a group's central commitments
2. The distortion of one another's positions because of the threat
3. A hardening of positions so that central assumptions about conflict become fixed for both parties
4. The development of fixed patterns of response that assume the conflict as a central and ongoing fact

Once the conflict reaches the fourth stage of development, agreement becomes very difficult to achieve.

Osgood (1962) suggests that moving away from frozen positions may begin with *gradual and reciprocal conciliatory initiatives* designed to reduce tension and build trust. The late Egyptian president Anwar Sadat used this technique when he flew to Jerusalem in 1977 prior to the 1978 Camp David Peace Accord meetings. In labor disputes, parties use this technique when they agree to relax a demand as a conciliatory gesture. "The aim of such initiatives is to enhance the trust of others to the point where productive communication and cooperation can begin" (Rubin et al., 1994, p. 163).

When open discussion meets intense resistance, resolving frozen conflicts could be approached through *covert problem solving.* This process involves disputants negotiating their differences through intermediaries in private sessions. Because intermediaries possess no power to make commitments and no need to engage in energy-consuming positional posturing, they can devote time to considering "supposals," or potential solutions to ending a stalemate. During the 1978 Camp David meetings, President Jimmy Carter shuttled back and forth between Israeli Prime Minister Menachem Begin and Sadat's cottages with supposals that eventually became the framework for a negotiated settlement.

Collaborative Approach to Resolving Conflict

Collaboration involves people working together for solutions that maximize the gains for all parties in the conflict. Approaching conflict from the perspective of collaboration depends on a fundamental, underlying principle identified by Chrislip and Larson (1994): "implicit trust that diverse people engaged in constructive ways and provided with the necessary information to make good decisions can be relied upon to create appropriate answers to the most pressing problems" (p. 14). This perspective is a profound shift for a competitive culture in which so many use intimidation, coercion, and litigation to force their way over others. Forcing may achieve partial success, but usually at high cost. Competitive strategies fail to address the long-term, underlying needs of relationships, organizations, or communities.

The following examples illustrate just a few of the many settings in which collaborative problem solving fuels innovative ways to manage conflict.

> Toyota's U.S. subsidiary established a problem-solving process that it called the Reversal Arbitration Board to handle disputes between the company and its dealers. The program reduced the number from a high of 178 in 1985 to a low of 3 in 1992 (Carver & Vondra, 1994).

> More than a dozen Massachusetts school communities developed teacher contracts and school policies through collaborative, interest-based bargaining. To date, the benefits of this nonadversarial approach include stronger teacher-administration relationships, higher quality contracts, and a better image in the community (Peace, 1994).

> In Ottawa, Canadian police, trained in facilitation, conducted community meetings designed to foster dialogue and creative brainstorming about fundamental causes and solutions to neighborhood crime (Hargrove, 1998).

Table 2.1 Conditions That Induce Collaboration or Competition

Collaboration	Competition
Open with information	Withholds information
High concern for welfare for self and others	High concern for self and low concern for others
Perceived similarity in beliefs and attitudes	Minimizes similarities of goals, beliefs, and attitudes
Trusting and friendly attitude	Suspicious or hostile attitude
Orientation toward mutual power	Seeks power over others
Respect for opposing interests	Lack of sensitivity to opposing interests
Readiness to be helpful	Use of coercion and threats
Focus on issues, interests, needs	Focus on personalities and rights

Deutsch (1991) identifies factors that influence the course of conflict (Table 2.1). He points out that conflict can move in either a cooperative and constructive path or a competitive and destructive path, depending on the parties' choice of action.

Understanding the elements and processes of the two paths, collaboration and competition, serves as a barometer for dealing with conflict in the most appropriate manner. Lower levels of conflict, when parties are more collaborative, may require only discussion, facilitation, or mediation. Higher levels of conflict, when collaboration is low and competition is high, may require collaborative hybrids such as mediation/arbitration or voluntary arbitration.

Fisher et al. (1994) offer suggestions about how to approach conflict from a collaborative perspective:

- ❑ Explore the perceptions of the other parties about the conflict.
- ❑ To gain empathy and a greater understanding, intellectually reverse roles.
- ❑ Look behind statements for underlying interests.
- ❑ Diagnose and analyze obstacles that prevent progress.
- ❑ Work on the problem together through creative inventing.

There is a variety of assisted and unassisted approaches to resolving conflict based on a collaborative perspective. Table 2.2 summarizes many of these approaches, which are described in detail in the chapters that follow. As the options move from negotiation to judicial processes, the choices become more formal, more costly, more distributive than integrative in outcome, and more adversarial, and the parties lose more control over terms of the settlement.

Collaborative Power

At first glance, power and collaboration appear to be opposing concepts. We are more familiar with negative displays of power than we are with positive dis-

Table 2.2 Collaborative Approaches to Resolving Conflict

Approach	Power of Parties to Influence Outcomes	Financial Cost	Ability to Preserve Relationship
Negotiation	High	Low	High
Mediation	High	Low	Moderate
Facilitation	High	Low	High
Nonbinding arbitration	Moderate	Moderate	Low
Binding arbitration	Moderate	Moderate	Low
Judicial processes	Low	High	Low

plays. When someone does not comply with the interests of another, the response may be a threat or demand that implies greater power. The goals of coercion or manipulation are to exert power over others. Supervisors may use the power of their role—"My way or no way"—to handle differences of opinion with staff. Litigation is a court process in which parties attempt to use the law to force the other party to comply with their interests. In extreme cases, a party may even resort to violence as a way to demonstrate power over others. These tactics for resolving conflict are not without cost. Keltner (1987) argues that the ineffective use of power "makes the world more brutish, escalates peaceful differences into violent conflict, brings on our own destruction more rapidly than otherwise, and creates social, psychological, and physical invalids" (p. 65).

The benefits of manipulation, litigation, and violence appear strong in the short term, but the long-term costs of loss of relationship, cooperation, and community are great. Collaborative power involves power *with* others to resolve differences and achieve interests. If we can create conditions in which others are highly motivated to share information, engage in give-and-take, and believe that our intentions for settlement are genuine, then there will be less need for them to retaliate or fuel conflict spirals.

Power with others involves an orientation based on principled negotiation. Discussion is based on reasons and explanations rather than manipulation and forcing. This approach values short-term tension in exchange for minimizing long-term pain. Collaborative power values the opinions and the interests of both parties as core elements for settlements. Sharing power means that we are just as willing to allow others to influence us as we desire to influence them. We may be firm on interests and needs, but we can be flexible about how we achieve them.

Craig and Craig (1974) describe this perspective as synergic power, in which the goal is "to increase the satisfaction of all participants by intentionally generating increased energy and creativity, all of which is used to co-create a more rewarding present and future" (p. 62). An orientation of collaborative power enables parties to focus more effort on joint problems and less effort on designing ways to force opponents into compliance. A longtime activist for peace, former Israeli Prime Minister Shimon Peres argues, "Whenever there are two positions in a negotiation, the solution will never be one of those two parties. A successful solution depends on finding a third position that must be created or discovered" (Hargrove, 1998, p. 223).

Conflict Styles

People approach differences of opinion and perceived interference from others in a variety of ways. Some people become aggressive and assertive. They will threaten and make demands. Others will become quiet and passive and avoid talking about their concerns.

The Dual Concern model (Table 2.3) explains how the needs of self and others interact in strategic approaches to conflict (Blake & Mouton, 1964; Filley, 1975). The model explains behaviors based on two independent variables—concern about one's own outcomes and concern about the outcomes of others. These two concerns become intertwined in decisions about the best choice for dealing with conflict.

The goals of avoiding and yielding approaches frequently involve preservation of the status quo or harmony at the present level. The competitive approach may pursue goals involving personal need at the expense of peace or perceived equity in the relationship. Each approach possesses benefits and costs in terms of meeting personal needs or preserving relationships.

People develop favored styles based on past family and work experiences. A person may be competitive at work yet be compliant and accommodating at home. In addition, the styles may be linked together. A person who is competing may get along well with a colleague as long as that colleague is accommodating. Conflict occurs when an issue of importance occurs and the accommodating colleague chooses to become competitive.

Factors that influence the choice of style include the importance of the issue to the party, contextual or cultural norms for how conflict should be approached, how one anticipates that others will react, and personal goals. The following five styles describe some of the most common ways that people approach conflict.

> *Avoiding*—One party denies that there is a conflict, changes topics and avoids discussion, and is noncommittal. This style is most effective in situations in which there is danger of physical violence, the issue is not important, there is no chance of achieving goals, or the complexity of the situation prevents solutions.
>
> *Accommodation*—One party sacrifices its interests and concerns while enabling others to achieve their interests. This style is effective in situations in which there is not much chance of achieving one's own interests, when the outcome is not important, or when there is a belief that satisfying one's own interests will in some way alter or damage the relationship.
>
> *Compromising*—Through concessions by all parties, each party settles for partial satisfaction of interests. This style is effective in situations that re-

Table 2.3 Dual Concern Model

	Concern About One's Own Outcome	Concern About the Outcomes for the Other
Avoiding	Low	Low
Yielding	Low	High
Competing	High	Low
Collaborative	High	High

quire quick resolution of issues, when other parties resist collaboration, when complete achievement of goals is not important, or when there will be no hard feelings for settling for less than expected.

Competitive—This style is characterized by aggressive, self-focused, forcing, verbally assertive, and uncooperative behaviors that strive to satisfy one party's interests at the expense of the interests of others. This style is effective in situations in which decisions must be made quickly, options are restricted, there is nothing to lose by pushing, other parties resist cooperation, and there is no concern about potential damage to the relationship.

Collaborative—This style is characterized by active listening and issue-focused, empathic communication that seeks to satisfy the interests and concerns of all parties. It is effective in situations in which power is reasonably balanced, the long-term relationship is valued, both parties display cooperative behaviors, and there is sufficient time and energy to create an integrative solution that will satisfy both parties.

Negotiation, mediation, and facilitation rely very much on collaboration or compromise to reach settlements. Arbitration and judicial processes expect parties to begin competitively. A neutral third party attempts to create conditions that will promote compromise or collaboration.

Comparison of Conflict Styles

In a study of 52 conflict cases involving middle managers, Phillips and Cheston (1979) compared the effectiveness of five conflict resolution styles: avoidance, forcing, accommodating, compromising, and problem solving. The researchers found that (a) problem solving was most effective in cases involving interpersonal communication and organizational issues; (b) forcing, though used twice as often as problem solving, had a 50% failure rate; and (c) avoidance, used as often as problem solving, had an 80% failure rate.

Other studies have reached similar conclusions. The collaborative, problem-solving style generally produces better decisions and greater satisfaction with the decisions produced (Lawrence & Lorsch, 1967; Tutzauer & Roloff, 1988;

Wells & Galanes, 1986). In addition, Conrad (1983) found that effective communicators are more likely to use a collaborative/problem-solving style, and less competent communicators will use competing or forcing styles.

Weeks (1992) described the most effective style for resolving conflict as a *conflict partnership*. This style emphasizes a "we, not I-versus-you orientation"; solves current problems in a way that protects the long-term relationship; and resolves conflict in a manner that parties can see that they have received something of benefit.

In a study that looked at 57 incidents in a social service agency, Tjosvold (1990) found that employees with cooperative goals were more likely to discuss specific problems and how to solve them, provide assistance and support, brainstorm options, and integrate new ideas into practice. Employees with uncooperative goals made decisions without consultation and were less likely to offer assistance to others. This supports Muldoon's (1996) contention that a collaborative approach begins with "starting with the destination in mind, a destination that is sufficiently challenging, urgent, and compelling to redirect the parties' aggressive energies away from each other" (p. 123).

Sillars and Parry (1982) wanted to know which nonverbal behaviors correlated most with three of the conflict styles: integrative (collaborative), distributive (competitive), and avoidance. They found that people who used a competitive style talked faster with less substance and used more one-line zingers in a hit-and-run fashion. Avoiders fidgeted, looked less at other people, and talked less. Collaborators tended to talk more, use more eye contact to display concern and interest, and engage in more dialogue. Newton and Burgoon (1990) linked the importance of these nonverbal messages to resolving conflict in their conclusion that there is greater satisfaction with relationship and conflict in styles that are involved and cooperative.

But knowing *how* to be collaborative may be only as important as knowing *when* to be collaborative. Phillips and Cheston (1979) found that problem solving is most effective in situations in which

- ❑ The parties are highly interdependent and have to work together in the future.
- ❑ There is a willingness to ignore power issues.
- ❑ Formal procedures for problem solving are available to parties.
- ❑ One or both people detect the conflict early and initiate problem solving before things get bad.
- ❑ Attention is focused on solving a common problem rather than defeating or adopting one person's preferred solution.

Hocker and Wilmot (1991) warn,

> If investment in the relationship or issue is low, then collaboration is not worth the effort, for it is time and energy consuming. Further, collaboration can be used in very manipulative ways. . . . Often high-power persons use pseudo-collaboration to maintain the power imbalance. (p. 125)

PROFESSIONAL PROFILE:
JOHN MARKS
Co-Founder and President, Search for Common Ground

Learning Through Engagement

The largest conflict management firm in the world takes a pragmatic approach to its work. Guiding principles of Search for Common Ground are the following:

- Even the most difficult problems can be resolved peacefully.
- Today's problems are too complex and interconnected to be solved on an adversarial basis.
- In most conflicts, common ground can be found in shared interests, principles, or concerns.
- Searching for the common ground can generate constructive movement and promote change.
- Understand the differences; act on the commonalities.

Introduction to the Practitioner

John Marks is the conflict manager/entrepreneur who founded Search for Common Ground in 1982 with two employees and a handful of supporters. In 1998, there were more than 125 staff members, thousands of people involved with the projects, and a direct outreach to millions through media programs. The organization has activities on four continents and offices in nine countries. For instance, Search for Common Ground staff have worked in Macedonia to help prevent the eruption of violence seen in other Balkan states, and they worked in Angola after the civil war there to offer alternative problem-solving methodologies. They sponsor dialogues in the United States that bring together pro-life and pro-choice advocates in an effort to find common ground. The conflicts that this organization tackles involve complex problems with roots in ethnic, environmental, economic, and political issues.

Before founding this peacemaking organization, John had other professional experiences with conflict management. Indeed, he estimates, "I'm on my fifth career!" Beginning as a foreign service officer with the U.S. Department of State, he resigned in protest over the war in Vietnam. John continued his efforts to end the war by working for New Jersey Senator Clifford Case. In that office, he assisted in drafting the Case-Church amendment, which eventually ended the war. His critique of the American security establishment was delivered in the book he co-authored, *The CIA and the Cult of Intelligence*, sales of which made him a best-selling author at age 31.

John recalls, "After 10 years of activism, I got to the point in my own life where I wanted to build a new system rather than tear down the old system. This was a long personal process, but I saw that I wanted to change the world from an adversarial to a nonadversarial place. So, I did this out of my vision of what was possible at that time. Someone I knew very well said that conflict resolution could end up as a system which improved law firm billings, or it could wind up as a new way of thinking. From the beginning, I've been interested in developing it as a new way of thinking. It's a transformational methodology that can change the way the world works." This vision led to the founding of Search for Common Ground. It continues to inform John's leadership as programs grow and develop.

Work of the Practitioner

Search for Common Ground is notable not only for its size and scope, but also because of the range of its methods. As John notes, "Virtually any function in society can be used to bridge differences. Currently, there are 18 tools used by staff to manage conflict. However, that list is not in concrete; it's one we're continually adding to, as opportunities present themselves. Every year, we figure out new ways to do the work, but they are all based on understanding the differences and acting on the commonalities." In addition to usual methods such as mediation, facilitation, training, and joint action projects, his organization uses the media extensively.

John's philosophy of media use involves countering the usual adversarial approach and, instead, framing contentious problems from a common ground perspective. His organization produces peace-oriented radio and television programs that include news, features, and soap operas. Recognizing that media coverage of disputes can ignite violence, Search for Common Ground has co-sponsored workshops for journalists in an effort to defuse inflammatory coverage. For instance, the center organizes interethnic teams of journalists who jointly investigate a subject and then co-author multipart series that are published simultaneously in papers that reach readers in conflicting areas.

John believes that community organizing within a nonadversarial framework can also be an important conflict prevention tool. He explains, "In Burundi, we thought it would be helpful to take a group of women leaders to meet with South African women, in order to understand their models and methods of conflict management. Out of that experience came the idea to establish the Women's Peace Centre, which supports Hutu and Tutsi women in peacemaking activities. The Centre has become an important component of our work in Burundi."

One of the more recent methods is the use of sports as a vehicle for discovering common ground. John enthuses, "Sports is a wonderful mechanism for conflict management! We hoped to improve relations between the U.S. and Iran, where no American group had been since the seizure of the U.S. embassy in 1979. After months of investigation, we found that wrestling could be a good way to launch nonofficial exchanges between the two countries, since wrestling is hugely popular in Iran. While the presence of any American team would have been criticized by hard-liners in Iran, wrestlers were protected by the unique role of wrestling in Iranian culture. A European ambassador told us that the decision to start conflict management with wrestling showed 'exquisite empathy' with the Iranian people."

Five wrestlers, including one former Olympic champion and two former world champions, served as sportsmen and citizen diplomats. The matches drew large crowds in Tehran, who cheered both the Iranians and the Americans. Americans present experienced positive sentiments from both the crowd and individual Iranians. On their return, President Clinton called John and the team to the White House to congratulate them. Mike McCurry, White House spokesperson, told reporters, "[The president is] drawing attention to an exchange that is maybe off the beaten path of diplomacy, but has something to say about the prospect and hope for more beneficial relations between peoples."

Opinions About ADR Issues

With regard to the training of practitioners in conflict management, John is very much the pragmatist: "I think that the best way to learn this field is through apprenticeship. I'm not convinced that a master's or a PhD is as useful. Courses in mediation and hands-on sorts of things are what are important. My sense is the way you learn is by doing. I think theory is not so important as the practice. Most of the theory is common sense. In my view, watching and practicing constitute the primary path to knowledge. There are scholars in the field whom I wouldn't let near an actual conflict. Also, there are certain people who are naturally good at conflict management." For conflict managers, qualifications are based on both nature and nurture.

John sees "learning from engagement" as the foundation of his success, as well as that of his organization. He finds, "It's important to become engaged, because then you see the possibilities. You need to be engaged to see what the prospects are of providing some relief to the problems. Virtually never is the process going to be the one that was envisioned at the beginning. Once we get a person on the ground, we see how to do things. I find that the best ideas come after the engagement." Obviously, flexibility and open-mindedness on the part of the learner are essential success components in learning through engagement.

John has maxims about conflict management that guide his work as a practitioner and as an institution builder. "One of the keys to me is making 'yesable' propositions, the concept from Roger Fisher and Bill Ury's book *Getting to Yes*. It took me about 5 years to internalize this concept. It seems to me that the way that one raises money, the way that one sets up a project, the way that one moves forward in this work is to make a series of 'yesable' propositions. That involves getting into the shoes of the other, and that's very important."

John's thinking about preparation emphasizes the extensive background work that is necessary to bring parties together in the frame of mind to find common ground. He believes that the key to conflict management is "making it happen, setting it up, creating the environment where people are willing to move forward. Most of the emphasis in the field of conflict management is put on the meetings once they start, and I think that that misses a major element in complicated social issues. It took a couple of years to set up the Iranian wrestling matches, working with insiders who offered the insights about the mythological aspects of wrestling to Iranians. It seems totally obvious now, but it wasn't at the time. And then, to identify and fund the American team took some doing." Effective facilitation of complex problems requires lengthy preparation.

John contends that the field of conflict management has not moved as far as it might because practitioners are not involved long enough to understand the issues in depth. "Most people work fee-for-services and do not have the time for learning through engagement. Who pays while someone is trying to set up a process? And academics who come in for short periods of time, who have to go back to whatever they're doing . . . the field loses something because they're not people who're able to focus in a continuing way on complex problems."

John and his organization observe the rule of "not parachuting," meaning that they try hard not to practice crisis management in situations where they have little experience or expertise. "We violate this rule from time to time, but we try to have people on the ground who are steeped in the problems. That cultural insight is incredibly important, both domestically and overseas. The idea that you can take an off-the-shelf process and drop it on a complex social problem is not a valid notion."

Preparation also involves skills and understanding. For instance, the staff person who wants to use media must understand the various media and their applications and technical requirements. Second, the staff person must also understand how media are used in a particular context. Different formats will elicit different responses. Third, what are the needs in the country, and how do you communicate? What are the ways of moving forward? It is also important that the neutrals be knowledgeable about Search for Common Ground philosophies and can see how to apply them in unfamiliar contexts. In John's words, "Successful consultants know where we come from and know where they are."

Adequate preparation depends on good problem-solving skills. John explains, "The first person we hire to go into a country needs the mentality of a supply sergeant. Being able to get things done in a difficult situation, negotiating licenses and permits, are just pure problem solving. The methodologies are not nearly so important as being able to problem solve within an unfamiliar context."

With 18 methods in the toolbox, there is no "typical" conflict management scenario. However, an example of media use in Liberia is instructive. Using radio in Monrovia, where 70% of the population is concentrated, local writers and producers generate weekly soap operas that feature the message of reconciliation. John reports, "A survey of listeners found that the programs were heard by 90% of the population, and that 75% of those who listened could repeat the message. By Madison Avenue standards, we are wildly successful. We're getting into the culture. Does that make Charles Taylor (current president) a better man? No. But you're creating an environment in which things can change."

What is success in such endeavors? It's particularly difficult to assess. John reminds us that, "Unfortunately, the methodologies of peacemaking are weaker than those of killing and violence. I've never heard of a case where someone who listened to one of our broadcasts dropped his Kalisnikov. Our approach is not that strong, but it can strengthen the immune system, it can change the environment." No one can prove that peacemaking efforts are directly responsible for prevention or reduction in violence, because no one knows what would have happened otherwise. Does that mean that they should be discontinued? Of course not.

Experience has convinced John and his staff that success is more likely in two contrasting situations. One is in countries such as Macedonia, where widespread violence has not yet occurred. Another is in countries such as Angola, where citizens are weary of civil war. These findings help guide where resources may be applied most usefully.

One of the toughest challenges John has faced has been the dialogues about abortion in the United States. "To find common ground between pro-choice and pro-life believers is hard. People in this country assume that there isn't any. There is a consensus in America that this conflict is irreconcilable. Work in Burundi was also very challenging, due to the number of killings. Would there have been even more without the work of Search for Common Ground? No one will ever know." John finds that managing such a large, globally based institution is a challenge in itself.

John's response to learning from mistakes might be predicted by his emphasis on learning from engagement. In his words, "We look in the morning, we revise at lunch. Feedback is embedded in our approach. The key is to look at what's working and to build on that." John also mentions that he has occasionally taken on a project against his gut instincts, only to watch it fail. With so many unknowables in his work, he has come to trust his intuition more.

As a change agent, John stresses the importance of staying with complex conflicts. For some conflict managers, success may be defined as that point at which the neutral withdraws, judging that the parties now have resolved their difficulties. In contrast, John and his organization have not withdrawn from countries where they have committed staff and resources. "In places where we have been deeply engaged, no one wants to say, 'Let's go home.' Unless the international community supplies conflict management, we suspect that violence will escalate. I'm not saying we'll stay forever, but we are there for the long term.

"We are trying to institutionalize our work so that locals can continue after we leave. That's very important. But particularly in divided societies, a third party is not a bad thing to be. For example, if Hutus and Tutsis are at each other's throats, who do you turn over your local radio station to? We *are* the space of common ground in these places." Even though there are few expatriates working in the overseas offices, it is their presence that ensures the continuation of peacekeeping projects.

John notes disagreements in the way practitioners approach conflict management. He wants the field to shift from solo work to more systemic approaches. He is concerned that the field draws individuals who are anarchists at heart and will therefore resist a systems approach. He wants to see less "parachuting" and more long-term commitment to difficult social and political conflicts. Finally, the field needs to move into a new thinking mode about how to practice conflict management so that it is transformational, and not just another professional "billing." John's work at Search for Common Ground provides a demonstration of the effectiveness of a committed, systemic approach to conflict management.

Professional Profile: Myra Isenhart
President, Organizational Communication, Inc.

Change Drives Conflict in Organizational Teams

One of the most popular applications of ADR in the workplace is the conflict management training that is done with intact teams. Much organizational production depends on the smooth functioning of work teams and the healthy interdependence of their members. The ability to manage the inevitable conflicts is a critical factor in the success of the team. Organizational systems that face pressures to make significant changes in real time must depend on shared agreements about how to resolve differences. Because of these dynamics, the demand for conflict management training of teams is strong.

Introduction to the Practitioner

Myra Warren Isenhart is a specialist in human communication; since the mid-1970s, she has been training and consulting in the application of communication to organizational settings. She combines this work with part-time teaching in higher education. She publishes in communication journals and speaks at conferences.

By the mid-1980s, Myra's consulting practice was shaped by the growing demand for conflict management skills, which outstripped that for other communication offerings. She received training in mediation and joined SPIDR and the board of the Conflict Center in Denver, Colorado. The collaborative methods of ADR seemed a natural fit with her communication background.

Work of the Practitioner

Myra works with teams of professionals or managers who are "stuck." Often, the first reaction of team members to conflict is to personalize the conflict; the consultant hears that "Harry/Harriet is a troublemaker." Team members observe someone enacting an organizational role in ways that make their lives difficult. The aspects of organizational structure and processes that drive that enactment are invisible, so the actor is blamed. For instance, management may spend much money and time organizing everyone into teams, but the reward structure is still based on individual performance. Is it any wonder that Harry/Harriet is not a "good team player"? Because the underlying problem is discontinuity between team and reward systems, any number of different members will exhibit the same "personality conflict."

Usually, a change of some kind creates the conflict: a new leader whose expectations are significantly different from those of the former leader; or perhaps the new expectations are not clear to team members, who are having difficulty with the leadership transition, but neither side can identify why. Other very common intrateam conflicts involve disputes over resources: Who gets the latest computer upgrade, the lion's share of support time, the raise, the promotion?

Team members are, by definition, interdependent; therefore, conflicts also arise from the impact that one person's work (or lack of it) has on others. Their negotiations about scheduling may be a source of conflict for similar reasons. Occasionally, team members interact outside of the workplace and bring those conflicts with them to the office. Other team members become involved as they are pressured to take sides with one team member or another.

In addition to conflicts generated within teams, Myra also works with disputes that arise when change results from the shift in organizational goals. This requires some alignment of team goals by its members. When the macro-level goals are not desirable to team members, or when their strategic implementation drives exhaustive team efforts, there will be conflict. Even more common is the situation in which changes coming down through the organization are not described in ways that are clear to those who must implement them. Team members may react to unclear changes, or multiple changes, by ignoring them until it is clear where the priorities are. In these cases, dispute resolution happens between the team leader and the executive whose duty it is to set and clarify those priorities.

Opinions About ADR Issues

Myra suggests that beginning practitioners need two basic tools. To begin with, they must have both a theoretical and a working knowledge of organizations. There are a number of different career paths that could provide this background. Myra notes, "I am grateful for my own experience conducting professional training in human communication, with its emphasis on interpersonal and small-group dynamics. The 25 years I've spent training and consulting as a communication specialist gives me a rich reserve of organizational conflict experiences, although I still receive surprises occasionally!" However, there are many paths to understanding organizational conflicts, most common among these being the study of psychology and human resources. Whatever the discipline, an understanding of systems theory is essential; "otherwise, you end up addressing the same conflict in different forms ad nauseam."

The second tool is expertise in conflict theory and management techniques. There are growing numbers of ways to garner this learning, through credit programs at universities, training provided by organizations experienced in dispute resolution, and mentoring under experienced conflict management practitioners. However, compared to the many professional entries into organizational systems, there are still relatively few opportunities to receive hands-on experience with feedback. And, some trainings are more substantive than others. Beginners who are seriously considering careers in this field would do well to consider a combination of for-credit education, training, and mentoring.

In addition to formal programs, Myra credits her experiences as trainer and consultant. "Over the years, though I was paid to deliver training, I was very aware that participants in my workshops, particularly in seminars lasting several days, were teaching me a great deal about the workings of various groups and organizations. Similarly, one of the reasons I continue to be stimulated by my consulting work in organizational development is that I have never encountered the same situation twice. Even with similar dynamics, there are always new insights to be developed from each client."

Experience that builds expertise is broader than that gained during working hours. Myra believes that "Many of us learn to be mediators from life experiences, even though we get gray hair instead of certificates. Anyone who has been married a length of time learns the basics of fair and unfair fighting. Anyone who has parented a toddler or a teenager knows something about dealing with anger management and setting boundaries. Anyone who has served on neighborhood associations or nonprofit boards has the raw material to be self-taught on group dynamics and the use of informal power. Whether or not we have the language of dispute resolution, we gain the experience to reflect on, and the language may be layered on later."

As co-author of this book, Myra can afford to be more provocative and inject the topic of gender *role* into the discussion of success factors. "I emphasize the word *role* to distinguish it from biological gender. It seems to me that being so-cialized feminine is an advantage in resolving disputes among team members." Experts such as Carol Gilligan (*In a Different Voice*) describe the feminine encul-turation as learning to be a good listener; to excel at decoding nonverbal cues; and to value collaboration, among other orientations. A significant minority of males are also enculturated with these skills and values. Those of us, male and female, who have had this early training have a head start on conflict manage-ment in the workplace.

Preparation time may vary for work groups, but Myra's goal is to hold sepa-rate, individual interviews with the team leader and members. The value de-rived rests not only in creating a representative picture of the dispute, the dispu-tants, and possible solutions, but also in establishing a relationship between the neutral person and the participants. "When we sit down in a group, each already has a personal comfort level with my approach and presence; we can move to-gether more readily when this level of certainty has been pre-established. Often, I find that team members use the private interviews to vent their feelings, and this also seems to help with later group problem solving."

Myra uses an interview protocol that varies from team to team, but usually includes such reflection questions as "How do you see the conflict? What part do you play in it? What are possible solutions?" She then collates the responses anonymously and gives this summary to the team at the first meeting. She re-ports that, "It usually clears the air for members to speak about what's really go-ing on. I have yet to find a team which didn't know, at some level, what is going on and how to fix it. My job is not to prescribe, but to evoke implicit knowledge."

Each team is unique. However, she feels that "it is *impossible* to overempha-size the importance of beginnings. First, I spend considerable effort making sure that everyone will be comfortable." "Comfortable" will include such topics as the timing (Fridays at the usual work hours generally work best), the location off-site, and access to breakout rooms. Second, in her introduction, she makes sure that everyone understands the ground rules of conflict management, and that all members are committed for a full day. Third, together, they build an agenda, reviewing the issues that surfaced in the interviews. Three sessions with a team is typical. She prefers to space out meetings so that members have an opportunity to practice and test solution ideas before meeting again.

In terms of the relationship between practitioners and teams, trust is funda-mental. Unless a group believes that the neutral person will respect its confi-dences and is not simply a tattle for management, conflict management is doomed to fail. In addition, all members must believe that the practitioner is completely neutral with regard to having favorites within the team. It helps if the trainer can demonstrate some lay understanding of their business. Although the human dynamics of teams have consistent patterns, each industry or profes-sion believes that its situation is unique.

For the team, there are several success ingredients. The first is that members must feel some pain. In Myra's experience, "If recognition of and concern about the problem is shown only by management, chances are that there may be little movement among team members." Second, the team must believe that considering options and working toward a conflict resolution is possible. Some teams have confronted difficulties and devised solutions, only to find that they will not be allowed the time or resources to pursue them. There must be a reasonable hope of making the changes agreed to.

For the practitioner, there must be comfort with using both analytical and empathic skills. Myra finds that "team conflicts arise often because it is not safe to express emotional content in the workplace. A practitioner who is not highly empathic or has trouble shifting into the psychological states of others will be a handicapped helper."

By definition, team members know their conflict much more intimately than does the neutral person. Analysis is less about data interpretation than it is about helping people to see their affairs in a different light. It helps to ask dumb-smart questions such as, "This conflict persists for a reason. Who (what units) benefit from it continuing?" In Myra's experience, reflection questions support success.

Challenges in this work come in several forms. Current statistics tell us that we are spending more time with our co-workers than we are with our families. The team is the organizational family in every sense of that concept. For instance, people transfer the orientation to authority that they learned as children into team settings. If members were encouraged to speak up and interact with a parent, they will repeat that behavior in the workgroup. If they were discouraged from interacting with authority figures, they will air their complaints in the rest rooms and the parking lot. Myra finds that "one of the most difficult tasks of introducing conflict management processes is that a significant number of team members are not bringing a healthy set of home-taught communication patterns to the workplace."

Another common challenge is the "upstairs" dysfunction. When there are problems "upstairs," organizational gravity will bring them down. Myra offers the following example: "Some of my toughest challenges have been trying to evoke changes when investigation shows that the trouble is with a management level above the team in question." In these circumstances, upper-level managers designate the problem elsewhere and may be remarkably resistant to making changes themselves.

Mistakes made are the flipside of Myra's emphasis on preparation and conduct of sessions. Sometimes, the nature of the conflict dictates that more progress will be made by including people who are not technically part of the team: support staff, resource people, and internal customers should be considered for inclusion in the group sessions. Mistakes also arise in the consultant's interpretation of the role: "Who is the (real) client? The manager who hires you? The team in conflict? Individuals without conflict management skills?"

The chief change that Myra notes is that there are many human resource personnel who are moving toward conflict management tools. In the past, it has been difficult for organizations to see the applications of ADR to teams, but she believes that appreciation is developing. In addition, she is aware of more interest in and respect for systems theory. As she interprets these trends, "These two changes are inextricably linked in my mind; as we adopt a systems approach to organizational conflict, we will be more successful in producing lasting and positive resolutions. To the extent that we can document results, those who fund dispute resolution in organizations are likely to be more receptive to its use."

Conflict managers working with teams will disagree on a few topics. Because of the varied paths by which practitioners enter the field, there are likely to be many areas of conceptual difference. Team consultants may disagree about how directive the third-person neutral should be. What work may properly be done by an internal versus external consultant will be debated by some. Conflict management in the changing workplace will always be complex!

Professional Profile: Bill Drake
Executive Director, Western Justice Center Foundation

Street Corner ADR: The South African Curb

There is global awareness of the value and importance of ADR. International applications are some of the most well-established and well-known uses of mediation. Former President Jimmy Carter is much in demand as a peacemaker when issues in dispute are salient to the United States. Governmental agencies such as the United Nations offer ADR services. Nonprofit organizations such as the Quakers and Search for Common Ground in Washington, DC provide education, build infrastructure, and co-mediate disputes with local leaders. Professional ADR meetings draw delegates from dozens of countries. In growing numbers, U.S. dispute resolution practitioners sell and donate their services overseas.

Any attempt to generalize findings on a global scale is obviously limited by the diversity of nationalities, cultures, and history with ADR. We approached these limitations by interviewing a practitioner who has long experience with both U.S. and South African ADR. South Africa escaped the bloodbath many expected at the government transition in 1994, in great part because of the dedicated peace efforts of its own citizens, along with some international assistance. The Peace Accords that created a framework for the first all-race elections in 1994 were negotiated among the white government and numerous opposition political parties. There are dozens of different ethnic and language groups represented in South Africa, many of whom have their own histories of intergroup conflict and violence. We reasoned that because ADR works in a situation with so many complications, there may be lessons for other nations as well.

Introduction to the Practitioner

Bill Drake brings a rich experience with complex disputes to international work. Trained as a city planner, he has held senior management positions with the National League of Cities and U.S. Conference of Mayors. For 9 years, he was Deputy Director of the National Institute for Dispute Resolution (NIDR); currently, he is the Executive Director of the Western Justice Center Foundation in Pasadena, California, overseeing research and development projects in conflict resolution, law, and justice. Bill's international experience includes repeated trips to South Africa, where he co-founded the African Centre for the Constructive Resolution of Disputes (ACCORD).

Bill was drawn into South African dispute resolution through the work he did at NIDR. He and a South African lawyer, Vasu Gouden, who was a senior fellow at NIDR while studying under a Fulbright grant, responded to the need for a conflict resolution organization in South Africa that would be credible to Africans, Indians, and colored people, collectively called *Black* under the apartheid laws. NIDR helped develop an organization called the African Centre for the Constructive Resolution of Disputes (ACCORD) and, in 1991, helped establish the new entity. He continues to advise ACCORD and conduct joint projects to build conflict resolution capacity in South Africa.

Work of the Practitioner

The work of this international practitioner has taken at least five directions. Bill tells us that "First, I have worked with South Africans on organizational development, using facilitation to build consensus around organizational structures and strategies." Many would call this conflict management systems design. In Bill's work, many stakeholders and meetings are necessary to achieve consensus.

Second, Bill has held official appointed positions. For example, prior to and during the first all-race elections that made Nelson Mandela president in 1994, Bill was named Senior Assistant to the International Supervisor of the State of Emergency in ZwaZulu Natal, a province that was under enormous threat of violence before the elections. Bill recounts, "This province was the epicenter of the conflict between the two largest black parties, the African National Congress (ANC) and the Inkatha Freedom Party (IFP-predominantly Zulu population). Parliament had established a state of emergency and formal powers in an attempt to control the violence expected before and after the election. No other province in the country was under a state of emergency. I met daily with a large working group to prevent and respond to violence, then went into the field to interview as needed. Among others, the working group included all of the military services, national and regional police officials, representatives of the Independent Election Commission as well as international observers and monitors of the elections."

A third way in which Bill managed conflict in South Africa is referred to there as going "on the ground," meaning he spent time in the field trying to assess what was actually happening. Bill identified both formal and informal leaders to assist him in managing conflict on the spot. As the title of this chapter suggests, Bill practiced mediation in situations where one must respond very quickly and independently, relying more on skill than legitimate authority. For example, Bill moved security forces into more visible positions in several polling places in order to reassure people about their safety when arriving at the polls to vote. (The military personnel were hiding, in effect, to avoid drive-by attacks on themselves.) When he observed Inkatha "warlords" in a remote rural polling place intimidating poll workers into letting Zulu youth vote illegally, he convened officials, concluded that no one present could control the situation, and called in by helicopter a crisis management team from the Independent Election Commission.

Fourth, conflict resolution in South Africa involved reframing conflict management in a climate where violence was the usual mode of problem solving. Many people had grown hopeless about a peaceful resolution of differences, so that "the practitioner's job often consisted of facilitating meetings in which people were helped to see their possible achievements and gain a sense of momentum toward a nonviolent solution." One example is Bill's co-facilitation of a national meeting of 100 leaders of political parties, African tribes, military services, and police agencies to plan for managing pre-election violence. Helping antagonists conduct a positive discussion when many of them believed each other's groups were killing their own members seemed to Bill like an impossible task. Yet he learned that there was a civility and grudging respect that permitted orderly discussion, once the dialogue was reframed as focusing on the future. One has to remember that for many political groups, violence was a consciously used weapon; it was not spontaneous.

Finally, Bill used his "street corner" skills in organizational as well as individual ways. Many of us remember the moving televised images of South Africans standing in long lines in rural areas, for days in some cases, many voting for the first time in their lives. Bill reminds us that "after the election, the process of ballot counting was complex and very controversial. In Durban, 100 different teams, totally 1,500 people per shift, were counting ballots around the clock. Not only were partisans insistent on gaining access to possibly influence the fairness of the process, but the counting house was besieged by thousands who believed the false rumor that they might be paid to count ballots."

Chaos was such that the official election commission staff fled, leaving Bill and several other conflict resolution experts who were called in to manage the crisis. The ad hoc team involved began effectively managing a mob outside, arranging for large numbers of election workers to enter and exit the building safely, and convening political parties and resolving political controversies inside the hall. "Street corner" ADR in the crisis involved resolving such questions as how to deal with contested ballots, fraudulent ballots, boxes stuffed with grass, and uncredentialed observers. Although the election commission had designed a process for dealing with such questions, no one left in the building was privy to it. The multiracial team managed by bringing the key leaders together calmly to resolve political issues; by moving in a positive, productive direction; by gradually dispersing the mob outside so that people could enter and exit the building, and so on. In a few days, the count was complete, and a very volatile situation was transformed.

Opinions About ADR Issues

Given Bill's "street corner" approach, it is not surprising that his approach to training puts more emphasis on experience than on education. Beyond the basic skill set of conflict resolution, along with the attendant values, attitudes, and sensibilities, Bill notes, "The rest of training must be open-ended, because it depends on where you practice, what the culture is like, and what language barriers exist. ADR international skills are circumstantial and contextual."

Generally speaking, Bill believes that "like many highly trained people, we in ADR overintellectualize what we do. Our work is really much simpler than it sounds, and more dependent on common sense and intuitive ability, which may be sharpened by training. We do a disservice to students when we imply that training is a direct vehicle to practice."

According to Bill, "Much cross-cultural training emphasizes differences, whereas ideal training would help practitioners understand what are the essential commonalities among people in a diverse culture. As a newcomer to the culture, you will never understand all the differences that separate people, such as language, symbols, gestures, etc. Successful practice of ADR depends on the ability to draw out the common threads which might link subgroups."

Bill found that two elements were helpful in his ability to function in South African culture. First, before his first trip, he spent a year and a half listening to South African colleagues in the United States and planning their common project. The value of mentoring and prior exposure paid off when he did arrive. Second, he spent enough time there over several years to allow himself to become immersed in the culture, history, and politics. "Despite invitations to do similar work in other African countries, I feel it is better to concentrate on one overseas assignment, becoming better acquainted and more helpful each time I go."

Bill's extensive experience is the significant factor in contributing to his success. In the field full-time for 17 years, he has been involved in programs, activities, research, and meetings that have characterized the development of conflict management in the United States. His training and experience as a facilitator in social conflict situations in the United States have been important.

Bill highlights a factor that many other practitioners do not: the face-to-face, real-world experience working professionally in the political sphere and related fields with the kinds of people who get involved in conflicts. This is true especially if there are public, political, ethnic, or racial issues embedded in the disputes. In his view, "Public disputes are difficult work, whether national or international, if you don't have a firsthand sense of the way people react in multiparty disputes."

Preparation means learning as much as possible in advance, realizing that "you're going to learn much of what you need to know when consultations and meetings begin. Readiness for international ADR is as much mental and attitudinal as it is substantive until you arrive. You can learn much through reading about background, history, and culture. Following an in-country newspaper is very helpful. Much international preparation follows the steps familiar to dispute resolution in North America. You plan and design meetings, negotiations, and trainings. It is critical to engage nationals in all these steps." Teams should model the multiracial composition of the nationals, especially in situations like South Africa, where there is little mixing among subgroups. Practicing collaborative behavior among ADR team members also models the behavior to be encouraged.

What is the typical international dispute resolution session? Although it is too varied to generalize, Bill does point out, "In South Africa, there are a number of racially diverse groups who tend to be politically contentious and who are accustomed to violence. However, members of these groups are willing to work when brought together. Surprisingly, the behavior of representatives of opposing groups is most civil in meetings, even when members of those same groups are killing each other in the evenings. There seems to be a certain formality in public, and, if constructive tones are set, there is a tradition of patience, listening, and being civil to one another."

Adopting the tempo of the other culture is essential for success. ADR practitioners must slow down and take into account African traditions such as storytelling. Our assumption about how to speak in meetings is to be brief and to the point, then pass the mike to the next speaker. In South Africa, people might gather together for a day or two and talk around the clock about a problem, hearing each other out, one by one, without interruption. Clearly, some basic assumptions about communication must be shifted to serve well in such a different context. Bill points out that "it is not helpful or wise to try to hurry a tribal chief along when he rises to speak."

The toughest challenge Bill identifies is not tempo, but information and understanding. He explains, "There is just so much going on, so many actors and organizations. In a place like South Africa, it's hard even to remember all the political parties, their platforms and their leaders. Gaining a mastery of history and events which bear on the disputes takes time." Therefore, it is not difficult to imagine that when he speaks of potential mistakes, he cites the tendency of some international practitioners to serve many countries. Bill emphasizes the gain in establishing relationships within one country, which may be nurtured by e-mail and phone in between visits. His view is that we owe a responsibility when we engage overseas and that we ought to be more modest about how effective we can be in a country we do not know well, particularly when we lack formal standing.

There are several important changes that Bill sees in the practice of international dispute resolution. First, there is more knowledge and receptiveness to mediation and peaceful consensus-based conflict resolution. The trend toward democratization means reformed legal systems, participatory democracy, and cultures where it is more natural to engage citizens in negotiation. This is happening not only in Africa, but in parts of Asia, South America and Latin America, Central America, Eastern Europe, and even Russia. Such development provides the context for ADR to flourish.

Second, there are more people claiming to be ADR practitioners. "Just now, there don't seem to be specialized careers in strictly international ADR, but that may become more common." Finally, in international trade, there is more interconnectedness, in the sense of relationship building in business and government. The supply of practitioners and the integration of international business should promote the spread of systems such as ADR.

The topics in dispute among practitioners named by Bill are familiar. He cites the question of how much (if any) familiarity the practitioners must have with the substance of the dispute. In addition, there is the question of how much cross-cultural awareness a conflict manager must have to deal with a dispute in another culture. Opinion differs widely on this matter.

Another disagreement relates to formality. Many U.S. mediators are trained in a formal, procedural, linear mediation model. Not all cultures subscribe to this approach. Able international conflict managers must be flexible in the way they think, frame issues, and engage in dialogue. Bill insists, "Cultural tailoring and shaping of the work is very important. You adapt what you do to whatever context or group of disputants you're working with. Sometimes, people with less training but more firsthand experience, natural interactive skills, and political sensitivity can adapt better than those who have practiced the Western model for some time."

On the sidewalk, not only in lofty international negotiation forums, international conflict managers do as much as they can at the time, realizing it will not be perfect. Natural ability may be shaped by training, but experience and in-depth knowledge of a particular culture are the essentials. Listening, a willingness to slow to the cultural tempo, concentration on one country, membership on multiracial teams—this is the composite material of Bill's sidewalk, where he walks the talk of international conflict management.

Chapter 3

Negotiation

In a situation where there is a chance for agreement, the way you negotiate can make a difference between coming to terms or not, or between an outcome that you find favorable and one that is merely acceptable. (Fisher, Ury, & Patton, 1993, p. 4)

Collaboration comes from two Latin roots—*cam* and *laborare*—which mean "to work together." It refers to the way people connect with one another, the way they work together in a mutually beneficial manner. Negotiation is the process that creates and fuels collaboration. Keltner (1987) refers to negotiation as a "peaceful procedure which reconciles and/or compromises differences and which depends on good faith and flexibility" (p. 68). It is the process that shapes United Nations agreements, that enabled Israel and Egypt at Camp David to end a centuries-old feud, and that enables people to live and work together harmoniously.

Negotiation is as much about a state of mind as it is a strategic choice for managing problems. Integrative negotiation is a constructive, problem-solving process, the goal of which is to maximize interests of both parties while protecting the relationship. Disputants who choose to negotiate begin in a spirit of co-operation and a climate of respect. Through the exchanging of information, they identify shared problems and interests. An attitude of integrative negotiation differs from bargaining (distributive negotiation) by the impact each has on disputants. The bargainer seeks to achieve goals at the expense of the other, plays games in order to gain an advantage in the processes, and coerces through demands or threats. A negotiator seeks to achieve a goal compatible with the goal of others and rarely uses threats or demands.

The bargainer approaches the resolution of differences or conflict with a different mind-set. He or she views issues with a narrow perspective and regards outcomes as fixed goals. The approach is positional, rigid, and insensitive to the interests of others. For example, in a mediation between teachers and administration in a public school, one of the teachers began the first meeting with a statement of her interests: "There is only one satisfactory solution to these problems, and that is to replace the administrators." Frequently, as in this situation, bargainers escalate conflict through personal attacks meant to weaken or neutralize competing interests. Bazerman and Neale (1992) call this mind-set the *mythical fixed pie*, where the bargainer sees a finite set of resources for which everyone must compete.

Integrative negotiation approaches conflict as a joint venture, an opportunity for mutual gain. Rubin (1991) describes this perspective as "enlightened self interest," where both parties see that it is in their best interests to help others achieve their goals (p. 4). Conflict is approached with an attitude of creativity (asking a lot of "what if" questions) and flexibility (looking for mutually beneficial trade-offs). In the school conflict described above, the mediator's response was, "Could we first look at the underlying issues that cause you to feel this way?" The angry teacher responded, "But the problem *is* the leadership." The mediator countered, "If we change the administration, you may get new administrators who do many of the same things you don't like. Wouldn't we be ahead by addressing the problems that make you unhappy?" The teacher agreed. Integrative negotiation seeks to build collaborative discussion so that in addition to meeting needs or interests, a process is created for resolving further problems. The goal is dialogue with mutually satisfying outcomes. Table 3.1 summarizes the differences between integrative and distributive negotiation.

Negotiation—A Good Option

Fisher and Ury (1981, pp. 4-6) point out that there are some good reasons for strategically choosing the mutual gains approach over the more competitive distributive approach:

1. Arguing over positions produces unwise agreements.
2. Arguing over positions is inefficient.
3. Arguing over positions endangers the ongoing relationship.

Strauss (1993) believes that the cultural trend toward win-win approaches is due to a phenomenon called *lateralization of power*. Issues are becoming more complex, authority is more distrusted or questioned, and there are more advocacy groups to support individuals who believe that they have not been treated fairly. Groups have greater capacity to block the plans of leaders or make decision making more difficult. Consensus-based, win-win discussions lateralize power between individuals or across organizations.

Table 3.1 Comparison Between Integrative and Distributive Negotiation

Integrative	*Distributive*
Collaborative	Competitive
Interest-focused discussion	Positional discussion
Problem solving	Forcing
Arguments based on merit	Bluff and intimidation
Valuing others	Devaluing of others
Win-win attitude	Win-lose attitude
Information sharing	Information hiding
Joint gains	Personal gains
Empathy and understanding	Self-focused
Joint interests	Self-interests
Power shared	Power over others

The Negotiation Process

Table 3.2 lists the phases of a negotiation process. Effective negotiation depends on the ability of parties early in the discussions to share a lot of information about needs, issues, and interests. Packages of trade-offs that meet all parties' needs depend on a high level of information sharing. Creativity and flexibility of parties generally produce the most enduring settlements.

Because negotiation reflects an attitude with which one approaches conflict, there must be core values or principles that characterize the perspective. Fisher and Ury (1981) provide insight about these in their discussion of core principles.

1. *Separate the people from the problem.* Blaming diverts energy from problem solving. Focusing on people polarizes and fuels face-saving behaviors and the need to resort to bargaining to equalize power. As people feel attacked, they build defensive walls that resist cooperation.

2. *Focus on interests, not positions.* Positions occur in statements such as, "Here's where I stand on this problem." It is difficult to persuade others to change positions. Instead, the goal should be to direct discussion toward the underlying concerns, needs, fears, and interests. To identify the underlying concerns, ask "Why?" "What leads you to say that?" or "What do you need?"

3. *Invent options for mutual gain.* Lax and Sebenius (1986) distinguish between creating and claiming value. Creating value involves sharing information so that disputants can develop trust, have as much information on the table as possible in order to create new possibilities, and discover trade-offs for mutual gain. Claiming value involves demands, exaggerations, minimizing the claims of others, and strategically concealing information. "Value creators see the essence of negotiating as expanding the pie. . . . This is aided by openness, clear communication, sharing information, creativity, an attitude of joint problem solving and cultivating common interests" (Lax & Sebenius, 1986, p. 37).

Table 3.2 Mutual Gains Negotiation Process

1. Get commitment to negotiate.
2. In prenegotiation, assess costs of no settlement.
3. Begin with an agreement on a definition of the problem.
4. Identify interests, concerns, and goals of all parties.
5. Discuss the most important issues first.
6. Explore alternatives and trade-offs without commitment.
7. Create packages that maximize gains for all parties.
8. Evaluate the costs and benefits of the packages.
9. Agree on a plan for implementation.
10. Formalize the agreement.

4. *Insist on using objective criteria.* If disputants can agree on objective, technical, or commonly accepted standards, there is less room for argument about what is fair. Used-car shopping involves Blue Book values, and house buying involves fair market value. In Human Resources, someone might ask, "What are the expectations of similar positions in other companies?" In a neighborhood dispute, the mediator might ask how similar problems were settled in other communities.

Factors That Promote Mutual Gains in Negotiation

Scholars agree on many of the behaviors that move negotiations on constructive paths for resolving disputes. The first strategy is the need to *build trust and share information.* Kimmel, Pruit, Magenau, Konar-Goldband, and Carnevale (1980) found that when people trust each other, they are less likely to engage in positional statements and threats. People are more likely to share information or express openness to trade-offs if trust is present. In a study that sampled opinions of 351 attorneys, Williams (1983) found that the most effective negotiators demonstrated cooperative patterns that include courteous and personable behavior, willingness to share information, statements with a realistic opening position, and the absence of threats.

Shapiro, Shepherd, and Cheraskin (1982) propose that trust in business negotiations occurs on three levels. The lowest level of trust is *deterrence.* Each party agrees to make small commitments. There are penalties for failure to live up to commitments. For example, in an environmental negotiation, trust in an agreement may depend on achieving reduction of toxic emissions with agreed-upon fines for failure to achieve goals. The second level of trust is based on *knowledge.* Disputants grow to trust each other as information is shared, uncertainties are resolved, or expectations and goals are explained. In workplace disputes, tensions between managers and employees tend to subside as expectations and responsibilities are clarified. The third, more advanced level of trust is called *identification.* This level is based on relationship. Confidence in the relationship is sufficient guarantee for parties to believe that commitments will be carried out. For negotiators, the issue may be less "Do I trust or don't I?" than "What do I need to guarantee my trust?"

Often, negotiators move from the sharing of information into disagreement about how interests should be met. For example, negotiations break down shortly after a federal regulator asks a farmer how he intends to comply with federal regulations about proper water usage for crops. Or an employee gets into an argument with her manager over uncompleted tasks. In such cases, negotiations break down because parties move to the generation of solutions too quickly.

A second strategy is to begin by *agreeing in principle.* Does the farmer understand that the federal regulations apply to him, or is the worker aware that she is responsible for the tasks in question? The more complex the issue, the more important it is for parties to first agree in principle before moving to problem solving.

A third strategy shared by most effective negotiators is the practice of asking *a lot of questions.* In fact, skilled negotiators ask, on average, twice as many questions when compared to average negotiators. Skilled negotiators devote 21% of their total negotiation behavior to asking questions. The questions uncover underlying issues, opportunities for options, and areas of potential agreement. In addition, questions create a perception that the negotiator is actively listening and is concerned about the interest and goals of the other parties. In a study of bank executives, Raiffa (1982) found that out of 34 behaviors demonstrated by negotiators, listening was one of the five most important. Effective negotiators do more listening, whereas average negotiators tend to do more arguing.

Jandt (1985) found that one of the most important skills of negotiators is the ability to mirror back tentative understanding. This accomplishes three goals. It makes sure that all parties are talking about the same issue, impresses others that the negotiator understands them, and encourages others to eliminate ambiguities (p. 227). Negotiators demonstrate understanding through paraphrasing, clarifying, and summarizing the contributions of others.

Many negotiators use a tactic called *tagging* to promote constructive discussion. Tagging involves calling attention to procedural or relationship behaviors that may inhibit or promote collaboration. For example, the negotiator may point out that bargaining tactics being used are discouraging one's willingness to cooperate; assumptions about motives may be inaccurate; or deviation from the agreed-upon process is causing the negotiations to bog down. At times, tagging may even involve positive aspects of the process. In these cases, the negotiator may point out the positive impact that small concessions had on cooperation, or how agreements thus far are creating a great deal of momentum toward settlement. Skilled negotiators use several tags per hour, about 6% of their total communication, compared to average negotiators, who tag about 1% of the time.

Scholars agree that planning is an essential element of most successful negotiations. One particular aspect of planning is the ability of negotiators to *generate many options* before problem-solving discussions even begin. Skilled negotiators generate five options or alternatives for every problem they can anticipate. Beginning a negotiation armed with an array of possibilities provides the negotiator more flexibility for generating a solution path or for imagining trade-offs. The rule that many negotiators follow is to be firm on goals but flexible on the means to achieve the goals.

Imagining many possibilities is linked to the practice of many negotiators of *packaging trade-offs* in their agreements. Rarely can a complex issue be reduced to a forced choice between two options. Negotiation usually involves many problems in which disputants value things differently. If the value difference is used to package mutually beneficial trade-offs, the parties achieve a balance between what they need and what they can live with. Negotiators can strategically package trade-offs based on necessity, timing for actions, tolerance to risk, kinds of investments, long-term versus short-term reward, or differences in preference.

Box 3.1 lists the opening positions and eventual trade-offs in the 1998 Communication Workers of America 15-day strike against U.S. West Communications. For the final settlement package, each side traded concessions and agreed to a union-management committee to explore and design mutually beneficial solutions for remaining issues before the next contract negotiations.

Rubin (1983b) points out, "Negotiators often find it tempting, particularly when discussions bog down and things appear not to be going the way they would like, to commit themselves to tough negotiation positions from which they swear they will never retreat" (p. 142). The assumption is that the hardened position will persuade the other party to be more flexible. This is a serious game of "chicken" in which the probability for failure increases dramatically.

Negotiators must be patient as they move toward a conflict's *break point*— that moment when parties who feel hopelessly stuck finally see possibilities for resolution. Following the sharing of information about interests and goals, tension increases to a point where parties feel like capitulating to bring the tension down or entrenching in positional statements. It is at this point, when all feels lost, that some of the most innovative, constructive solutions will occur. In negotiation training, we ask students to be patient, remain hopeful and collaborative, in spite of unbearable tension, and look for the break point at which new possibilities will emerge spontaneously.

Figure 3.1 graphically illustrates the escalation of conflict and how it then frequently moves to collaborative discussion. In the U.S. West contract negotiations, many factors collided to create the break point. The agreement occurred several days following the death of a child during a 911 power outage, one day before workers would lose their health insurance benefits, and one day before institution of a new 10-digit dialing system for the U.S. West phone area.

BOX 3.1
Example of Trade-offs in the Resolution of U.S. West Dispute

Management Proposal	*Union Proposal*	*Final Agreement*
1. Employees required to meet performance standards. Better performers can make as much as $15,000 per year in bonuses. Company needs greater quality control measures.	1. Employees penalized by not meeting standards when weather inhibits. Too much control by managers over standards. Against all such proposals.	1. Pay for performance will be voluntary. But managers allowed to monitor workers' calls to check performance. Joint committee will design new performance proposal.
2. Overtime required for 7,100 technicians during periods of peak use, power outages, and storms. It must also be required for new hires and transfers.	2. Downsizing has created too much work for too few workers. Against mandatory overtime.	2. Mandatory overtime capped at 16 hours until 2001. At that time, cap reduces to 8 hours. All workers guaranteed two 5-day work weeks per month.
3. Limit five health insurance plan options to two. Deductibles will be required on coverages and larger employee contributions.	3. No changes.	3. $25 per month individual contribution and $70 for family. Deductibles will be collected on vision and dental. Joint committee will evaluate future health insurance plans.

Issues That Influence Our Ability to Negotiate

Harvard professor Howard Raiffa (1982) identifies a number of factors that will influence a person's ability to negotiate an issue effectively.

1. To what extent are the parties monolithic? If the other side is composed of many people, they may not be in agreement about the issues or may look unfocused in their discussion with you. This lack of unity may be reflected in familiar tactics such as good cop-bad cop, with which you are subtly manipulated.

2. Is there more than one issue? Multiple issues create the need for a package agreement. There will be trade-offs in which parties get enough of what they want on some issues and take less on other issues. "When there are several issues to be jointly determined through negotiation, the negotiating partners have

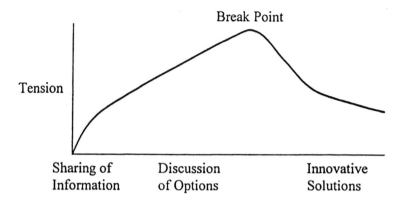

Figure 3.1.

an opportunity to considerably enlarge the pie before cutting it into shares for each side to enjoy" (Raiffa, 1982, p. 14).

3. Are there time constraints? Time can be used to motivate parties to be more cooperative if waiting will increase costs. In the school mediation discussed earlier, there was little progress in the first three group meetings. In the fourth meeting, the mediator began with the statement, "If we can't make progress today, my efforts here will be ended. You'll need to begin again with someone else leading you." About one-half hour from the end of the session, the groups broke their stalemate and accomplished more than they had in similar discussions for the past 4 years.

4. Do the group norms favor negotiation? Individuals who have learned to stall in order to get their way will continue to use that tactic as long as it works. In settings where individuals snipe insults at each other during discussions, it is difficult to develop full cooperation or trust. In groups that have a history of nonparticipation, there may be a hidden assumption that no matter what the leaders agree to publicly, they will not really change their behavior. Assumptions such as this make negotiation difficult. Some professional mediators find that in training, a significant percentage of helping individuals negotiate a mutually beneficial settlement of issues as discussions evolve. In one school mediation, during a group meeting, one of the administrators made an attacking comment toward one of the teachers. The mediator pointed out the behavior, adding, "If we are going to talk to each other that way, this process is going to take much longer. Unprofessional communication sabotages our efforts to build trust and cooperation." If there is a history of antagonism, group norms such as distrust, dishonesty, strategic posturing, unwillingness to share information, and poor listening will work against negotiation efforts.

5. Do disputants want an agreement? Willingness to cooperate with a negotiating attitude depends on having a shared goal of desiring an agreement. Contrast the difference between the car buyer who can walk away from a discussion with a dealer, and a teachers' union discussing wage increases with representatives from the state. The car buyer does not have to agree to anything. The teachers or state representatives may delay a negotiation process, but eventually, there must be an agreement. If one of the disputants has a better alternative to a negotiated settlement (more commonly known as Best Alternative to a Negotiated Agreement, or BATNA), there is less motivation to collaborate, engage in trade-offs, or be flexible. One component of negotiation is persuading disputants that they will get a better settlement in the current discussions than they will if they wait for future discussions or rely on litigation. An agreement now prevents future inconvenience or cost.

Defining Success

Success in negotiation depends on many factors. Some might not settle for anything less than achievement of goals, no matter how aspiring. Others value relationship, a minimum of stress, a fair settlement for all parties, or a foundation for future discussions. Fisher and Ury (1981) define success as an efficient process that produces satisfying results for all parties and preserves or enhances the working relationship. Susskind and Cruikshank (1987) define success as a fair, wise, and stable settlement reached in an efficient manner. They describe *efficient* as a process that uses time constructively and provides sufficient opportunity for trades.

A successful negotiation uses a process in which all parties have confidence in the results. The process involves parties who have a stake in the outcome and authority for making decisions about the issues. Too many negotiations have been sabotaged by participants who lack the authority to engage in agreements. Fisher and Ury's emphasis on relationship is important in situations where continuing discussions are necessary, such as in disputes that involve community, family, public policy, or ongoing business negotiations. As Jandt (1985) summarizes,

> The goal of any negotiation should not be merely to get to yes—not merely to bend the other party to your will by whatever means you can—but rather to get past yes by resolving the conflict in a way that serves the best interests of both parties and encourages a harmonious, long-term relationship. (p. 143)

Factors That Inhibit Effective Negotiation

The way that a negotiator frames or describes a problem frequently influences the willingness of disputants to engage in integrated negotiation. If the problem appears too complex or too overwhelming, disputants may say, "Why bother?" If disputants are allowed to maintain a blaming perspective and frame the problem as a person, there may be little motivation to engage in concessions or trade-offs. For example, in a corporate dispute, supervisors were unwilling to negotiate with their manager until the mediator suggested, "If your management chooses to replace your manager, what will stop them from replacing some of you as well?" The group became significantly more cooperative when they thought about the impact of their unwillingness to negotiate. Bazerman and Neale (1992) summarize, "To negotiate rationally, you must remember that the way in which a problem is framed or presented can dramatically alter how you perceive the value or acceptability of your alternatives" (p. 38). Box 3.2 depicts how union and management in the 1998 U.S. West strike framed issues. One of the greatest challenges facing negotiators is how they might frame issues in a collaborative, nonpolarizing manner.

Rubin (1983a) describes a phenomenon called *entrapment,* in which disputants become overcommitted to a course of action despite negative impacts. Devotion to precedents, investment of time or money, unrealistic assessment of value, or rigid aspirations can all lead disputants to refuse cooperation in spite of the losses they will incur. They become psychologically anchored to positions. The more that others try to force cooperation through threats or intimidation, the deeper they become entrenched. Competitive irrationality occurs when two disputants become polarized, psychologically anchored, and entrenched. The outcome is a destructive spiral in which neither party gains much. Rubin suggests the following as possibilities for removing anchors as barriers: listening for hidden agendas, reminding parties of the cost of no settlement, returning to objective standards and away from arbitrary aspirations, dividing involvement into lesser commitments, reframing the nature of the problem, or providing the esteem needs that others may require.

Selective perception will often inhibit negotiation. People see in the data what they want to see or hear in the words what they want to hear because it confirms their preexisting bias. Lewicki, Litterer, Mintan, and Saunders (1994) point out that negotiations are prone to bias in perceptions of the situation, the range of possible outcomes, and the likelihood of achieving the outcomes (p. 106). An important priority for the negotiator is the reduction of inaccurate perceptions or incorrect assumptions. It is not the actual differences in needs or interests, but people's perceptions of them, that largely determine the course of the negotiation. An important moment in the development of perceptions occurs as early as the opening statements of a negotiation. Research suggests that the more open, nonthreatening, and cooperative the opening statement made by the negotiator, the more trust and cooperation are expressed by the other parties (Michelini, 1971; Oskamp, 1970). Throughout the discussions, the negotiator must be aware that the statements expressing collaboration influence the selective perceptions of disputing parties.

There are many assumptions that can turn out to be incorrect as information is shared. At times, these may sabotage discussions. Negotiators make assumptions about the other party's commitment, options, resources, and motives. A few of the mistaken assumptions that occasionally create roadblocks to constructive paths in negotiation are the following:

BOX 3.2
Example of Framing Issues in a Polarizing Manner

Union Spokespeople	*U.S. West Management*
We're in a war. We've got to fight strategically.	We're dumbfounded. The union is turning its back.
The company is using a big lie strategy.	Once again, they're trying to tell a big lie rather than dealing with the issues at the table.
They want to take the negative road and gut our contract and expect us to take it.	They're playing fast and loose with the facts.
The company is engaged in a campaign of deceit with no intention of negotiating an end to the dispute.	They're trying to win the get-tough contest.

- ❏ What is good for me is bad for the other party.
- ❏ We agree on what the problem is.
- ❏ The other party is not as stubborn as I.
- ❏ Engaging in contentious tactics, such as bluffing, coercing, or manipulating, is worth the risk.
- ❏ It is only the tangible resources that count in negotiations.
- ❏ We have exhausted the possibilities for creatively solving these problems.
- ❏ Undermining the arguments of the other side will get me what I want.

Prenegotiation

A great deal of successful negotiation relies on information gathering that occurs before a negotiation begins. Many in the ADR field regard this phase as critical for later success. Stein (1989) argues that prenegotiation matters because it "permits the participants to learn about the preconditions for and possibilities of both a negotiated agreement and an alternative management of the relationship" (p. 459). Prenegotiation may uncover relationship problems that, if resolved before discussions, enhance the potential for success. Prenegotiation may reveal underlying problems (such as the financing of a solution) that could be researched before negotiations begin. Prenegotiation enables disputants to send up trial balloons about negotiating ranges and reservation points without publicly committing to solutions (Stein, 1989).

Saunders (1985) describes prenegotiation as the actual first phase of negotiations. In this phase, parties define the problem, develop a commitment to negotiate, and make arrangements for negotiations. Zartman (1989) significantly extends Saunders's insights. He views prenegotiation as an opportunity to begin transforming adversarial attitudes and positioning into more cooperative orientations. Based on principles discussed in Zartman's work, we might add the following tasks to possibilities that can occur in the prenegotiation phase:

- Parties identify negotiation as a policy option and communicate this intention to the other parties who might be involved.
- Parties shift from unilateral solutions to multilateral or mutual gains solutions.
- Parties move from adversarial behaviors to cooperative behaviors.
- Parties begin to believe that trade-offs might facilitate solutions.
- Parties evaluate costs of concessions and failure to reach a settlement before commitments need to be made.
- Parties consolidate support within their constituent groups.
- Stakeholders are selected who provide the best potential for settlement.
- Parties change the dynamics of the conflict by initiating a cease-fire for the duration of the discussions.

Who should do the prenegotiation? In unassisted negotiation, a representative from each group could meet and explore possibilities. In assisted negotiations, the facilitator or mediator could shuttle back and forth between parties.

Destructive Tactics

Occasionally, negotiators will encounter people who approach the negotiations from a distributive perspective. They see the world as eat-or-be-eaten. From this perspective, they engage in tactics that some people call dirty tricks and others call unethical behavior. For example, they may choreograph the negotiation setting. They seat the other party in a lower chair facing a window with bright sunlight. They may stretch out negotiations for hours to wear the other parties down so that the others will agree to anything just to go home. More destructive games include saying one thing publicly and the opposite privately. Or, they may communicate a willingness to negotiate when their goal is to stall. Amy (1987) warns that many people "celebrate the fact that it [negotiation] is a simple and informal process that the common citizen can participate in . . . but there is the danger that novices can easily be taken to the cleaners by more experienced opponents" (pp. 101-102).

One way to prevent being taken advantage of is to understand some of the deceptive games that unethical negotiators play. Fisher and Ury (1981) measure the ethics of negotiation tactics by asking if the tactics pass the test of reciprocity.

If tactics benefit only one side or place one party at a significant disadvantage, then they fail the test.

Dealing with tactics designed for deception or manipulation requires firm, reasonable responses. Begin by tagging the game you are seeing played. For example, "It appears that you and your partner are not in agreement about your goals or needs. This is giving me ambiguous messages. Perhaps we can take a break, and the two of you can reach some agreement about what you want." Second, you may want to warn the other side that deceptive tactics are not without cost. They may delay or prevent achieving agreement. You will stay involved in discussions as long as you believe they are being honest and genuine with you.

A few of the dirty tricks that negotiators have encountered include the following:

- *Good guy/bad guy.* One party appears friendly and cooperative. The other is adversarial and makes extreme demands. Psychologically, you will be more receptive to the requests for information and concessions by the friendlier partner. Later, you find that you have been manipulated. A variation is the good guy asking you for concessions to please the much less flexible partner.

- *Bad faith negotiating.* The negotiator expresses a commitment to collaborate and to find solutions, but in actuality, all the person is doing is stalling for time or exploring for information that might be used to advantage at a later time. A variation is the negotiator who initially agrees to points in a settlement, but later reopens each one. The goal is to get greater concessions. The other party reasons, "I've come too far to let this get in the way," so agrees to the concessions.

- *Lack of authority.* The person with whom you negotiate lacks the power to make decisions. So, all agreements must be approved by a third party with whom you are not able to have discussions. One party is kept off balance by an inability to keep commitments or changes in agreements. In addition, negotiators may be more receptive to getting any agreement they can just to complete the negotiations. If the issue is lack of authority, you might request speaking directly with someone who can make decisions about the issues. In many disputes, negotiators begin with the question, "Before we begin, let me first ask, Do you have the power to make or implement decisions if we reach an agreement?"

- *Inaccurate data.* It is the negotiator's responsibility to fully explore and question the information on which a deal will rest. Inaccurate or misrepresented information is, at some point, a component of most negotiations and can place one side at a significant disadvantage. If the deceptive tactic is a misrepresentation of information, you might ask for an impartial third party to generate more data or interpret the data for you. You might ask for objective standards or precedents with these kinds of issues.

- *Many for one.* One party makes small, inconsequential concessions early in the negotiations. As the negotiations progress, this negotiator approaches issues of concern with the attitude of "You owe me." The negotiator asks for a major concession as payback for all the concessions already made to you.

- *Information overload.* The negotiator provides so much information that others feel overwhelmed. They may not question the data because there is too much to read or understand. They may grant more power to the provider because he or she knows so much about the subject. Information overload can be used to stall negotiations or manipulate parties in a particular direction. Amy (1987) warns,

"Hidden in the masses of information will be deliberate errors, self-serving assumptions, and contradictory material" (p. 103). When inundated with data, you may want to ask for a recess to examine the data or submit the data to someone you trust to interpret it for you.

Lewicki and Litterer (1985) discuss other kinds of behavior that might be regarded as unethical or dirty tricks, including lies about information; using gifts or bribes to get opponents to soften their position; using spies to learn about confidential information; undermining opponents in the eyes of their constituency; trying to demean or humiliate an opponent through public charges; or misrepresenting credentials, reputation, or expertise (p. 326).

Massachusetts Institute of Technology professor Lawrence Susskind recommends that we not engage in reciprocal dirty tricks when we encounter them. Just because others have left the high road of ethical behavior does not mean that we must leave it as well. We always have the power to walk away or say "no" to whatever possibilities are before us. Our response should be to point out the disruptive nature of the tactics and return to a discussion about ground rules. After trust has been broken, one may need to require confidence-building measures, such as small moves or concessions, on which one can build new trust.

Deadlocks

There are times when negotiators find that parties remain positional and will not budge. One of the parties refuses to make small concessions, and creative options remain elusive. Skopec and Kiely (1994) make several suggestions about how to unfreeze deadlocked negotiations:

1. *Limit the scope of the problem.* At times, the complexity of a problem overwhelms the thinking of negotiators. Break the big problem into manageable parts, where trade-offs may be more obvious.

2. *State the other side's case.* Frequently, negotiations become a debate in which parties assume defensive postures. Unfreezing these positions can be sometimes accomplished by "stepping to their side," as Bill Ury describes it, and seeing the issue from their perspective.

3. *Focus on areas of agreement.* Negotiation discussions can become preoccupied with areas of disagreement or conflict. Summarize areas of progress and agreements, thus far, which become a foundation for a deeper level of cooperation.

4. *Take a break.* Listening, probing for information, analyzing data, and managing disagreement consume an enormous amount of energy. Occasionally, deadlock may be the result of fatigue or stress. Request a time-out for a breather or caucus in order to renew fading energy.

5. *Seek additional information.* Deadlocks are frequently caused by inaccurate assumptions that influence thinking or lack of information about alternatives. Asking for additional information from the other party or additional research about the subject may reopen the stalemate.

Professional Profile: Lawrence Susskind
Founder and President of the Consensus Building Institute

Consensus Building in Assisted Negotiations

Introduction to the Practitioner

In the arena of multiparty, multi-issue disputes, few names are better known than Larry Susskind's. Trained as an urban planner at Harvard and MIT, he entered the fray of public disputes with a clear mandate to engage citizens in participatory decision making. Unfortunately, the mandate did not come with directions, that is, Larry began his career before the theory and principles of how to engage large numbers of disputants effectively had been worked out. The more people he brought on board, the more problems there were!

Consequently, Larry went to work on the problem of what success means in multiparty disputes. He worked on how to produce an agreement that reflects the concerns of many stakeholders. He began thinking and writing about how the planner works as a broker between government and citizen action groups. As he worked on these problems, he discovered that people in labor and international relations had already explored the role of negotiation broker.

Larry joined an effort organized by Roger Fisher at Harvard Law School to unite people who were working on public disputes. The members of this group were focused on building theory from their practice of negotiation. Eventually this group coalesced into the Program on Negotiation. While continuing to teach at MIT, Larry became the Program's first director. He has continued to be involved with the Program and to develop theory informed by practice.

The concern with theory often leads to a demand for clarity in the definition of terms. According to Larry, "Those playing the role of neutral in public disputes prefer the term 'consensus building' to 'alternative dispute resolution.' While ADR may serve in some areas where the alternative to a settlement is strictly litigation, this is too narrow a term to cover multi-stakeholder disputes, where the alternative may be a strike or a war." Consensus building is a broader description that applies to the use of interest-based negotiation in varied situations.

Work of the Practitioner

Susskind is, in fact, president of the Consensus Building Institute in Cambridge, Massachusetts. At that independent, nonprofit institute, he applies interest-based negotiations in five ways. First, if clients request it, they are offered training in mutual gains negotiation. Second, clients who are already engaged in a dispute are given ideas about what the practice of negotiation entails and what role a neutral might play. Third, clients who have a pattern of repeated disputes are led through a process of conflict management design. Many consultants would conceptualize their client base in one of these three ways.

Fourth, and much less usual, Larry explains, "Evaluations are performed on negotiation outcomes. The Consensus Building Institute uses personal interviews to ascertain whether the parties are satisfied with negotiation outcomes, whether the outcomes are efficient relative to their BATNAs, and what the relationships between disputants are most likely to be in the future. What the Institute does *not* do is count the 'settlements' or assess through pencil-and-paper surveys."

Through these evaluations, theory is refined and new teachings are created. The Institute makes its findings public through a quarterly newsletter, "Consensus"; see its web page for back issues (cbi-web.org), or e-mail for further information (consensus@igc.org). Finally, the Institute offers training and takes on approximately 15 interns each semester. Most, but by no means all, of these students are registered at Harvard or MIT.

Opinions About ADR Issues

For those students of consensus building not interning at the Institute, what skills are recommended? Larry stresses the importance of first learning unassisted negotiation. In his opinion, "It is most important that future practitioners learn the theory behind the mutual gains approach. And let there be no mistake—it is not necessary to be an attorney to assist with public dispute negotiation. To the contrary, law school often produces 'trained incapacity' for this kind of practice."

Larry cites several factors underlying his success with public disputes. First, he is an academic, and as such, he appreciates the importance of a practice informed by theory. If and when the practice does not work, the theory must be reworked. Next, Larry appreciates the strength he has as a team member: "I do not expect to succeed alone in multi-issue disputes, but my knowledge of mutual gains is complemented by team members who are experts on content issues and the context of the dispute. Team members refine and customize interest-based negotiation to fit a particular dispute."

Finally, Larry pursues continuing improvement through reflection on his practice, that is to say, subjecting trial and error in negotiations to careful criticism. He conducts these reflections within his own negotiation team, with clients, and with a peer group. He feels strongly that progress in consensus building depends on the willingness of negotiators to document their experiences and share them with other practitioners.

Preparation, or prenegotiation, is the most critical phase for negotiators. Larry asserts, "No conflict should be addressed until the assisting neutral has met privately with representatives from each of the stakeholder groups." The neutral then assesses the conflict and summarizes the findings. A plan is proposed, based on what type of conflict is diagnosed, what timing is considered appropriate, and what resources are required to implement. Preserving anonymity, the unattributed findings and the proposed plan are shared with the key stakeholders. The question for those involved becomes, "Would you participate in such an interest-based negotiation?" Based on participant input, the draft plan is improved, and the neutral best suited to assist this dispute is selected.

Risk controversies are typical for Larry's practice in assisted negotiation. The dispute may center on siting controversial facilities or substances, changing policies, creating standards, or crisis management. There are usually 50-60 parties involved who negotiate over the course of 1½ to 2 years. Ordinarily, the key stakeholders meet monthly, with committee work taking place between meetings. The process usually concludes with a written agreement that often takes months to complete.

Larry often uses a parallel approach with public negotiations. For instance, when working toward an international agreement with 160 countries on the issue of climate change, there are public sessions in which speakers maintain their country's position. Larry tells us that, "Concurrently, I am privately working with the key stakeholders. In an off-the-record process, I am leading participants through the basic steps of mutual gains, beginning with prenegotiation, identifying interests, generating options, and drafting an agreement. In this example, because of the number of participants and the complexity of the problem, this negotiation may take a very long time."

What accounts for success in public negotiations? As noted earlier, careful conduct of prenegotiation or the assessment stage is fundamental. Also, there must be adequate representation by key stakeholders. Neutrals must have ascertained who should be at the table, and participating stakeholders must enjoy credibility within their groups. In addition, a skilled mediation team must be on board and functioning well together. Finally, the public negotiation must be financed adequately. With reference to the climate change negotiation discussed above, each informal workshop costs hundreds of thousands of dollars. Unless sufficient resources are provided, such large, multi-issue gatherings will not achieve their potential.

On the other hand, Larry reminds us that stakeholders may bring challenges as well. "When key stakeholders have no background with consensus building, they often fear entering into negotiation for fear of diluting their authority. If their experience with distributive negotiation is a zero-sum model, they only understand competition, not collaboration. Enormous effort by neutrals is required to convince them that they will have a hand in shaping any proposal for settlement and can always walk away from the table."

Another serious challenge arises when the heat of conflict clouds clear thinking. Getting people in the midst of high emotion to agree on using a neutral can be quite difficult. When opinions are sharply polarized, agreeing with the other side on anything, including the desirability of assisted negotiation, is problematic.

Larry says, "Dealing with the press is a huge headache. To begin with, few journalists have a precise knowledge of consensus building and cover negotiations with muddled understanding of what the neutral is attempting to do. In addition, most journalists do not share the sense of 'educative responsibility.' Most reporters do not conceive of their job as introducing the public to consensus building. On the contrary, they are looking to fill in the names of the stereotypical 'good guy vs. bad guy' story line."

Larry's reflective learning process ensures that he has considered his mistakes and learned from them. Interestingly, they all relate to that critically important prenegotiation period. He recounts mistakes that were "client inspired," that is, acquiescence to pressures from clients. For instance, "I was persuaded by one client that time pressures were so critical that the assessment phase should be skipped—with consequent difficulties which would have been foreseen in a careful diagnosis." In another instance, he feels he did not work hard enough to engage a key stakeholder to participate in the negotiation. As a result, the excluded stakeholder was able to undermine the implementation of the final agreement. Finally, he made a mistake in proceeding when a client was unwilling to commit adequate finances, and Larry ended up volunteering a substantial amount of time.

With regard to changes in the practice of public negotiations, Larry sees tremendous growth. "From a $500,000 business only 5 years ago, the Consensus Building Institute is now worth many times that amount. This trend is international; there are at least 50 countries that are applying consensus building to public disputes. There is no indication that this spread is slowing."

Training and education have institutionalized the demand for and the supply of assisting neutrals. For instance, state offices of dispute resolution have become commonplace in a rather brief period, with public dispute management growing faster than other sectors. However, because of the growing opportunities for training, the supply of neutrals is growing faster than the demand for them. As mentioned earlier, there has been growth in the theoretical underpinnings that support practice.

Although growth is common in many areas of public dispute negotiation, there are a number of debates among its practitioners. Primary is the controversy over the role and responsibility of the neutral. Larry says, "I subscribe to an activist approach, taking those actions which will move negotiations for-w ... it stakeholders or helping them raise the

on the need for assessment. Some negotia-
is pressed for time. As mentioned earlier,
ent is fundamental to success.

oach to the press. Some try to manage re-
negotiations whenever possible and sug-
from stakeholders. Larry subscribes to a
hy of working with the press is 'engage-
erstand the media's needs and accommo-
so had success separating publishers and
on are likely to differ.

ow to measure success in the management
nce to practical success factors, such as the
scussion of evaluations performed by the
are whether or not the parties are satisfied
or not the outcomes are efficient, and what
likely to be in the future.

ut the notion that neutrals should aim for
ticipants should walk away from the con-
rnalistic and manipulative to me. I am con-
e of success creates unreasonable expecta-
le labels his own approach to measuring
ic.

n of these debates, there is no debating the
ed the practice of public dispute manage-
nd theory building. He has been an institu-
tual gains negotiation is a field that has
ohistication. Larry Susskind can take pride
tributions to assisted negotiations.

rofile: Mark Udall
se of Representatives

In a legislative body, the ability to find common ground is the sine qua non of creating acceptable law. State and national legislatures depend on the aptitude for and the practice of negotiation. Power bases for legislative negotiators include seniority, policy expertise, relationships with fellow legislators, and a basic understanding of how bills are passed. Legislators who possess these power sources can shape and promote bills that are more likely to pass.

Experienced politicians regard politics as the art of the possible, practicing that art by informing themselves of the facts, developing an understanding of the multiple perspectives from which opposition is likely to come, and shaping compromises that will be acceptable to all. Most bills are shaped in the back rooms through reliance on these and other applications of the art. By the time a bill reaches the committee level, attitudes toward it have hardened, and further negotiation is seldom possible.

Successful legislators maintain collegiality (at least in public), do not take opposition to their positions personally, and know when to collaborate and when to push back. The level of maturity demanded for legislative accomplishment is high and somewhat paradoxical; to win office, legislators must demonstrate that they tower over opponents in wisdom and ability. To operate, they must be able to keep their egos in close check, especially if they represent the minority party.

Introduction to the Practitioner

For many years, Mark Udall served as a representative from the minority party of the Colorado state legislature. Currently, he serves as U.S. congressman representing Colorado. Mark is the son of Morris Udall, a longtime congressman from Arizona who ran second to Jimmy Carter in the 1976 Democratic primaries. In addition, he is the nephew of Stewart Udall, the popular Secretary of the Interior in the Kennedy and Johnson cabinets. Stewart's son and Mark's cousin, Tom Udall, was the Attorney General of New Mexico; later, he was elected to Congress from that state. In addition to his own experience in Colorado, Mark has a strong family history of experience and relationships upon which to draw.

Mark notes that negotiation skills may be developed through a variety of experiences. Although the Rocky Mountains are located far from the state capitol, "Some of my most formative learning about negotiation took place when I was a student on a Colorado Outward Bound course. On those courses, students are required to come to consensus on decisions which affect them all, such as whether to attempt a peak climb given weather conditions. This is a 'no king' situation, where multiple stakeholders and the lack of formal hierarchy are conditions which require group negotiation skills."

Later, Mark returned to Outward Bound as an instructor, course director, and, ultimately, school director. In that position, he often negotiated with multiple stakeholders such as field and office staff, trustees, and contractors. He notes the importance of collaborative decision making in long-term planning for the organization, where both the content and the relationship-building aspects are critical. These experiences prepared him well for the content/relationship work he does as a legislator with colleagues, members of the executive branch, citizen's groups, and lobbyists. His concern for protection of the environment and the family tradition of public service prompted him to run for office.

Work of the Practitioner

In terms of recommending training, Mark believes in on-the-job training for using ADR in the legislative arena. There is some assistance through seminars held by the National Council of State Legislatures (NCSL), and he emphasizes the need for extensive personal experience with participative leadership. However, in the end, "there is no way around 'immersion dunking' for the novice legislator."

Mark believes that his own strengths lie in several areas. "Foremost, I build relationships with the people I work with, beyond work issues. I find a way to respect my colleagues, regardless of where they are on the political spectrum, since it's impossible to anticipate when or where mutual interests might develop." He cites the example of cosponsoring a bill with a fellow legislator who had a 100% record of voting against environmental legislation, freedom of reproductive choice, and other issues Mark has consistently supported. However, they came together on supporting (successfully) a bill to equalize medical payments for drugs that treat mental illness.

Second, Mark is deeply engaged in the value of this work and stimulated by the multiple issues that are embedded in it. He notes his ability to focus on the merits of an issue, as opposed to personalizing the conflict. Although the legislative setting may be unique, the factors that predispose successful negotiation are the same as in other arenas.

"Preparation for negotiation in a legislative session requires a great deal of research on the content of the bill, as well as the anticipated support or opposition of the many stakeholders who may have an interest. Lobbyists are often useful; even those who represent the other side may have facts and figures which build perspective. Citizens and advocacy groups often make significant contributions to my understanding and ability to move a bill forward."

Mark described a bill, typical of those he has sponsored, which proposed an increase in the fee ($30-$45) levied on out-of-state hunters. The number of hunters had risen dramatically, and one purpose of this bill was to let market regulation achieve some reduction. Another goal was to bring Colorado's fee close to that demanded by neighboring states. There were many meetings involving landowners, hunters, environmental organizations, and state and local wildlife departments. Mark would not recommend the bill unless there was 100% consensus among these groups and their representatives. Eventually, the bill was successful, largely because of many meetings in which the various interests were served.

The essential success elements were listed in the beginning of this chapter: knowing multiple perspectives, avoiding being wedded to a position as opposed to an interest (carry, don't marry a bill), and checking one's ego. "Specific skills which are associated with success are writing amendments to satisfy reservations; speaking articulately for one's point; and possessing expertise in a particular content area, such as environmental preservation. Relationship building begins and ends the list. Without it, all the other skills are devalued."

The challenges of applying ADR in the legislature have also been mentioned: finding common ground, knowing when to collaborate and when to push back, and having a reduced power base by belonging to the minority party. Even though he notes it as a strength, Mark admits to feeling challenged by the temptation to take some conflicts personally.

Having served two terms in the state legislature, Mark is clear about the learning curve that precedes the skills and practices mentioned above. "As a freshman legislator, I did not know the 'players' (his fellow legislators) or 'the rules' (the practices mentioned above that precede the passage of a successful bill). My freshman mistakes were an inevitable part of the learning process, which are less to be regretted than to be learned from." He reflects on his naïveté as a legislative beginner, and he remarks on how tough the process is; even the most powerful members get "rolled" occasionally. His mistakes were those of the freshman legislator who must learn the process and the players in the trenches.

Opinions About ADR Issues

Changes? Mark is impressed that even the "good ol' boys" are overheard using the terms and concepts of principled negotiation. It may be that consensus values have infiltrated all institutions, including legislatures. Are there disagreements? It is hard to imagine how our legislative system could operate without negotiation and some degree of consensual decision making. However, it is still win or lose when the final vote is taken.

Mark speculates that negotiation in a legislative session is more difficult than most, because there is "no king." Without a final decision-making authority, negotiation will be less structured and more diffuse than other organizational applications of ADR. As long as legislators remember to carry, not marry, the bill, they will often be successful, but "carry" describes a set of skills that is sophisticated and demands a heightened maturity. Fortunately, Mark Udall can not only describe the process, but practice it in a citizen forum.

Professional Profile: Mike Jenkins
Community Development Coordinator, San Diego

The Search for Creative Options

Introduction to the Practitioner

ADR practitioners in business, professional, and family settings use principled negotiation in various ways and at various times in their cases. Mike Jenkins is one person who uses principled negotiation every day with business, government, and citizens. He has been involved in economic development for more than 20 years, putting him squarely into the arena of multiple players and multiple interests. He is the Business Development Coordinator for the City of San Diego, California. Mike also teaches negotiation at the University of San Diego School of Law.

Work of the Practitioner

Mike says, "The thrust of my work is to encourage and oversee economic development for the city." Working with many partners in large projects, Mike must manage with scant government resources, yet many governmental regulations. Success depends on his ability to foster collaboration; discover common interests behind diverse positions; and generate creative options to cope with local, state, and federal regulations. Principled negotiation is his tool in this complex and difficult arena.

Opinions About ADR Issues

For training the beginning negotiator, Mike emphasizes the need to shift paradigms, from the "hard bargainer" posture to reframing the negotiation as a win-win communication. Given the importance he assigns to retooling the usual competitive approach, it is not surprising that he puts a premium on acquiring and polishing communication skills such as listening and understanding others. "I have been successful because I listen carefully, and also because I can be open-minded about how to get there." Often, Mike finds that success is associated with encouraging others to be more flexible and creative as well.

Preparing for a specific negotiation is seldom possible for Mike, partly because time does not allow and partly because he has repeated experience with a few key issues. When he does need to prepare, he uses his personal network to check references, and he also explores web pages. When some of his staff are also involved in a negotiation, Mike will spend some time coaching them before they begin. General preparation involves staying on top of local business issues and changes in laws and regulations, as well as maintaining important colleague contacts.

A typical negotiation session for Mike might be to offer an "off the shelf" incentive program to a business; this occurs in his practice approximately 40% of the time. For instance, he has some standard questions that help him assess the viability of a project, such as, "Do they qualify?" "Is the time frame realistic?" "What market are they attempting to tap?" "In what sense is this a unique product?" and "What amount of sales tax would be generated by this project if it were successful?"

The remaining 60% of his sessions are unique. In multiparty negotiations, it is often difficult to determine who has control of different parts of the project. Mike may be the principal negotiator, or he may facilitate the discussion. If he is facilitating, he will pay particular attention to hidden agenda and emotional issues.

"Conveying to the other parties what the city's regulations are and why they exist is often a critical element in the success of a negotiation. Sometimes, success depends on the business being forthright about its interests." A frequent challenge to conducting a successful negotiation is business representatives who have hostile, antigovernment perspectives. Those who project this attitude onto city government representatives can be difficult to deal with. Mike cited his earlier reactions to such hostility when asked about mistakes. Understandably, it is difficult to remain calm and in control when an attack feels personal. He claims that, "I have learned from experience to depersonalize these attacks and focus on common goals."

Another different but discouraging challenge comes when the parties have worked out an agreement in principle, but then laws are changed that affect the substance of the agreement. Many hours of negotiation are lost, the sense of progress is inhibited, and the timing of the project is delayed. A related hitch might be the assignment of dollar amounts before a general agreement is concluded. "In my experience, the astute negotiator waits until the agreement in principle is achieved before he or she fixes prices. Otherwise, the general agreement may be more difficult to obtain."

Mike reports that changes in the field of negotiation involve the growth of teaching principled negotiation. Most notably, three law schools in the San Diego area are teaching negotiation, mediation, and the law relative to ADR. These courses are relatively recent additions.

Mike points to the persistence of the "hard bargainer" approach to negotiation as another reason why agreements are sometimes not achieved. Although adoption of principled negotiation is growing among professionals, there is still debate about whether it can be as successful as proponents hope. On this issue, we may be certain of one thing: Mike Jenkins will continue to practice, teach, and champion the cause of principled negotiation.

Chapter 4

Mediation

Create a space where it is safe for people to speak about what is important and meaningful. (Ellinor & Gerard, 1998, p. 180)

When problem solving or negotiations break down, disputants frequently seek the help of a third party to help them resolve their differences. In one of the earliest recorded mediations, Moses went to the top of Mount Sinai to intercede between the early Israelites and God. During the Middle Ages, the Catholic Church served as a prominent center for mediation activity in Western Europe. In early colonial American history, Puritans and Quakers used both voluntary and involuntary dispute resolution processes to manage conflict in their communities. In 1879, representatives from the Iroquois, Delaware, Cherokee, Choctaw, and Osage Indian tribes met in a ceremony called the "Medicine Wheel," in which they engaged in a process for discussing differences.

Since the 1970s, the percentage of cases going to trial has been in a steady decline, largely because of the growing number of cases settled out of court. Contributing to this decline are *Fortune* 500 companies, who currently have a formalized agreement that they will not take each other to court without first attempting mediation. Ten companies in the food industry, including General Mills, Ralston Purina, and Kellogg, have agreed to mediate any trademark, packaging, or managing disputes that occur among them. They cited corporate image and customer good will as the primary reasons behind the agreement (Singer, 1994).

In a survey of 1,500 firms, the General Accounting Office found that 90% of U.S.-based firms with 100 or more employees routinely used some form of ADR process to resolve disputes (74.2% negotiation, 47% mediation, 9.9% arbitration). In an analysis of 449 cases, distributed among contract disputes (36%), personal injury (36%), property damage (2%), environmental issues (1%), and other (13%), Brett, Bargness, and Goldberg (1996) found an overall success rate of 78% for mediations. Compared to arbitration, mediation was less expensive, both in time and money, and was perceived as fairer by disputing parties. Many companies, including GE, Toyota, Wells Fargo, Chrysler, Citibank, and Coors, have established their own mediation systems to handle employee or customer problems.

The U.S. Environmental Protection Agency (EPA) institutionalized mediation in the late 1980s. Since 1991, the number of mediated cases has tripled. In a study of 177 cases involving environmental disputes between 1970 and 1990, University of Colorado researchers found that the companies who collaborate with the EPA come out financially ahead of companies that choose litigation ("The Price of Being Green," 1998, p. 14G).

The Civil Justice Reform Act, passed in 1990, directs all federal courts to consider the use of ADR to reduce the costs and delays of litigation. From 1990 to 1995, the Administrative Dispute Resolution Act required all federal agencies to "offer prompt, expeditious and inexpensive means of resolving disputes as an alternative to litigation in the federal courts"; provide employees with ADR training; and develop policies for the use of ADR. Currently, the U.S. Department of Labor has used mediators to resolve labor-management disputes through the Commission of Conciliation, later renamed the Federal Mediation and Conciliation Service. Currently, there are more than 20,000 trained mediators who serve in community mediation centers in 48 U.S. states. Former Harvard President Derek Bok (1983) says that the challenge of the decades ahead

> will lie in tapping human inclinations toward collaboration and compromise rather than stirring our proclivities for competition and rivalry. If lawyers are not leaders in marshaling cooperation and discovering mechanisms which allow it to flourish, they will not be at the center of the most creative social experiment of our time. (p. 12)

Mediation Is . . .

Mediation is a process in which a third party—who is impartial, has no stake in the outcome, and has no power to impose a decision—guides disputants through a nonadversarial discussion process that has as its goal the settling of disputes. Goldberg, Sander, and Rogers (1992) point out that "mediation is usually a by-product of failure—the inability of disputants to work out their own differences. Each party typically comes to mediation locked in a position that the other(s) will not accept" (p. 105). Success of mediation depends on the disputants' willingness to accept the mediator's role as a process expert for resolving differences, as well as disputants' willingness to share information that might lead to a mutually beneficial agreement. Bush and Folger (1994) add, "The mediation process contains within it a unique potential for transforming people—engendering moral growth—by helping them wrestle with difficult circumstances and bridge human differences, in the very midst of conflict" (p. 2).

The mediation session provides a setting that alters how outcomes are achieved. First, the mediation setting serves as a *safe context* for sharing information that might not otherwise be shared. Disputants feel protected as the mediator minimizes threatening behavior, regulates the length of time people talk, and specifies the manner in which disputants treat each other. Second, the mediation context *changes the focus of discussion* from positional statements to interest statements that express needs, concerns, and fears. Discussions based on merits of choices have a greater potential for creating durable and long-lasting solutions than do discussions characterized by defensive positions and blaming. Additionally, the focus changes as each party expresses commitment to engage in assisted negotiation. Agreement to participate in mediation symbolically communicates to other parties a willingness to resolve differences.

Third, the mediation context provides a setting in which a neutral party who is emotionally uninvolved with the dispute is able to *identify and clarify the central or underlying issues* of a complex situation. The thinking of quarreling parties often becomes distorted by their emotional involvement. They become overwhelmed by the complexity of the situation, and this prevents them from seeing ways out of a stalemate. As an impartial third party, the mediator provides an objective, outsider's look at what is keeping parties stuck in destructive, unproductive patterns of conflict. A fourth factor is the absence of a leader who might impose a solution on the disputants. Guided by a process expert, the disputants have an *opportunity to assume greater responsibility* for finding ways to resolve differences. Because disputants make significant contributions to potential solutions, there is greater possibility that they will suspend hostilities or implement an agreement to which they contributed.

Donahue (1991) describes four phases that occur in third-party interventions in which agreements are likely to occur. Mediators begin with a period of *orientation* in which parties learn about the process, the ground rules, and the role of the mediator. From orientation, parties move to *sharing background information*. In this phase, parties tell their stories and state their goals for the process. This is followed by the *processing of issues,* in which parties respond to points of difference, provide reasoning about why they favor particular options, and clarify underlying issues that may have been overlooked earlier in the discussion. The final phase involves *proposal development*, in which disputants actively negotiate differences, engage in trade-offs, compromise, and accommodate.

Mediation Goals

Interviews with mediators reveal a variety of goals. Cupach and Canary (1997) point out, "While there is agreement concerning the basic principles that define mediation, the goal of the process is a matter of some dispute" (p. 207). Mediator styles range from very *directive,* when the goal is reaching an agreement, to *nondirective,* which emphasizes dialogue, relationship, and organizational change. Of importance is awareness that the mediator's choice of goals has concrete effects on techniques chosen.

The most common goal of mediators is reaching an agreement that will *resolve differences* or end conflict. Mediators from a wide range of disciplines view problem solving as the ideal orientation for managing conflict. Scholars emphasize the importance of this orientation in business management (Blake & Mouton, 1964; Pruitt & Lewis, 1977), psychology (Likert & Likert, 1976; Pruitt & Rubin, 1986), communication (Borisoff & Victor, 1989; Putnam & Poole, 1987), and law (Fisher & Ury, 1981). Mediators focus on problem-solving work in contexts such as families, labor unions, businesses, governmental groups, and churches. Through assisted negotiation, parties resolve differences and form agreements about specific, well-defined problems. The goal is an efficiently produced *agreement, either in principle or formally written,* that will be both durable and beneficial to disputants. Table 4.1 summarizes the range of goals frequently chosen by mediators.

In a review of literature about successful mediations, Folger et al. (1993) found that mediators often play a major role in *breaking attack/defend communication cycles* that create stalemates. The task here is to manage the discussion between disputants in a way that minimizes threats and fears. Among the ways that mediators accomplish this task are (a) emphasizing their impartial role, (b) equalizing the parties' communication by performing in a referee-like role, and (c) reframing disputants' hostile or blaming language (Tracy & Spradlin, 1994). The assumption is that if the destructive cycle can be broken, the parties possess sufficient skill to resolve conflict. Mediator Brian Muldoon (1996) describes this task as one of dynamic containment, where hostilities between disputants are stabilized so that basic dynamics that fuel the conflict can be changed. He argues that this is accomplished by changing the conflict into a dispute and then turning the dispute into negotiating a deal.

Facilitating dialogue is a third goal expressed by mediators. Mediators with this focus describe their work as facilitated negotiation. The task is to help disputants figure out for themselves what the problem is, what they want to do about it, and how they might prevent the problem from recurring. In addition, the task is to reframe communication from "either-or" to "both-and" and from "me" to "we." Mediation changes the way people relate to each other. These mediators emphasize process, communication, and the importance of relationship. Kolb and Associates (1994) report that

> They see themselves as behind-the-scenes catalysts or orchestrators of the parties' own coping and problem solving skills . . . [who] foster in the parties a more immediate sense of ownership and a better foundation for dealing with each other in the future. (p. 477)

The most far-reaching of the goals expressed by mediators is *facilitating organizational change.* This is a difficult, complex, and hard-to-measure goal. Kolb and Associates (1994) describe these mediators as facilitators of change who es-

Table 4.1 The Range of Mediation Goals

Facilitate organizational change	Create process for dialogue	Break destructive cycles	Agreement in principle	Formal written agreement

pouse transformational vision. These mediators work in settings such as community groups, international relations, and large organizations. The goal is to create fundamental changes in people or processes so that conflict is managed more effectively.

Mediators will often have primary and secondary goals. For some, reaching an agreement is primary, although they hope that they can create dialogue that prevents future problems. Other mediators downplay achievement of specific agreements and speak of the importance of creating dialogue for building relationships and trust. But these same mediators may list as a secondary goal the breaking of destructive cycles or an agreement about how decisions will be made or conflict resolved. Context often directs the choice of primary or secondary goals. For example, in the case of violence, an agreement to suspend hostility must be first but may be followed by an emphasis on dialogue or altering the interaction patterns. In environmental mediation, a primary goal may be to establish dialogue between parties, with a secondary goal of progress toward an agreement in principle.

Conditions Necessary for Mediation

There are many variables that influence the mediator's ability to successfully mediate a conflict. Among them are the skills and past experience of the mediator. But there is also a set of conditions that brings the disputants to mediation, and this can influence the success of the process. The following list summarizes a few of the factors that must be present for mediation to have a high potential for success.

- ❑ The parties have reached a stalemate or crisis and are willing to allow a third party to help them resolve the dispute.
- ❑ The parties express a willingness to engage in collaborative discussion about the issues.
- ❑ The interests or goals of the parties are interdependent so that they can help themselves by helping each other.
- ❑ Participation is voluntary, and parties have the power to create a mutually agreeable settlement.
- ❑ Disputants are willing to suspend hostilities, threats, and intimidation during the mediation process.

❑   All parties who contribute to the dynamics of the conflict will be included in the discussions.

❑   The mediator is regarded as acceptable to all parties.

Sander and Goldberg (1994) propose that mediation will be most successful when disputants want to minimize financial costs that may be incurred with legal remedies, prefer a speedy settlement, favor a private and confidential setting, and want to maintain a relationship with the other party. The mediation process gives disputants greater control over the options and outcomes than might otherwise be available. Parties are less likely to settle when fundamental issues of principle are involved, when there are differing interpretations of facts or laws, when the dispute is linked to other disputes, or when there is the prospect of a large payoff (Sander & Goldberg, 1994).

Political science professor Douglas Amy (1987) proposes that in larger mediations involving many parties or in public disputes, successful mediations are more likely to occur in situations where

❑   Disputants begin with common values or interests

❑   There exists a relative balance of power between parties

❑   The dispute is confined to a small geographic area with a well-defined group of participants

❑   The dispute is not confined to either-or choices

❑   Disputants genuinely want to reach an agreement.

Although Amy's criteria are targeted at large groups, the conditions may apply to many of the other settings where mediation occurs as well.

Core Values or Principles

There are a number of principles that guide successful mediators. The following list summarizes studies that looked at values most common to the best mediators.

Impartiality—Inevitably, mediators bring their own biases and predispositions, but these beliefs need not unduly influence the course of a mediation. Mediators may not be neutral, but they can be perceived as impartial. Disputants will demonstrate more guarded communication with mediators whom they regard with suspicion. Susskind and Cruikshank (1987) conclude that "the mediator must submerge his or her sense of what is best and focus instead on the disputing parties' own measure of success" (p. 163).

Empathy—Parties who feel judged will become defensive, which is a barrier to achieving integrative solutions. The best mediators display empathy at appropriate points to let parties know that their concerns matter. When parties feel heard, there is a greater chance that they will be candid with their contributions and more confident about the process. Goldberg et al. (1992) suggest, "An empathic mediator conveys respect to the parties, doesn't register approval or disapproval of what is being said, refrains from providing unsolicited advice and does not interrupt" (p. 106). In an analysis of labor mediators, Honeyman (1988) concluded that each of the mediators in his study took steps to establish empathy with disputants and displayed a willingness to hear parties talk about matters of concern, both related to and not related to the case at hand.

Effectiveness as a Questioner—Successful mediators are adept at asking probing and clarifying questions. They ask insightful questions that uncover concerns and interests that underlie positional statements. Questions are used to teach rather than lecture (Susskind & Cruikshank, 1987), expose inconsistency rather than openly confront, and demonstrate understanding rather than argue.

Valued Reputation—Two related attributes of the best mediators are good reputations and demonstrated records of success. Once a mediator loses a reputation for being fair, honest, genuinely concerned, and impartial, it takes a lot of work to rebuild it. For selecting a qualified mediator, Susskind and Cruikshank (1987) list as criteria background, affiliation, record, and reputation.

Confidentiality—The ability to function effectively heavily relies on the ability to honor the confidentiality of information shared by disputants. This includes information shared privately in a caucus and information shared with others in the community after the mediation is completed. A mediator serves as a safe listener and one with whom parties can share information that they would not otherwise share publicly. Exceptions to this principle occur in situations where child abuse is revealed or laws have been broken.

Process Skills—Because the level of conflict is high when parties come to mediation, disputing parties expect the mediator to use processes that manage tension and destructive conflict behaviors. Haynes (1994) explains, "The more coherent and organized the process, the easier it is for participants to arrive at solutions that are mutually appropriate for them" (p. 1). Yarborough and Wilmot (1995) extend this point further to conclude, "How well the mediator conducts the process helps determine whether or not the parties reach agreement, the durability of the agreement and the satisfaction of the disputing parties" (p. 8).

In a study that involved characteristics of mediators in labor disputes, Landsberger (1956) found that successful mediators also possessed

- An appropriate sense of humor
- The ability to act unobtrusively in conflict
- The ability to create the perception of "being with" disputing parties and being concerned about their well-being
- Persistence and patience
- Specific knowledge about the subject area in which they are mediating.

Mediators demonstrate a wide range of skills for helping people resolve their conflict. But lest mediators believe that success depends entirely on how well they do, they must be aware of an additional factor. Rubin and Brown (1975) point out that the mere presence of a third party who is independent of parties in a dispute serves as a significant factor in the settling of disputes. Often, the role of a third party is to get parties talking *constructively*, and then get out of the way while *they* resolve their differences.

Mediator Roles

There has been a great deal of research about the roles of a mediator. The types of intervention and needs of disputing parties often guide which roles take precedence. Some of the most important roles served by mediators include the following:

- Legitimizer who encourages parties to recognize the right of others to be involved in negotiations
- Agent of reality who helps build a reasonable and implementable settlement and who questions and challenges parties who have unrealistic goals
- Process facilitator who structures and guides the mediation session
- Catalyst who stimulates discussion and who encourages parties to see problems from a variety of viewpoints
- Trainer who educates parties about the processes
- Resource expander who links parties to outside experts and resources that might aid the process (based on roles suggested by the American Arbitration Association).

In addition, a mediator frequently serves as a *motivator* who encourages parties to keep negotiating or who identifies incentives to preserve momentum. There is a variety of opinion about how far mediators should go in order to motivate. Some remind parties of the cost of no settlement. Others orchestrate small concessions or pressure parties to look more closely at particular alternatives. Mediators who are more settlement-oriented may feel a need to intervene more than mediators who see their task as promoting dialogue.

As a *communication bridge*, the mediator serves as a conduit for the safe passage of information between disputants. At times, this means reframing emotionally charged, toxic language that might further polarize disputing parties. At other times, this might mean shuttling between parties as a messenger. Moore (1996) recommends that mediators reduce adversarial language by "referring to conflicts as problems, positions as viewpoints, parties as your group, and negotiations as discussions in order to depolarize and neutralize value-laden and conflict-oriented terminology" (p. 181). In addition, complaints can be reframed as requests and "my interests" can be reframed to "our interests." Goldberg et al. (1992) recommends encouraging parties to understand each other's views and clarifying differences of perceptions about interests and goals. The ability to manage the communication process may be the single most important skill that determines mediator effectiveness.

Mediation involves a series of discussions within which parties negotiate an end to disputes or satisfaction of their interests. Within this discussion process, a mediator may serve in the role of *procedural marshal* (Karambayya & Brett, 1989). As marshal, the mediator maintains boundaries between disputants so that threats and power imbalances are discouraged. Davis and Salem (1984) propose that it is the mediator's responsibility to interrupt intimidating behaviors that

Table 4.2 Mediation Process

1. Introductions
   —Explain mediation and mediator's role
   —Introduce parties
   —Establish ground rules
   —Agree on an agenda
2. Share information
   —Review context of problem
   —Hear parties tell their stories
   —Share and clarify interests
3. Generate options
   —Engage in negotiations and trade-offs
   —Select best option
4. Draft agreement
5. Decide on how agreement shall be implemented
6. Make plans for later evaluation after implementation

might inhibit constructive discussion. Table 4.2 describes the typical phases of a mediation process.

Mediation Process

Introductions

In the first phase of a mediation, the mediator builds confidence and encourages commitment to the mediation process. This is accomplished by explaining the goals and expectations of a collaborative process, the role of the mediator, and the ground rules that will guide discussions. Two of the strengths of the mediator's role are the mediator's impartiality and the confidentiality of discussions. These factors should be emphasized in the opening statement. Typical ground rules for a mediation might be the following:

- ❏ Only one person speaks at a time.
- ❏ No interruptions while someone else is speaking.
- ❏ No personal attacks will be allowed.
- ❏ Information shared during the mediation session will be treated as confidential.

When deemed necessary by mediator or parties, a private caucus may be requested. The ground rules offer predictability and safety for discussions. After the mediator shares them, they should be followed with two questions: "Are there any further rules that you would like to add?" and "Will you agree to abide by these principles during our session together?"

During the opening statements, the mediator will also emphasize the informal nature of discussions. There are no tape recorders or formal minutes. Discussions are expected to be honest, open, and problem solving.

The mediator will ask participants to agree on an agenda. There are at least four ways that a mediator might establish an agenda:

1. Following a list of concerns that were presented to him or her by the parties prior to mediating the session
2. Discussing concerns one at a time, as they are identified, during the problem-solving phase
3. After all interests are identified, having parties rank them in terms of importance, to be discussed in an order closest to shared priorities
4. Having parties alternate presentation of issues of highest priority

To get buy-in for the process, it is essential for mediators to involve parties in establishing the agenda. Yarborough and Wilmot (1995) state, "It has been our experience that framing and ordering the agenda set the stage for transforming negative conflict into a productive experience. Agreeing on priorities begins the process of cooperation that disputes have undermined" (p. 120).

Information Sharing

Discussing a problem in terms of fears, concerns, and interests is certainly the center of a mediation. This phase (described by many as the storytelling phase) offers the mediator the opportunity to model active listening for parties and encourage constructive negotiation about the issues. It is during this time that the mediator will attempt to expose underlying interests that parties, until now, have been reluctant to disclose.

Occasionally, the problem-solving phase includes the venting of emotions. One case involved a board of vice presidents that had resisted working together. There was such an emotional wall that it was difficult to identify the problems that prevented them from working together effectively. After several hours of little progress, the intermediary offered, "We've gone round and round these issues, and we don't seem to be making any progress. What's really going on here?" (This is a tagging response; see Chapter 2). One of the vice presidents spoke of her anger toward another. Then another talked about frustration with the lack of cooperation. During 30 minutes of venting, it sounded as if they needed a therapist, not a mediator. But when the venting was over, they engaged in constructive communication and began to function as a team. Venting addresses a need identified by Folger and Poole (1984) of unearthing the historical roots of a problem. In the case of the vice presidents, a past event contaminated present discussions.

Interests that are shared in discussion may fall into one of four domains: procedural, substantive, relational, or philosophical. Occasionally, a roadblock may occur if the mediator or parties do not recognize these different needs. Procedural concerns involve beliefs about the way things should be done, and some parties will not engage in talk about substance interests until they trust that the process will meet their expectations. Substantive interests involve tangible items such as money, the placement of a fence, cessation of a behavior, or changes to an existing agreement. Frequently, there are intangible interests that fall within a third domain of interests, relationship. A party may be seeking respect, a sign that he or she is being heard, or a belief that he or she will have greater power in the relationship.

Philosophical interests occur when people believe they have to prove a point before they will listen to anything further. They want other parties to demonstrate respect for a principle or value before they are willing to go on with discussions. For example, a husband in a marital dispute responded to a request for more sharing of the housework with, "I just want you to understand what it means for me as a male." This may be a difficult request for the wife, but her respect for the principle might increase his willingness to listen to discussion about division of the housework. In an environmental mediation, an environmentalist may require that other parties acknowledge his or her value for regarding the land as sacred before moving on to discussion about how to use the land.

Occasionally, when philosophical discussion gets in the way of dealing with concrete issues, the mediator will have to redirect the discussion. At times, philosophical discussion might even serve as a stalling tactic to prevent discussion of more immediate issues.

Yarborough and Wilmot (1995) propose questions that might be useful for mediators in probing for interests:

- What will it take for you to cooperate?
- How would you like to be treated?
- What problem(s) are we trying to solve?
- What concerns you most?
- What are two other ways you can get what you want?
- Before this conflict started, what did you want?
- What would help you feel good? (p. 129)

Ideally, mediators would like all interests presented before moving to the next phase of mediation. In most mediations, parties will propose options well before the mediator is ready. Rarely do phases go exactly the way they are presented in books. If solutions come too soon, they should be saved by charting them on a flip chart or white board. This affirms the contribution but prevents diversion from the initial agenda.

Generating Options

By now, parties have sufficiently clarified the problems, identified their interests, and established common ground for reaching a mutually acceptable solution and are ready to explore alternatives for resolving problems or satisfying interests. In the initial phase of this segment, the mediator must explain the difference between developing options and selecting the best options—two distinct steps in the process.

The group has a significant, strategic choice about how it wants to develop a set of options that might meet its current needs. Among the choices are the following:

1. As a group, brainstorm options. Build on the synergy already achieved.
2. Each of the parties, individually, develops a list of possibilities and brings them to the next meeting for consideration.
3. Divide the problem and delegate parts to task forces who will return to the next session with sets of options that address interests of the group.
4. Look to outside experts who can provide sound advice.
5. A member of the group researches and returns with a set of options.

For complex issues and technical issues, Options 3-5 provide information that the group needs to make an informed decision. For less complex issues, or in groups that already possess sufficient expertise about the problems, Option 1 or 2 might be the best choice for developing options.

After all options have been generated, the parties will need to consider how they wish to discuss the issues. The strategic choices parallel the agenda-setting phase. Disputants may evaluate options one at a time or withhold discussion until all possibilities have been suggested.

Selection of the best option will involve choosing criteria with which to evaluate the choices. The criteria may be, "Is this option fair for both of us?" "Is the proposal cost-effective, legally feasible, or financially in our best interest?" "Can I live with this settlement long term, or is short term good enough?" Occasionally in corporate or public disputes, the options involve many complex choices and need to be organized for parties. For example, in an environmental mediation, task forces were asked to bring back lists of options that included discussion of advantages and disadvantages. The mediator then took the lists and created a matrix that evaluated each option based on the criteria proposed by the group. The matrix enabled the group to visually see and weigh the options. The matrix resembled Table 4.3.

During this phase, parties may engage in *logrolling*, in which they trade factors of differing importance (Pruitt & Lewis, 1977). In the above dispute, one party may agree that it could live with the negative impacts on animal habitats but wants the final option to be one with positive impacts on water quality and agriculture. *Bridging* occurs when parties create a totally new option out of the information, interests, and goals presented. For example, in the above example, parties may see a way to prevent soil erosion and protect animal habitats by using innovative business technologies to mine gravel from the river.

Reaching an acceptable package of solutions may require synthesizing parts of several options, establishing limits on some options, or dropping others all together. Moore (1996) describes this phase as *incremental convergence*, where "par-

Table 4.3 Illustration of Matrix of Options in a Mediation: Russian River Enhancement Plan

Option	Long-Term Benefits	Short-Term Benefits	Agricultural Impacts	Soil Erosion	Animal Habitat Impacts	Water Quality Effects
One	No	Yes	min	min	+	+
Two	No	Yes	min	+	min	+
Three	No	Yes	+	+	min	min
Four	No	No	+	min	+	+
Five	Yes	No	min	+	+	min
Six	Yes	Yes	+	min	+	+

ties make gradual concessions within the bargaining range until they reach a mutually satisfying compromise position" (p. 281).

Drafting an Agreement

After agreeing to the best course of action for resolving the dispute or achieving goals, the parties may draft a *memorandum of understanding* that summarizes their agreements. This final document should include the following:

1. Identify people by full names.
2. Be specific about who will do what, when, how, and where.
3. Reduce ambiguity of implementation by listing each key provision in separately numbered paragraphs.
4. Identify specific steps and times for implementing the agreement.
5. Establish a monitoring system for measuring successful compliance.
6. Omit any mention of blame, failure, or guilt.
7. Explain penalties for failure to fulfill terms of the agreement.
8. Establish provisions to accommodate future changes.

The Sunny Hills Memorandum of Understanding (mythical school name), illustrated in Box 4.1, demonstrates a settlement agreement that was created following a series of discussions about inconsistencies in enforcing school rules for student discipline. Differences of opinion about rules escalated into a discussion about how decisions are made and clarity about roles for enforcing proper behavior.

Drafting the agreement in a form that serves as a legally binding document does not guarantee compliance. The strength of the document will rest in how well the agreement meets the interests of the disputing parties. The goal is to have parties leave the process thinking that it is in their best interests to fulfill the terms of this agreement.

BOX 4.1
Illustration of a School Memorandum of Agreement:
The Sunny Hills Faculty-Administration Agreement

1. On August 8th at 9:00 a.m., all staff will meet with an outside trainer to discuss student discipline options. The school counselor is tasked with arranging for the facilitator. The faculty discipline committee will monitor the selection of this candidate and the agenda for the meeting. The senior administrator shall make schedule and room arrangements and notify all faculty about plans.

2. On September 1, at 1 p.m., all staff will receive training in decision making. The human resource director for the school district has agreed to provide information about processes that successful schools are using. The goal is to implement an effective system by the end of fall semester. The senior administrator is tasked with scheduling her for that date. The backup date for this program will be October 8.

3. To monitor the response and effectiveness of these first two programs, the school counselors will distribute a survey during the first week of November. A task force of faculty, administration, and staff will compose questions for the survey. Results will be distributed to all employees. Specific problems that require further action will be the subject of January's faculty meeting.

4. As a symbolic gesture to demonstrate support for colleagues and help with break or noon discipline problems, all staff during fall semester commit themselves to be more visible in the halls during these high peak times. Teams from the different grade levels will monitor the responses of their members to this commitment.

5. Because dispersal of information is a continuing concern for faculty and staff, senior administration will make sure that every employee has an e-mail account and that all relevant information is regularly disseminated. The chair of the faculty will monitor compliance and report monthly about progress on this issue.

6. Failure to cooperate with group agreements for handling discipline problems, managing staff conflict, or contributing to decision-making processes will be reflected in annual performance evaluations. The school district staff has agreed to monitor the school administration's compliance.

The Caucus

Occasionally, problems develop in a mediation that create barriers. For example, despite reminders about the ground rules, one party continues to interrupt, threaten, or intimidate others. In such a case, any party or the mediator may request a private, confidential meeting (a caucus) to discuss the problem. In this private session, the mediator may ask the offending member to stop the behavior or ask for information about why the behavior persists. In addition to breaking destructive cycles such as this, a caucus can be used to do the following:

- Reduce tension that might be building up during the mediation
- Move parties away from positional orientations and toward problem-solving orientations
- Weigh the acceptability of options
- Clarify interests or goals that change during discussion
- Explain the costs of no settlement and identify the benefits of cooperation
- Interrupt a stalemate
- Allow venting of emotions that might be destructive if done in the session

Providing that the mediator included an explanation about the purpose and principles of caucusing during the opening statements, a caucus may be initiated at any time by any of the parties. Although there is no general rule as to how long a caucus should be,

> common practice and courtesy dictate that if a caucus is to take more than an hour, a formal break should be called in negotiations so that the party with whom the caucus is not being held is not kept waiting. (Moore, 1996, p. 323)

During the caucus, the mediator may need to discuss with a party how to explain to the other parties the purpose and results of the caucus.

To demonstrate impartiality and reduce distrust, the mediator should check in with the noncaucusing party prior to reconvening the session. No information uncovered during the caucus should be revealed unless the parties who shared the information grant permission.

Professional Profile: Barbara Ashley Phillips
Co-Founder of America West Institute

The Mediator's Credo: When I Listen, People Talk

Introduction to the Practitioner

Barbara Ashley Phillips is representative of those who were early adherents of mediation. Having practiced law for 20 years, she was searching for "a better way." In 1981, she organized a training program so that she and others could learn the process. Currently, she mediates commercial, construction, personal injury, product liability, professional liability, malpractice, accounting, and partnership issues. Her career path is typical in the sense that most mediators come to alternative dispute resolution from a practice in other areas. Law, social work, psychotherapy, and human communication are very common areas from which mediators are drawn.

If you want to understand Barbara's approach to mediation fully, read *Finding Common Ground: A Field Guide to Mediation*. It is a classic for new and experienced practitioners alike. If you want to attend one of her presentations at conferences of the Society of Professionals in Dispute Resolution, wear comfortable shoes; it is likely to be standing room only. Her experience and sense of presence are compelling to her colleagues.

Barbara's ability to communicate the "magic of mediation" explains both why she is so sought after at professional meetings and why she was chosen for this interview. She sees mediation as the natural way for people to move on with what is important in their lives, rather than simply clinging to the past. For instance, conflicts may become protracted because people are not ready to forego the benefits of being the victim. In her words, "Until people can be brought to the point where they are ready to claim the much greater benefits of not being victims, they won't move on. The process of mediation is a natural way for people to move on in that it brings people to a new story about what happened and where we go from here. Mediation is forward looking."

Work of the Practitioner

Barbara's approach in creating this new story relies on communication skills such as listening, "read back," translating, and organizing. She says, "Intense listening is the most powerful relationship one can have with another human being. By 'read back,' I mean acknowledging what you heard, only shaping it in constructive ways." Other mediators might call this reframing. "Translating" means expressing the emotional content that is implicit (but unexpressed) in the speech of disputants. Finally, she assists by organizing less coherent thoughts into a structure, or new story. The combination of these approaches allows a neutral third party to break through stalemates of disputants who may be too embedded in the issues to be using relevant communication skills.

In addressing how beginners should approach the acquisition of mediation skills, Barbara sees the typical 40-hour mediator training as "absolutely rock bottom minimum." Whenever possible, it is helpful to take different trainings. She stresses the value of mentoring in professional development. Aspiring mediators develop their skills by being assigned to share in responsibility with a more experienced mediator. Observation and feedback by the senior mediator are critical for the development of effective practitioners. Mediation training flourishes in a mentoring relationship.

Given her characterization of communication skills as the "magic of mediation," it will be no surprise that Barbara feels that she is most successful when she is deeply listening. She is emphatic on this point: "In this way, trust is built up between the mediator and the parties. The effective mediator knows how to build it and how to regain it should the need arise. The management of building and maintaining trust is a major function of the mediator's work."

Barbara prepares for mediations by meeting and talking with the principals before the mediation. In this way, she can build an agenda that incorporates something that each has said, so that they are already participants before they ever open their mouths. In terms of written material, Barbara notes, "I am guided by the traditions of mediation; I don't need to know how I would decide as judge. Therefore, I scan quickly through the material (sometimes boxes and boxes of it) for the peaks and valleys."

The mediation begins by naming the matter and confirming with all participants that they are there to work as long as is required, sometimes into the night. Barbara then covers logistics and previews the sequence of events in a typical mediation session. Her goal is to develop a common basis of understanding of information received. She highlights the issues that seem to be the peaks in the dispute. Barbara first employs the read back process here, feeding back her understanding of the dispute, but with a more constructive frame.

If there is a major issue that has not been covered, she will ask the lawyers to describe that issue. She will be sure that in so doing, they do not ask for commitments from the other side up front, because that would be destructive.

At the first joint session, Barbara explains the caucusing process. She explains the rationale for a mediator caucusing with disputants separately:

1. It is a chance for her to listen to anything disputants might not have wanted to say in joint session, but want her to know.

2. It is a chance to tell disputants things she sees as hurdles or problems in their positions.
3. It is a chance to develop options for resolution without name tags on them.

At a caucus, the mediator can deal with the situation in which disputants may come to mediation with no intention of moving at all. This could happen for a variety of reasons: Among others, they may be mandated into mediation, or they want to give the appearance of cooperation. Barbara explains, "My approach is to point out to them in caucus that the purpose of mediation is to find out what are the alternatives to litigation. The only way this can happen is for each side to have enough movement to get the other to move to where it's ultimately going. Otherwise, the mediation is a waste of time." The effect of this approach is that the intractable side often becomes curious. Parties consider, "What is it that I'd be passing up if I decided not to resolve here?" Thus, the caucus becomes a place where even the obdurate are motivated to explore their options.

Opinions About ADR Issues

Barbara defines success as, "When you've opened people's eyes to the various options which they may not have known before." She emphasizes that success is not getting a settlement, although this standard has been used often by researchers attempting to determine which mediations are successful and which ones fail. Barbara reminds us that a settlement may be a destructive one, or that, after options have been explored, going to court may emerge as a better option than any settlement the disputants have offered. In her view, as long as mediators have delivered the most credible process of which they are capable, they cannot fail. Failure in mediation is linked to the awareness of options, not the finalization of a settlement.

Barbara's toughest challenges have come when parties give the mediator too much trust and want her to tell them what to do. In her opinion, "It's consistent with the process that disputants in mediation must have a sense of their own power and responsibility as problem solvers. It's also important they see that the mediator doesn't have a private agenda to resolve. The ethical underpinnings of mediation depend on neutrality. The temptation to judge for others must be resisted."

Barbara's trust in the process of mediation and her commitment to it are reinforced by her response to the question about mistakes and what she has learned from them. One mistake she notes is assuming that she understood what a party's needs were. In her view, "My mistake was not listening long enough to comprehend what the party was communicating. Thinking that you already understand, being a 'smarty pants,' is what can get mediators into trouble."

The change in the field that most concerns Barbara is the increasing demand for standardization and/or certification. She holds that, "Beyond ethical mandates, which have great intrinsic value, we don't understand enough about the process of mediation and how it may be played out in different areas by various practitioners. As soon as we begin writing standards, we truncate the development of the field. My hope is that we will delay finalizing standards until we have enough maturity as a field to write wise and wholesome standards."

Mediators disagree about the extent to which the neutral party should evaluate issues in the dispute. Barbara feels strongly that traditional mediation dictates a facilitative role for the mediator. In her opinion, "To establish a subgroup of mediators who practice what they call 'evaluative mediation' would confuse the public, the disputants, and the mediators themselves. Traditional mediation is facilitative, that is, strong on process but not directive as to outcomes."

Finally, Barbara is encouraged by the wide adoption of mediation, even among practitioners who originally favored third-party judgments exclusively. She has watched attorneys come to mediation for the first time, expecting to experience a sort of glorified settlement conference. They soon aspire to a much higher level of functioning, or traditional mediation. Despite extensive training in adversarial procedures, they are usually attracted to mediation fairly quickly. In her view, the field maintains itself through the integrity of the process.

Ultimately, the goal of mediators is for disputants to develop expertise based on experience with mediation. In that scenario, mediators become invisible to the process, and third-party neutrals will seldom be needed. In an era where we are pumping our own gas, writing our own wedding vows, and generally taking more responsibility for the important decisions in our lives, we may all become mediators. Where Barbara's writing, training, and consulting is present, this scenario is already coming to life.

Professional Profile: Lenny Marcus
Program Director, Harvard School of Public Health

This Will Never Happen Again

Health care in the 1990s is a minefield of tangled relationships and shifting accountabilities. Medical professionals and management are operating under incredible pressure to deliver quality care based on limited resources. Representatives of insurance companies have their own survival and compliance with governmental regulations at risk. Patients and their families, even when satisfied, bring a high level of emotionality to conflicts within the medical system. It seems most appropriate that ADR processes have established a foothold in the health care arena.

Among the numerous examples of ADR applications are the following:

- HMOs set up dispute resolution systems to reduce the intensity of conflict between medical professionals and lower the number of staff complaints that result in formal grievance procedures.
- Health care systems sign agreements to use ADR procedures with each other and with suppliers so that they avoid litigation and unwanted publicity whenever possible.
- Hospitals, physicians, and insurance companies use both mediation and arbitration to resolve disputes with patients and their representatives.

Those who work as neutrals in physician-patient conflicts find that so often, the unhappy patient (or patient's family) is not seeking to grow rich at the expense of a physician, hospital, or insurance company. Most frequently, the motive is to receive an apology, hear an explanation of what went wrong, and be assured that no one else will suffer the same misfortune.

The need for dialogue and interpretation is best satisfied in the nonadversarial setting of an ADR procedure. Although there will always be some egregious examples of incompetence that are suited for litigation, a great many of the malpractice allegations may be resolved in a personal understanding of what happened and why. Procedures that guard against the repetition of unwanted consequences assure the patient and family that whatever suffering occurred was acknowledged and taken into account for future caregiving.

Introduction to the Practitioner

Lenny Marcus is a believer in the application of ADR to health care conflicts. As director of the Program for Health Care Negotiation and Conflict Resolution at the Harvard School of Public Health, he has taken a leading role in creating this interface. As an entrepreneur, practitioner, teacher, writer, and consultant, Lenny is a tireless advocate for ADR in the health care arena.

In 1986, Lenny received a prestigious Kellogg National Leadership Fellowship. After some training, Kellogg fellows are assigned to research and propose a project of community benefit in an area that is new to them. Having received his doctorate in health sciences from Brandeis, Lenny decided to pursue his interest in conflict management; although this was a new area of study for him, it would readily complement his focus on health care.

So, Lenny did what any of us would have done—he picked up the phone and called Abba Eban, then foreign minister of Israel, for a consultation! He reasoned that Israel was one of the hottest spots for conflict in the world, and that, as leader, Eban would have valuable information to share. Whether Eban would have the time or interest in consulting with Lenny was not a consideration. Indeed, the statesman had both, inviting Lenny to his home for a "fireside chat."

Following this inspired mentoring, Lenny received his formal training in dispute resolution through George Mason University. Convinced that health care was an arena ripe for ADR, he developed a model to apply. At the Harvard School of Public Health, he has a grant from the Hewlett Foundation to develop a curriculum, research agenda, and conceptual and applied framework for the field. However, it is primarily as a practitioner that Lenny offers us his thoughts on ADR and health care.

Clearly, Lenny has many skills, and he has a strong sense of the particular skills needed for practicing ADR in health care settings. Lenny says, "One must know both the substance of the dispute as well as ADR techniques. Familiarity with medical vocabulary and procedures is essential for success. Contextual background advances the possibilities for the neutral person to be helpful and makes the mediator more credible in the eyes of the clients."

Work of the Practitioner

Lenny prepares for a medical practice mediation by testing whether the parties are sincerely interested in settlement. He asks questions such as, "What are your choices?" and "What would be the consequences of that choice?" Before the mediation, he will have discussed the issue with each side. Arriving early to check the seating, he begins by asking the family to explain its position, then asks the physician to explain what happened in his or her view. It is at this point that Lenny and others find out whether the family's actual interests consist of explanation, apology if appropriate, and assurance that mistakes will not be repeated.

Lenny stresses that "trust is the essential for success." He believes that the neutral is being scrutinized by both parties for signs of favoring one side or the other, preferring one solution over another. The mediator must establish his or her legitimacy with the parties, who are, and are feeling, very vulnerable. Lenny states, "A good deal of symbolism and drama are involved in creating this space where parties feel safe because they trust the competence and fairness of the mediator."

There are two challenges that Lenny cites. One is the broad need to build support for ADR in health care settings. The other and greatest challenge is "dealing with those who are not emotionally balanced and therefore unable to assess their own best interests. The inability of one or more parties to make rational decisions is anxiety-provoking for a mediator."

There are several mistakes with which Lenny is familiar. One is the propensity to jump to conclusions. The parties are in conflict, usually for the first time. The mediator may have observed a similar situation many times. Holding back and letting them come to their own conclusions is sometimes difficult.

Opinions About ADR Issues

Mediators also may err by becoming too invested in settling. In Lenny's thinking, "Calculating the 'success rate' for cases or mediators amplifies the frequency of this error; some cases are better off not settled." Pressure to achieve a high average of settlements does not necessarily serve the parties' best interests.

Changes in the application of ADR to health care reflect the growth of this area. There is noticeably more willingness to engage in ADR as conflicts within the area grow. The formation of commissions within many health care systems suggests that this is a widespread trend. Whereas many people tend to focus on individual disputes, Lenny sees great potential in developing a system to prevent conflicts.

Disagreements among ADR practitioners tend to center on the question of whether mediators need a health care background to be effective. Lenny's opinion is that they do. His vision for the future is to redefine the way patients view conflicts within the health care system. "I want them to see disputes as normal, to learn to negotiate them by expressing different needs, and to make mediation widely available." Given the trends in the area and Lenny's capacity as a change maker, we have no doubt that this will come to pass.

Professional Profile: Joan Kelly
Executive Director, Northern California Mediation Center

A Safe Setting for Clear Communication

Family mediation developed in the late 1970s as a response to the failure of the adversarial court system to deal with divorce issues in a satisfactory manner. Divorce lawyers, social workers, and psychologists sought settlements for child custody and property issues that would be less adversarial and more durable. Many feel that mediation offers them the tools that make this progress possible; research supports their feelings.

Numerous studies show that settlement rates in custody and divorce mediations range from 60% to 85%. Not only are the rates encouraging, but there are other advantages as well. Mediated settlements are achieved more quickly and cost-effectively, compared to those arranged through the court system. Rates of client satisfaction are high, and, so far, settlement outcomes do not appear to differ significantly whether they are achieved through mediation, attorney negotiations, or judicial decree. Most importantly, participants leave with a sense of mastery over their family problems, as well as exposure to a problem-solving method that, if reapplied, should reduce future anger and resentment associated with conflict.

As more courts and private clients seek these benefits, family mediation has become an umbrella for a growing number of disputes that lend themselves to facilitated negotiation. In addition to comprehensive divorce mediations, which would include issues of property, support, and child custody, separation agreements prior to divorce and the modification of custody and parenting plans postdivorce may be mediated. Even married couples who have complex conflicts over finances but no intention of divorcing sometimes bring these conflicts to mediation. Two small but growing areas of family mediation are parent-child and elder care.

Parent-child mediation most often involves one or two parents and adolescents who are acting out: truancy, drug abuse, running away, and so on. This mediation has a problem-solving orientation; its goal is to help a family identify and cope with sources of conflict. Elder care mediation addresses the growing number of seniors who require extensive care, along with responsible family members who may not agree on the nature of that care or the best way to provide it.

Other types of disputes that may come to family mediators are adoptions and child protection. In adoption mediations, the birth parent and adoptive parents arrange how they will interact after the birth and adoption. Settlements usually reflect agreements around supervised visitation, communication about and with the child, financial responsibilities, and any bases for invalidation of the agreement. In child protection mediations, the planning process between the client and the social service caseworker is the focus. Typical goals are to define the nature of visiting contacts between parent and child while the child is in foster care, develop a placement and reunification plan, and clarify future requirements for the parents.

Introduction to the Practitioner

Family mediation is a growth area in terms of numbers of clients and practitioners as well as the types of disputes that may be suitable for mediation. One practitioner who has played a key role in this growth is Dr. Joan Kelly, currently Executive Director of the Northern California Mediation Center. A graduate of Yale University's clinical psychology PhD program, Joan researched divorce and family adjustment from 1970-1980; she has been researching mediation from 1982 to the present. Although she has published extensively, she is perhaps best known for her book, *Surviving the Breakup: How Children and Parents Cope With Divorce.*

Joan originally began her professional life as an academician and psychotherapist and still practices clinically. However, most of her time is devoted to mediating with families and organizations, providing training, research, and writing. Joan has also assisted with the professionalization of family mediation through her work with associations. She has been president of both the Northern California Mediation Association and the International Academy of Family Mediators. She speaks and trains family mediators from Scotland to Australia. Joan has been honored with many awards from professional associations.

According to Joan, "There are a number of necessary trainings for beginning practitioners of family mediation. Beginners should come prepared to invest considerable time and money in becoming competent family mediators. Extensive training in mediation (60-100 hours) should include training in conflict theory and conflict management."

Joan stresses that communication training is a must. For example, mediators must know how to reframe hostile remarks, understand both spoken and tacit messages, and project empathy. Specifically, "beginning mediators would do well to attend professional meetings, while practicing mediators must continue their education through internships, co-mediation, consultation, or other means." Clearly, the skill base for family mediators is extensive.

Joan emphasizes the importance of relevant experience, such as familiarity with family law on the part of attorneys or of child development on the part of therapists. For instance, those who conduct parent-teen mediations must know the laws on truancy—not to give advice, but to inform. The competencies that attorneys and mental health professionals possess already are necessary but not sufficient preparation for mediation. Although some of the communication skills are part of a mental health professional's training, mediation requires that they be used from the stance of a neutral, not a therapist. Mediation training and supervised experience are required to develop a skilled mediator, no matter what other expertise exists.

In addition to training and experience, Joan believes that her success relates to certain personal qualities, such as patience, a calm demeanor, and a tough skin. The latter is important because family mediation often involves working with angry people expressing strong feelings. She also cites critical analytic and reasoning abilities. She maintains, "The best family mediators have an eye for detail and a preference for sharp focus. Issues of property and custody often involve complex matters that bog down disputants; a mediator who is attentive to those details and knows how to manage them will be of great assistance."

Work of the Practitioner

Preparation for the first session of a divorce mediation is done partly by the mediation center's secretary, who collects an intake form from each party. In a typical divorce case, Joan will review these forms before beginning the first session with a contracting phase. She explains the mediation process, discusses the ground rules, and determines the clients' situation and readiness to mediate. Joan discovers their view of which issues mediation should cover. Once the fee is established and a joint decision to proceed is made, parties will sign an agreement to mediate. In a typical divorce case, this will ensure confidentiality and protect the mediator from being subpoenaed in future litigation.

In the next phase, a family mediator constructs an agenda. Joan asks the following questions: Are there any urgent issues? Any crises that must be dealt with first? What are areas of agreement, and which issues need resolution? What are assets and liabilities? What documentation is needed? Then, Joan starts working on specific issues, attempting to bring out underlying interests.

By the end of the first session, all should agree on what the issues are, and the mediator frames them in ways that can be negotiated. Sessions for divorce mediation run no longer than 2 hours and vary in number from 2 to 10 meetings, depending on the degree of difficulty in reaching settlement and the complexity of issues. Most other family mediations require one to three sessions.

In later sessions, Joan will assist the parties in generating and testing options. As they move toward resolution, she will integrate their thoughts into a "Memorandum of Understanding." Then, they will each have the option of reviewing the draft settlement with attorneys before signing off on a legally binding agreement.

With respect to successful family mediation, Joan states, "There are three factors. First, the parties must be willing to try and reach agreement. They must be invested in a process that requires them to at least consider the needs of the other. Often, this is a tall order for a period when anger and resentment toward the other are running high."

Second, in divorce cases, the mediator must be competent in related technicalities. If the parties are not familiar with legal issues that impinge on their settlement, the mediator should educate them so that they can make informed decisions. There may be tax considerations that arise in the same way. Mediator competence in no way implies acting as attorney or accountant, but in pointing out the common considerations that divorcing couples will not have encountered before.

Third, the manner in which the mediator treats the clients is critical to success. Joan states, "Especially in divorce cases, the mediator will be successful by being evenhanded, by giving both parties opportunities to express themselves. This may mean controlling a spouse who attempts to dominate, for instance, by interrupting angry or abusive communication. The successful family mediator creates a safe setting for clear communication."

Joan notes the challenge of dealing with individuals who feel angry and betrayed. Those who are emotionally disturbed or who present complex personality problems are not prime candidates for mediation. In Joan's experience, "I have had difficulty mediating with families whose children show the results of years of poor parenting. In such situations, agreements tend to be unstable, and parent counseling or therapy would be more likely to produce lasting results. However, the mediator should not mix the two processes, but certainly can suggest therapy where it appears indicated."

Her own challenges have been to sometimes "hang in" too long with tough cases. For instance, a verbally abusive husband may accuse the mediator who interrupts him of being biased toward his wife. There are some families who are not candidates for mediation, and the experienced practitioner knows when to quit.

Opinions About ADR Issues

Changes that Joan identifies relate to the expansion of the field. Also, Joan is concerned that "lawyers are taking over family mediation in some states. If that trend were to spread, the field of family mediation would lose the blend of law and mental health that has thus far enriched it."

Disagreements among professionals involve the following questions: Is there a need for licensure? What is the role of the mediator? On a continuum from most passive (it is their problem) to most active (tell them when their plan will not work), where is mediation most effective? According to Joan, there is a large middle ground between the extremely active and the extremely passive positions. She believes in providing all relevant information up front, as well as suggesting options when they are appropriate. She definitely believes that mediation and therapy should remain separate processes.

Professional Profile: Speed Leas
Co-Founder of the Alban Institute

True Believers Must Fight to Remain Faithful

Whatever your own experience of fighting in the family or at work, it is unlikely you will have experienced conflicts more difficult than those in church settings. There are many factors that contribute to this difficulty; conflicts that arise because of differences in theology, liturgical practice, and proscribed behavior generally do not lend themselves to compromise or collaboration. For example, in mainline Protestant churches in the United States, questions such as the sexual preferences of ordained ministers arouse strong feelings and divide congregations. Strong feelings about church leaders can be projections of individual needs and tastes that are unlikely to be resolved by ADR techniques. Although it also would be fascinating to observe church conflicts among other denominations, including those that are not Judeo-Christian, this interview focuses on mainline Protestant.

Church observers note that congregational members often deny the presence of conflict. More than most, members are likely to feel that conflict is at odds with the perfection they seek and therefore are unwilling to acknowledge it, cope with it above board, and plan rationally for its resolution. The typically unspoken assumption is that if they were really good people, working in good institutions under divine guidance, conflict simply would not exist.

In addition, certain belief systems, such as inerrancy, which is the belief that everything in the Bible is true, lead people away from listening to multiple points of view. There is a right way and a wrong way. Therefore, to agree to a settlement that includes some "wrong" clauses would mean being faithless to one's revealed truth. This orientation is difficult to integrate with the view that different disputants will bring different, but legitimate, perspectives to ADR approaches. Speed Leas, co-founder of the Alban Institute, offers the paradox that became this section's title, "True believers must fight to remain faithful." When one believes that one knows *the* truth, it will be seen as a higher value than collaboration and settlement with others who are not similarly informed.

Church conflicts do not have to involve true believers to be difficult, for there are structural factors that affect conflict management in congregations. Speed points out, "Similar to other nonprofits, there can be a strong tacit power block in churches of those who do not hold formal office, but exert considerable influence through years of networking and volunteer services. Since informal leaders may believe they are accountable to no one, conflicts may pit those with formal authority against those who have power but little or no formal authority. Church members always have the alternative of leaving and joining a different congregation or parish."

Introduction to the Practitioner

Conflicts such as these would send most ADR practitioners running for cover. They have comprised the working life of Speed Leas for 35 years. Educated at the University of California at Berkeley and Yale Divinity School, Speed serves as senior consultant to the Alban Institute. Founded in 1974, the Alban Institute consults with faith communities, primarily those that are mainline Protestant. It conducts action research, brokers consultants and trainers, and provides publications and continuing education.

At this point, Speed's work is approximately 60% mediation within a given church, 30% teaching courses at the Alban Institute and other seminaries, and 10% writing. He has published frequently, and his best known book is probably *Moving Your Church Through Conflict*. Those who have used his books and observed him as a speaker or trainer know him as a thoughtful, direct, and practically oriented authority on church conflicts.

These traits were evident in Speed's recommendations for beginning practitioners. First, he stresses, "Self-management is most important. Mediators must do their best to control their own anxiety should they be under attack, especially since most of the church meetings will be public. Second, practitioners must be expert with group process. This implies both intellectual and practical understandings of the twists and turns that groups in conflict will take."

Third, practitioners should be well grounded in mediation, knowing how conflict affects individuals and organizations. Speed says, "Identifying interests and helping people negotiate are especially important. Mediators should be solid with regard to organizational development and family systems." As mentioned earlier, the informal or tacit power structure of a church is a critical piece of the conflict. In his words, "The practitioner must be able to identify who's in charge even though their names won't appear on the organizational chart." Speed himself has a certificate in Organizational Development and has received training from the National Training Laboratory.

Speed suggests that his experience with different denominations and knowledge of their different authority systems has prepared him well for intervening in church conflicts. Also, he has extensive experience as a mediator. He stresses the importance of learning from the relevant literatures (conflict management, organizational development, and family systems especially). He also notes the great contribution that mentors can make to the development of church mediators.

Work of the Practitioner

Speed's most typical case involves a faith community trying to decide whether its pastor should stay or go. Usually, an official representative of that church system initiates the call to him. He prepares by asking generic questions such as, "How many members are involved, who are the key players, what are the critical issues? How broadly is the conflict known?" Over the course of several days, Speed conducts individual interviews with key actors and group interviews with others. He reviews written materials that might provide insight into the history and the structure of the conflicts.

When Speed has synthesized this information, he makes a proposal to the client about how to proceed. He calls this "recontracting." Most often, he will ask the legally responsible group, such as a parish council or vestry, to authorize an ad hoc group to deal with this conflict. This new group has three duties: to establish the criteria for what a good job of leadership consists of, to describe how the pastor is measuring up to these criteria, and to outline a plan for improvement. He will suggest that this same group reevaluate the pastor in 9-12 months. There should be parallel activities for leaders from the congregation, that is, an independent group should set criteria, evaluate, and recommend as well.

"ADR is still an art, not a science," is the preface for Speed's response to what is essential for success in church interventions. In other words, no one can predict exactly what will work in any given situation. Speed does name several elements that are critical: "hope, time commitment on the part of disputants, and having all involved willing to participate." The Alban Institute research shows the following results from interventions:

- Thirty percent of the time, the dispute stalemates or actually becomes worse.
- Twenty-eight percent of the time, there is a decision made about the pastor but no improvement in congregational relationships.
- Forty-two percent of the time, there is both a decision about the pastor and an improvement in relationships.

The toughest challenge is the one suggested by this section's title. Speed explains, "People believe they've been told the Truth, sometimes by God Himself. These may well be people of real integrity, believing wholeheartedly. Their positions are intransigent. They cannot stop fighting, because to do so would be an act of unfaithfulness."

With regard to mistakes and what has been learned from them, Speed returns to one of the critical components of an effective intervenor he named earlier, self-management. He finds that he has the most trouble when he becomes angry at clients. For instance, faith community members who complain bitterly about their pastor in private interviews sometimes deny there is any problem when the time comes for a joint session. The intervenor will surely have strong feelings in such a situation, but he or she must learn to share those feelings appropriately, or deal with them otherwise without being competitive or punishing.

Overcommitment is another mistake Speed names. This will sound familiar to organizational development practitioners. Speed puts it this way, "In the euphoria of peace, the intervenor may encourage faith community members and leaders to plan more than they have the time or resources to accomplish. This will, of course, lead to frustration on everyone's part."

The major change in ADR that Speed identifies is "the movement from being a practice of techniques to a field of practice. We are still in the Dark Ages with regard to the importance of systems theory in our work. We are not clearly asking ourselves and each other basic questions such as, 'How can people work together regularly and still tolerate low levels of conflict?' "

Opinions About ADR Issues

Practitioners in church interventions disagree about at least three areas. First, to what degree are systems transformable? We will not make a contribution unless we are realistic about which changes are possible. Projecting an idealistic organization is not helpful.

Second, there is disagreement about the confidentiality of information shared with the intervenor. Speed encourages disputants not to keep secrets, because he sees secrecy so often as part of the problem. Others want to preserve the confidentiality of the relationship with the neutral, taking a stance that they feel is more gentle.

Finally, there are major differences in effective church interventions related to race and ethnicity. For instance, Speed challenges the "whiteness" of ADR practices. In his view, "white ADR doesn't know how to apply its techniques in an African-American community. Members of that community tend to be much more direct, up front, in-your-face with each other. Current practice needs to be examined for its cultural bias." In this as in other challenging tasks, you may be sure that Speed will be present, asking tough questions, identifying underlying issues, and reconciling church members.

Professional Profile: Marjorie Corman Aaron
Mediator for Commercial Disputes

Mapping the Dynamics of a Dispute

Introduction to the Practitioner

Successful mediation of civil issues depends on a wide variety of skills. The understanding of legal implications and the ability to analyze cases are among those that are valuable. It is also critical for the mediator to be able to see both perspectives and help the disputants to craft a solution that they may not have considered. This is true even when the disputes are legal matters and the mediator is an attorney. Marjorie Corman Aaron is an attorney-mediator who believes that using a variety of skills is especially important when the disputes are legal and the mediator is an attorney.

Marjorie is a private practitioner who also teaches. A graduate of Harvard Law School, she has practiced civil litigation, served as an assistant district attorney, taught, and published widely. Until recently leaving the Boston area, she was Executive Director of the Program on Negotiation at Harvard Law School, a panel mediator for a Massachusetts court, and a former vice president of Endispute. Her current practice is in Cincinnati, Ohio.

Like many other attorney-mediators, Marjorie was attracted to mediation because litigation seemed "a terribly circuitous way to achieve settlements. We pretended to prepare a case for trial when we knew it was a fiction, that 90%-95% of the time we were really going to settle the case." Her current caseload is quite varied, although she does not do divorce mediations.

The skills needed for a beginning mediator include a deep understanding of negotiation. Ideally, mediators would have both experience and formal training in negotiation. Obviously, in-depth training in mediation skills is called for. In Marjorie's view, "It's important, particularly for lawyers coming into mediation, that they understand the skills of a mediator may include persuasion and legal analysis, but that's only a small part of it. What a mediator really needs to be good at is empathizing with the parties, seeing what it looks like from their perspective, gaining their trust, being creative. . . . That's a whole range of skills that sometimes lawyers or judges don't have which they need to develop."

Marjorie's own mastery of the skills leads to her own success. She is a quick study, able to analyze a legal and factual situation and see to the heart of the case.

Because of this, she is able to engage the lawyers involved in a discussion of the strengths and weaknesses of the case. Because of her experience and acuity, the lawyers are not able to "pull the wool over my eyes."

A second success factor is that Marjorie can readily connect with the people involved, both parties and lawyers. She confesses, "I'm a chit-chatter and it's easy for me to find something in common with folks and to build trust." Parties understand that she appreciates the significance of the dispute for them and will help them think through the problem. She is also adept at helping them to come to decisions that move them toward solutions.

Work of the Practitioner

Marjorie prepares for mediations by talking to people from both sides prior to the first session, if at all possible. Basically, she is trying to determine what the case is about. In her words, "What's in controversy? What do they agree on? What nut are they trying to crack?" It is important to her to understand the issues, and she reads key documents to have that sense. However, she stresses the importance of knowing what the personalities are like, what the tensions and dynamics are. She notes, "It's helpful for me to know what kind of tone needs to be set, what kind of things I can do in a joint session, what kind of things I can't, where I can push them and where I can't." This combination of issues and personal dynamics results in a mental map of the dispute.

Meeting the disputants first is a feature of Marjorie's private mediation work. When she mediates on a courthouse panel, there are rules that govern the process, and preparation is seldom an option. In those cases, she begins with a joint session, explaining ground rules and expectations for the mediation process and discovering what the issues are. She may or may not use a caucus, depending on the case.

A tool that Marjorie often uses is "Decision Analysis." During the mediation, the mediator builds a decision tree structure and assigns probabilities or values to each issue on the tree. For instance, typical questions in a civil case might be, "What are possible outcomes of a summary judgment? What could happen at a trial? Is the admissibility of any evidence in doubt? How would that affect the trial outcome? What are the damages likely to be?" Through questioning and discussion, the mediator sets up a neutral framework for discussion and decision making.

Providing an evaluation is a delicate task that is inherently risky for the mediation process. However, Marjorie uses it carefully, explaining to parties and counsel the logic of it, assisting them in an analysis of their alternatives, using their assessments of various probabilities. She presents the results in private caucus so that the side less favored by the evaluation outcome does not lose face. Decision analysis may also be computer-generated, which assists in distancing the parties from the dispute and transforming it from a battle to a business problem.

Marjorie notes the importance of mediator optimism. She recommends saying to the parties (and meaning it), "We can do this. I've done cases that seemed much farther apart than this." Mediators must remember that parties often come having tried for resolution and failed. In addition, Marjorie stresses the importance of creativity for mediators, "the ability to help people come up with ideas that are on a different track." Mediators must be energetic and comfortable with conflict. Too many go into mediation because they value peacefulness: "Parties are mad; they're not happy with each other. You have to be able to deal with that."

Employment cases are especially challenging to do. Marjorie explains, "A lot of them cry out for mediation, and I think they are incredibly difficult because people have so much invested in their work emotionally. Employment cases are challenging but incredibly satisfying when they work."

Another interesting challenge is that discovering the truth will not necessarily move a mediation toward resolution. Marjorie mediated a case in which there was a tragic misreading by one party of the communication from another party. As a result, a cycle of destruction began. Even when the mediator was able to discover the true intent, and a disputant recognized the possibility of her misinterpretation, she rejected the finding "because it was too personally painful to realize that she had made such a huge mistake. It was better for her psychologically to think that the other side was a villain. The challenging moment for me was the realization that a joint arrival at truth doesn't always help." She stresses that this is not a typical mediation outcome.

With regard to mistakes, Marjorie holds that, "Over time, I have learned that empathy is as important as analysis." By empathy, she means demonstrating that the mediator has listened, understood, and connected to disputants as people.

Opinions About ADR Issues

The changes that Marjorie sees concern the increased understanding of mediation. "People don't mix up mediation and arbitration the way they used to 10 years ago. When I ask who's been in a mediation before, more often than not, folks have—at least the lawyers." Judges also have more familiarity with the process. The dark side of this phenomenon is that "There's less naïveté, so now people do more 'spinning the mediator,' trying to work the mediator in a way they didn't do before."

There are a number of topics about which attorney-mediators disagree. "Is mediation the practice of law? Can a lawyer represent someone who was a party to a mediation? Can nonlawyer-mediators provide certain kinds of advice or opinions in the course of mediation?"

Another hot topic is whether evaluation is a legitimate part of mediation. Marjorie definitely thinks it is. "I don't think every mediator has to evaluate, and I don't think every mediation requires an evaluation. It's better if the parties come to evaluate what their alternatives are by themselves, but if parties to a mediation are at an impasse because they both have an entirely divergent view of what is likely to happen at trial, then it's appropriate for the mediator to tell them what he or she thinks. They can accept it, reject it, or be influenced by it or not. At least the mediator has been willing to offer her analyses to bridge an otherwise unbridgeable gap."

Marjorie argues that as long as mediators are advised to "provide the parties with a dose of reality" or "ask probing questions," they are leading toward a vision of what will happen if the dispute goes to trial. She states, "You're putting a question at the end of what is really an expression of your opinion. I think it is more manipulative. If it will be helpful, at some point I ask, 'OK, do you want to know what I think?' Then I tell them directly. If I'm just kind of suggesting it with little probings along the way, I have the opportunity to be more manipulative, like a hidden agenda, or an editorial writer posing as a reporter."

This is a thoughtful critique of some very standard advice to mediators (ask probing questions). It is clear that Marjorie Corman Aaron has carefully analyzed this and many other aspects of the mediation process in her practice of civil mediation, teaching, and writing. It is just as evident that she feels very strongly about the intuitive process and how it interacts with the "nut to be cracked." These two coordinates are the basis of her approach to mapping disputes. Marjorie's dispute map is both comprehensive and useful.

Chapter 5

Facilitation

A facilitator's job is to help the group have a productive meeting. A facilitator is an impartial process guide who is responsible for managing the discussion so that parties can focus their attention on substantive issues and achieve their goals. (Carpenter & Kennedy, 1988, p. 107)

Communities, organizations, and governments depend on groups to solve problems that individuals cannot solve alone. In the United States, it is estimated that there are more than 11 million meetings a day. Over a lifetime, people will spend about 1 year of their lives in meetings. Yet Poole and DeSanctis (1990) found that as high as 50% of the industry meetings they sampled did not use effective procedures. People complain, "It dragged on and on"; "I had more important things to do"; "We kept getting interrupted"; or, "As usual, a couple of people did all the talking, and they weren't the right people." Delbeq, van de Ven, and Gustafson (1975) found that unfacilitated, freely interacting groups often fall below their potential performance primarily because discussions degenerate into a battle in which winning the discussion is more important than finding the best course of action.

Groups can be an effective forum for creating synergy about ideas, identifying new options, or facilitating support for decision choices. Or, groups can be a source of disappointment as members suppress open discussion or sabotage constructive processes. Problem-solving groups require a process champion, a facilitator, to design and monitor discussion that is focused and productive.

Historical Roots of Facilitation

The art of facilitation may be one of the oldest forms of conflict management. More than 20,000 years ago, scouts led discussions with hunters about which way to travel. Around campfires, shamans led discussions about solving tribal problems. In the *Iliad,* we read of Agamemnon calling the wisest of warriors together and facilitating discussion about the best way to defeat enemies.

The modern practice of facilitation has intellectual roots in the work of educator John Dewey in the early 1900s. Dewey (1910) described reflective thinking as a model to systematize thought processes in problem solving. Briefly, the process involves the following:

1. Describe the difficulty.
2. Locate and define the problems.
3. List possible solutions.
4. Explain your reasoning.
5. Verify or reject conclusions based on further observation.

In the 1940s, scholars looked at the impact of leadership communication and style on group processes. A few of the conclusions they came to include the following:

1. Authoritarian leaders produce more, but the effect weakens when the leaders leave the room.
2. Democratic groups produce at a consistently higher rate, demonstrate a higher level of cohesiveness, and express more satisfaction with the work produced.
3. The influence of leaders who emerge in the group may be different from that of leaders who are assigned to the group.
4. Leaders have responsibilities for managing both tasks and relationships in groups.

In the 1950s and 1960s, scholars looked at procedures for organizing group discussion. Brainstorming served as a technique to generate as many ideas as possible without evaluation. Buzz groups divided large meetings into smaller work groups that focused on target questions presented by the facilitator. Two group techniques, Nominal Group and Delphi, were created to control tangential discussions or polarizing emotional interactions. The Nominal Group technique reduces group tension by beginning with written comments that solicit ideas about a problem. After all ideas are gathered, group members rank ideas and then discuss them. The Delphi method involves asking members to write their opinions about the nature of a problem, possible solutions, and the value of their solution before presenting results to the whole group. These methods are covered in more detail later in the chapter.

In the 1970s and 1980s, empirical research verified that many procedures used in group facilitation had a significant impact on group outcomes. For example, Nelson, Petelle, and Monroe (1974) found that brainstorming processes produced a higher quantity and quality of ideas than did other methods of discussion. Jarboe (1988) demonstrated that the use of the Nominal Group technique produced a greater number of ideas than did reflective thinking. Scholars found that highly verbal, interactive, decision-making groups produced better decisions than did those using procedures that allowed limited verbal interaction among members. Members in groups, trained in creative problem solving, participated more, criticized ideas less, generated more ideas, smiled more, and supported the ideas of others more (Firestein, 1990).

Facilitation Is . . .

The word *facilitation* derives from the Latin word *facilis*, which means to make easy, to free from difficulties, or to promote or move forward. A few contemporary definitions of facilitation describe how to move a group forward or make its discussion easier for members:

> Group facilitation is a process in which a person who is acceptable to all members of the group, substantively neutral, and has no decision making authority intervenes to help a group improve the way it identifies and solves problems and makes decisions, in order to increase the group's effectiveness. (Schwartz, 1994, p. 4)

> Facilitation is any meeting technique, procedure, or practice that makes it easier for groups to interact and/or accomplish their goals. Meeting procedures are sets of rules or guidelines which specify how a group should organize its process to achieve a particular goal. (Frey, 1995, p. 4)

> Facilitation involves the assistance of an individual, who is impartial toward the issues or topics under discussion . . . [who] provides procedural directions as to how the group can move efficiently through the problem solving steps of the meeting and arrive at the jointly agreed upon goal. (Center for Dispute Resolution, Boulder, CO)

> Facilitation is a process through which a person helps others complete their work and improve the way they work together. (Weaver & Farrell, 1997, p. 3)

Common to the definitions of facilitation is the role of a person who serves as an impartial or neutral discussion leader, who guides a group through a specified set of procedures for the purpose of accomplishing a purpose or goal, and who enforces ground rules that manage verbal interactions between group members. Harvard professor Roger Porter (1980) describes this role as an *honest broker*, someone who guarantees that the process is fair and does not disadvantage spokespeople with different perspectives.

Facilitation and mediation frequently overlap in terms of expectations, skills, and role. Table 5.1 attempts to clarify some of the distinctions between these two related functions.

Both facilitators and mediators are impartial leaders, trained in conflict resolution, who help parties make decisions or negotiate solutions to problems through dialogue. A key difference between facilitators and mediators is the em-

Table 5.1 Comparisons Between Facilitation and Mediation

	Facilitation	Mediation
Size of groups	Large: 12-200	Small: 2-20
Problems	Complex or unclear	Clear, more defined
Level of conflict	Low to moderate	Moderate to high
Polarization of parties	Low to moderate	Moderate to high
Emphasis on group process	High	Low
Goals	Dialogue for problem solving and decision making	Dialogue that produces written agreement
Context	Generally public	Generally private
Use of caucus	Rare	Common

phasis that facilitators place on group processes to create consensus. Some will choreograph seating, discussion methods, and participation if it will promote greater group discussion. Susskind and Cruikshank (1987) describe a negotiation where a facilitator used many techniques to promote collaborative discussion of issues: brainstorming, role-playing, opinion surveying, and collaborative image building. It is common in a single session for a facilitator to use two or three different methods for group discussion. An additional key difference is one of goals. Because conflict is less polarized, the facilitator creates processes that promote an ongoing, collaborative relationship. Often, this cannot be a realistic goal for mediators. For example, it is difficult to imagine discussions between Israel and several Middle East nations without a mediator present, despite the fact that these peoples have been neighbors for thousands of years. The goal of the facilitator is to use knowledge about how groups function to help people engage in productive problem-solving and decision-making discussions.

Situations That Require Facilitation

Not all groups require facilitators. The services of an outside facilitator may not be needed when groups involve highly skilled members, trained and respected leaders, or issues that are emotionally neutral or relatively unimportant. Groups that have high consensus about goals and problems are also less likely to need facilitation. But many situations require outside intervention, such as neighborhood meetings, organizations where trust is low or honest communication suppressed, public meetings where the problems are complex and unclear, or industry settings where conflict management skills are weak. Facilitation is the most useful option when:

1. Problems are complex.
2. There exists no more than a minimum of polarization of group members.
3. People with expertise about the issues express a willingness to participate in discussion about the issues.
4. Solutions to the problems are not better solved through unilateral decision-making processes.
5. The group is willing to accept ownership of its discussion processes and the outcomes of the discussion.

The purpose of a facilitated meeting must be clear to participants, or else discussion will fragment or degenerate. Discussion methods and goals differ among neighborhood meetings wanting to bring issues to the surface, corporations wanting to make decisions, or work groups trying to solve problems. Purposes influence the facilitator's choice of setting, participants, discussion methods, and expectations.

Core Values for Facilitators

Values about human behavior guide perceptions, priorities, expectations, and communication behaviors of the facilitator. A belief that a particular group of people is difficult to work with can serve as a self-fulfilling prophecy for failure. Argyris and Schön (1974) suggest three core values that can serve as a positive force in the work of a facilitator:

1. People share and understand information that is relevant to them.
2. People have free and informed choice so that they define their own objectives and methods for achieving them.
3. People feel responsible for decisions they make and find their choices intrinsically compelling.

In many groups, problem-solving processes are sabotaged by members who withhold valuable information. They may have a personal stake in decision outcomes, believe that sharing information may make them lose face in the group, or treat information as power. The facilitator should approach the meeting believing that all group members should have the opportunity to freely share information that is relevant to their interests. The process should provide sufficient safety so that participants want to share information because they have a stake in the outcomes.

If we are asking group members to accept responsibility for group outcomes, then we must create an environment where there is free and informed choice. The facilitator guides a process that prevents coercion, manipulation, or side deals (meetings after the meeting). Quality decisions rarely occur in groups where participants say what they believe the leader wants to hear, or where there is a lack of freedom to express differences of opinion. Group think frequently occurs in groups where insufficient information is shared or where a few members dominate discussion. The effective facilitator works coopera- tively with group members to establish mutually agreed-upon objectives, time commitments, agenda, and procedures. Heider (1986) admonishes, "Remember that you are facilitating another person's process. It is not your process. Do not intrude. Do not control. Do not force your own needs and insights into the fore- ground" (p. 33).

Facilitator Responsibilities

The role of the facilitator is to manage environmental factors that inhibit partici- pation, provide a set of procedures that helps the group achieve its purpose or reach its goals, and create a group climate that encourages and supports con- structive relationships. Each of the three sets of responsibilities influences recep- tiveness in the other domains (see Figure 5.1). A great facilitator can provide a wonderful set of procedures and yet be sabotaged by a cold room or poor seat- ing. A facilitator can have ideal meeting conditions and provide well-focused procedures but fail because group members could not get along.

Environmental Responsibilities

The effectiveness or success of a group is highly influenced by the environ- ment in which discussion takes place. Meetings immediately after lunch, at the end of a busy day, during a period of high work demand, or on Friday afternoon might not get the same level of participation as those at other times. Meetings held in a meeting room next to the supervisor's office may inhibit free expres- sion about problems. Rooms that are too hot or too cold will reduce participa- tion. Seating arrangements influence how much people speak and to whom they speak. A flip chart set before the group symbolizes the working nature for the group and moves the focus off of people and toward problems listed on the chart. A facilitator is responsible for monitoring and managing the environmen- tal factors that discourage communication and group progress.

The size of the room in relation to the number of participants also influences participation. Performance on complex or unclear tasks suffers in rooms where members feel crowded. Similarly, a room that is too spacious creates the possi- bility of distractions and diminishes perceptions of group cohesiveness. Ideally, the room should be small enough to promote interaction and cohesiveness yet large enough to accomplish tasks.

Time can serve as either a positive or a negative reinforcement for group production. If the time allotted for accomplishing objectives is perceived as too short, people will not fully consider all information. If time is open-ended or perceived as too long, the group will move at a disappointingly slow pace or demonstrate inability to focus on issues.

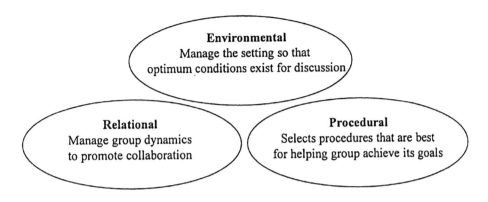

Figure 5.1. Facilitator Responsibilites

Procedural (Task) Responsibilities

Participants in meetings frequently complain, "We kept getting off of the subject"; "A few people did all the talking"; or, "I'm not sure what the purpose of the meeting was." Poole (1991) explains that procedures perform a very important function in group processes. The positive benefits of procedures include the following:

- Protecting the group against its own bad habits
- Balancing member participation
- Helping surface and manage conflict
- Building on the diversity and strengths of the group
- Guarding the process with an objective set of ground rules

Constructive procedures serve the function of preventing discussion from degenerating into a proliferation of unsolvable issues or deviation into tangential or irrelevant issues that sidetrack the group's focus. In addition, a facilitator who leads a group through predictive, constructive processes minimizes the impact of power games or status differences of group members. As a process champion, the facilitator monitors the balance of discussion so that all viewpoints are included. In a somewhat unusual way of explaining, Poole (1991) concludes that the effectiveness of procedures is their ability to make groups uncomfortable. Procedures make participants go against the grain of the way they are used to discussing issues. Procedures "counteract sloppy thinking and ineffective work habits which are part and parcel of everyday group interaction" (Poole, 1991, p. 66).

The following list summarizes some of the procedures for which the facilitator is responsible:

❑   Set time limits for the meeting
❑   Establish ground rules that promote full, equal participation
❑   Help group establish its goals or objectives
❑   Identify outcomes that the group would like to see for the meeting
❑   Describe discussion plan that increases the likelihood that objectives will be achieved
❑   Keep the group focused on objectives
❑   Periodically summarize the group's progress.

In general, meetings that have more conflict, time restrictions, or unclear goals will require more enforcement of ground rules and procedures. Meetings with greater clarity of tasks and goals or more skilled participants will permit more variation from established procedures.

The quantity or loftiness of the goals can affect outcomes. If the group members perceive that there is too much expected, they may adopt an attitude of "Why bother?" If the goal is perceived as too trivial, they will not devote attention to group discussion. Similarly, if a group is presented with too much information, members may feel overwhelmed by the task and be less focused.

When stress is high in groups, the members frequently demonstrate impulsiveness about solving the problem. They move toward solutions too fast without defining the problem clearly or considering all options. They will devote too much attention to superficial information and display less flexibility or imagination with regard to options. If the cause of the stress is environmental (setting, seating, timing), the facilitator will need to make changes. If the source of the stress is external, the facilitator may want to alter the agenda momentarily and surface the issue.

Social (Relationship) Responsibilities

One of the most difficult factors for facilitators to manage is how participants in a facilitated meeting get along. Often, members bring a history of noncooperation or past group failures to the meeting. These can be obstacles for a facilitator to overcome. A first principle for facilitators is to model the kind of behavior that is expected of participants. Effective facilitators encourage honest feedback, listen as others speak, demonstrate respect for all members, and affirm member contributions even if in disagreement with them. The effective facilitator is willing to admit mistakes and models adaptability as conditions change. When conflict occurs, the facilitator models constructive behavior by negotiating perceptions about issues and choices for courses of action.

A facilitator cannot make group members cooperate, but she or he can facilitate a climate that encourages cooperation. A few of the ways facilitators promote healthy relationships in groups are as follows:

❑   Focus on issues and ideas instead of people
❑   Point out agreement on issues as they occur
❑   Clarify misunderstanding

- ❏ Reframe toxic comments
- ❏ Regulate participation so that conflicting members do not dominate discussion
- ❏ Use techniques that alter polarizing or destructive discussion
- ❏ Step back and look at the group from a metacommunication perspective: "Let's see how we're talking about these issues"
- ❏ Call for a break or caucus to reduce tension
- ❏ Manage the amount of time devoted to emotionally charged issues

Facilitators must be aware of relationship patterns that range from highly coercive (my way or no way) to collaborative (together, we can do anything). Occasionally, a facilitator must assume the role of a teacher and point out more effective ways to reach goals. Ideally, the facilitator would like to see a high level of collaboration, which involves commitment to a goal that supersedes individual goals, willingness to put aside personal differences for the purpose of working together, and acceptance of responsibility for the group's outcomes.

The Facilitation Process

1. After agreeing to do facilitation, attempt to do premeeting assessment. Identify and prioritize the issues that the group believes to be most important.
2. Arrange the setting, seating, and timing in a way that maximizes participant attendance, participation, and energy.
3. Arrive early. Before the meeting, mingle with participants to develop a sense of trust and confidence in your leadership.
4. Clarify the purpose and goals for the meeting and your role as facilitator.
5. Establish ground rules for the group discussion to which all can agree. An example of the ground rules used by facilitators is as follows:

   Listen to understand, not to rebuke
   Do not interrupt others
   Do not engage in side conversations while others are speaking
   Refrain from using abusive language
   Disagree, but do not be disagreeable
   Deal with it here and not after the meeting
   Do not engage in personal attacks
   Try to stay focused on the subject; tangential discussions will cost everyone time.

6. Identify outcomes that the group would like from the meeting. For example, will the outcome be a list of issues to be discussed further later, a recommendation to be passed to someone of authority, or an action item for which someone in the group will take responsibility?
7. Agree on an agenda for the meeting. Issues of greatest priority should be dealt with first. Later issues sometimes become irrelevant as major issues are solved.
8. As the group is led through discussion:

   Facilitate agreement on an accurate description of the problem
   Prioritize the issues and focus on one at a time
   Suggest that unrelated topics that are introduced be tagged for later discussion
   Help people remain aware of time limits for meeting
   Track insights, agreements, and conclusions on a flip chart

Involve all members in discussion
Clarify and summarize to facilitate understanding

9. As time for the meeting nears an end, summarize the group's progress and seek agreement about the next step the group would like to take.

Facilitator Group Techniques

A facilitator without group discussion techniques is as limited as a mechanic without tools. Some techniques are designed to focus on identification of problems and others on evaluation of alternatives. Some techniques encourage free expression of ideas, whereas others prevent interactions until the issues are clearly defined. Let us survey a few of the frequently used techniques.

Problem census—The goal of this technique is the identification of problems. In round-robin fashion, each member is asked to present one problem or question. This process continues until members believe that all problems have been identified. Items are then listed and prioritized. Members will vote on their top two, three, or four choices (depending on quantity of items). Lower-ranked items are deleted. Members vote on the items a second time. This final prioritized list is discussed in depth.

Brainstorming—The goal of this technique is to stimulate group creativity. The group begins by identifying a problem. For a set time, members are encouraged to quickly volunteer ideas, without criticism or evaluation, until all ideas have been shared. After the preset time elapses, the facilitator asks the group to identify the ideas that have the most possibility, and members engage in discussion.

Delphi—This is a group technique that manages conflict by severely limiting interaction. Participants complete an initial questionnaire with open-ended questions that are designed to get ideas about issues. There is no discussion. After a break, all group members receive a second questionnaire with a summary of the ideas and are asked, based on specified criteria, to rate or evaluate each idea. Another break occurs. During the next session, a third survey reports themes, frequencies, or consensus identified in the second survey. Members are asked to revise their earlier ratings or ideas in light of the consensus view or to justify their dissenting opinion. Results are once again distributed. A final questionnaire is distributed asking for a last ranking. At this point, the facilitator may put the results together in a final report or facilitate group discussion about conclusions generated by the results. The Delphi method works especially well in settings in which group members are dispersed. Decisions can be made through the mail, fax, or e-mail.

Nominal group—This is a technique for increasing group participation. Participants individually write down ideas. The ideas are collected and recorded on a centrally placed flip chart. Names are not associated with the ideas placed on the flip chart. Without evaluation, the group may question or explain each of the ideas on the list. The group may rank the ideas in order of importance, and a thorough discussion follows. The result is a rank-ordered list of suggestions.

Samoan circle—The goal of this technique is to identify problems involving policy choices. Four chairs that face each other are placed in the center of a group. A problem of common concern is written on a flip chart or board that faces members. The facilitator shares the rules: Only members who sit in one of the chairs are allowed to participate in the discussion. In order to join the discussion, observers may stand next to one of the participants in the chairs and wait for an appropriate moment to become a member of the circle. The member who gives up the chair becomes an observer. No communication occurs between members in the chairs and the outside observers, although one of the members of the circle may request that one of the observers come and become a member of the circle. The facilitator monitors respect for the ground rules and records insights produced by the group on the flip chart.

Risk—This technique is useful for evaluating solutions. The facilitator presents a detailed explanation for a solution to a problem confronting the group. This solution may follow hours of meetings discussing the issue. In round-robin fashion, members are asked to brainstorm risk, problems, or fears that might result from the solution being implemented. After this initial meeting, a list of the potential problems is sent to all members, who are asked to add further concerns or refinements to what has already been offered. A list with these revisions becomes the agenda for the next meeting.

Blending Facilitation With Mediation

Occasionally, the two roles of facilitator and mediator are exercised by the same intervenor. For example, Spangle was asked to serve as facilitator for the monthly meetings of a 25-member community advisory board who monitored the cleanup of a toxic waste site. Members of the board described their discussions as antagonistic and highly polarized. Because they did not trust each other, they rarely reached consensus on issues. He knew that to be effective, he needed to mediate conflict between members before he could make progress facilitating the public monthly meetings. The board needed a facilitator who could also mediate.

Similarly, after years of fighting, a church group decided to seek outside help. An assessment found that four coalitions of members continually contended for power. This group dynamic explained why their congregational meetings became fragmented and unproductive. In order to be effective facilitating the public congregational meetings, a facilitator would also have to serve in the role of mediator who privately resolved differences between the coalitions.

Facilitation Traps

A common roadblock to group progress is the participant who sabotages discussion by introducing issues tangential to the agenda. These members have difficulty remaining focused on issues of priority for the group. Some have suggested that this is a strategy for achieving a hidden agenda. The facilitator must be consistently on guard against this trap. A corner of the white board or flip chart should be devoted to saving or parking the tangential issues for discussion at a later time.

A second trap is movement toward solutions too quickly. Pressures of time, need for quick fixes, past failures, or lack of energy to devote to the issue create this trap. For these groups, the facilitator can present the problem-solving process as a short-term pain but long-term gain. If more time is devoted to identifying, defining, and prioritizing, participants can deal with deeper issues that are frequently time-consuming. Additionally, members learn to work together more effectively, creating less need for such meetings in the future.

A third trap for facilitators is the victim-rescuer triangulation (see Chapter 2). The facilitator will hear participants tell stories about how they are victims to an unrelenting persecutor. These participants will blame people outside their group for their problems and personalize the issues. Facilitators are vulnerable to assuming an emotional role as rescuer in the triangle. The potential outcomes for facilitators who assume this role are (a) the discussion deteriorates into an unproductive gripe session, (b) the facilitator loses the ability to move the group toward goals and objectives, or (c) the leadership notices that the facilitator has lost neutrality and replaces the facilitator. To be successful in groups with a victim mentality, the facilitator must strive to maintain an issue-focused, process-responsible, neutral role.

A fourth trap occurs when meeting participants begin verbally attacking and blaming each other for problems. No one appears to be listening or trying to understand others. The trap can be managed by stepping back and diagramming on a flip chart the pattern of interactions observed operating in the group. After the group members visibly see how they look, ask, "What would you like to do with this? What do we need to do to be productive?" The group is given the opportunity to diagnosis its own communication problems.

Achieving Closure

Achieving consensus about problems or solutions is often a goal of groups. Often, in spite of worthwhile objections, group members will consider a vote with the majority on an issue as a test of loyalty. We want to discourage this kind of thinking.

Realistically, 100% agreement on any issue is difficult to attain. Early in the process, the facilitator can explain the meaning of consensus as 85% support by

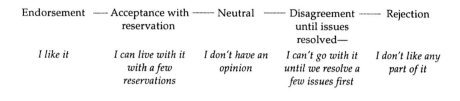

Figure 5.2. Gradients of Agreement

members on any issue. Members do not have to agree on everything to move forward. In fact, by establishing an understanding of consensus at 85%, we allow for discussion through and after the decision-making process. Allowing for differences of opinion and "agreement with reservation" or "step aside" allow the group to remain vigilant about the choices they make and aware that they may need to refine, adapt, or change decisions as new information comes in. Lack of total agreement on an issue does not mean a group cannot move forward with confidence.

Kaner (1996) recommends that groups approach agreements with a better vocabulary. He recommends that we look at gradients of agreement rather than forced choice, "You either totally accept it or you don't." Figure 5.2 illustrates the continuum of positions with which a person could describe how he or she feels about a decision.

With all of the positions except for full rejection, participants are expressing room to negotiate. *Disagreement until issues resolved* is frequently viewed by groups as full rejection, but that is an inaccurate conclusion. Facilitators should ask, "Under what conditions could you accept, or at least give consideration to, the current proposal?"

The final step for the facilitator is to help the group achieve closure. The issues may not be resolved, but the time for the end of the meeting has come. The facilitator's final tasks include the following:

- ❑ Summarize progress thus far
- ❑ Clarify agreements made as a group
- ❑ Encourage people to follow through on agreements
- ❑ Help the group decide on the next step it would like to take
- ❑ Arrange to provide a summary of the meeting or offer the flip charts to a member who agrees to create a summary for the group

---

Professional Profile: Christopher Moore
Co-Founder of Center for Dispute Resolution

ADR and Public Disputes: Consensus Decision Making

Introduction to the Practitioner

One of the most skilled, experienced, and highly successful practitioners of facilitation in public interest disputes is Dr. Christopher W. Moore, a partner of CDR Associates (Collaborative Decision Resources, formerly the Center for Dispute Resolution) in Boulder, Colorado. The first major intervention of Chris's career, conducted only a year after he graduated from college, illustrates one of his continuing areas of interest and practice, public dispute resolution. The conflict involved a confrontation between members of the Black Panthers Party, a group of militant African Americans, and the Philadelphia police in the 1970s. Despite inflamed racial and community tensions, a team of conflict managers from the Friends Peace Committee, of which Chris was a member, helped prevent an outbreak of racial violence so common in U.S. cities during that period.

Even as a recent college graduate, Chris could see the potential for using collaborative processes to resolve public disputes. But to realize this potential, he saw the need for potential intermediaries to learn more about negotiation, facilitation, mediation, and conflict management strategy design procedures and how they could be applied in addressing multiparty conflicts. To obtain these skills, he worked for a decade as a community organizer, was trained as a mediator by the Federal Mediation and Conciliation Service and the American Arbitration Association, and went on to earn a PhD in political sociology from Rutgers University.

Chris says he chose political sociology because it enabled him to study in-depth democratic methods of decision making. He said, "The use of ADR in the public context promotes a more sophisticated form of consensus decision making that takes into consideration all concerned parties' interests and strives to build a public consensus on critical issues."

Most of his research in graduate school focused on procedures for the analysis and effective resolution of disputes. His dissertation later evolved into a book, *The Mediation Process: Practical Strategies for Resolving Conflict*, which has been through several editions and is one of the most widely known titles among ADR practitioners in the field.

In addition to research and writing, Chris has been an avid conflict management practitioner and trainer. After working for 2 years as an environmental mediator and trainer at ACCORD (an environmental dispute resolution center in Boulder, Colorado that operated during the late 1970s and 1980s), Chris moved on to become one of four founding partners of CDR Associates. CDR is an international decision-making and conflict management firm that specializes in collaborative approaches and multiparty problem-solving procedures to address organizational, public, and environmental disputes. CDR's early operation included two paid staff, a one-room office with a room divider, two desks, and one black telephone. Today, CDR has more than 20 full-time staff, 15 consultants, close to a $3 million budget, and works in more than 20 countries around the globe.

Work of the Practitioner

The work that Chris does for CDR has several components. Sometimes, he acts as the facilitator in large, complex disputes. His nationwide practice involves many public disputes in the environmental arena, including water, air, mining, urban growth, and habitat protection issues. Often, he will work with a team of neutrals in these large disputes.

Serving as an intermediary in public disputes has also resulted in travel to a number of international locations, where he has facilitated or mediated disputes including, but not limited to, environmental issues. He has conducted numerous capacity-building training programs. Some of his clients include the United Nations, for whom he has worked on Middle East peace and water issues; the Organization of American States, where he focused on assisting with the implementation of the national peace accords that ended Guatemala's civil war; various parties in South Africa, with an emphasis on issues related to ending apartheid; and governmental and nongovernmental organizations (NGOs) in Bulgaria, where he worked with various ethnic groups on promoting multicultural cooperation and ethnic dispute resolution.

The work of the public interest practitioner may also include dispute system design. Chris states, "I work for the private sector, government agencies, and NGOs to establish new systems and procedures that will prevent destructive disputes from developing. My goal is to address and resolve those which do erupt, before they become intractable. I help organizations prepare for effective negotiations, particularly on issues where public and private interests overlap, and prepare local mediators to assist parties to amicably resolve their differences." His dispute system design work has been both in North America and abroad. In the former, he has assisted in the design of new personnel systems for organizations such as Levi Strauss and Company and the Royal Canadian Mounted Police. Internationally, he has worked with groups such as the Ministries of Justice of Haiti and Sri Lanka, the Department of Local Government in the Philippines, and the Ministry of Environment and NGOs in Indonesia to develop nationwide mediation systems to resolve civil and environmental conflicts.

Chris notes two separate paths for prospective practitioners to learn procedures and skills needed to be an effective intermediary in public disputes. One route involves participating in a short-term public training program on multiparty conflict resolution, followed by an apprenticeship with a practicing mediator or a mediation firm where a novice can gain hands-on experience and receive mentoring. The second route involves formal university training in dispute resolution, which can provide a good theoretical basis for practice. If the latter route is pursued, graduates will often need to obtain case experience elsewhere in order to make them more marketable to either clients or firms in the field. Chris asserts, "There are few training programs in public dispute resolution, and these are generally offered by practitioners or university faculty with some experience in the field. A 40-hour program is the minimum that a prospective practitioner should take, with even more hours being highly desirable. Educational programs should focus on the dynamics of conflict and its resolution, approaches to negotiation and problem-solving facilitation and mediation procedures, ethical dilemmas posed by interventions, and substantive background in the trainee's prospective area of practice."

Chris responded to the question of what makes an effective practitioner by talking about CDR culture. "Cultural traits of intermediaries include a broad interest in many topics, being a quick study in learning and grasping new information, an understanding of communication theory and processes, being articulate, and sensitivity to the psychological aspects of disputes and a solid understanding of dispute resolution strategies and procedures. My colleagues also have a very high level of stamina, value a fair process, are caring, and have an ability to relate to people from highly diverse backgrounds."

Preparation for a specific public interest facilitation usually involves beginning with a convening process. This procedure, and subsequent meetings, are generally sponsored by a governmental body. During the convening, the facilitator, who is often a contractor to an agency, identifies key parties, their issues and interests, conflict dynamics, and options for agreement that disputants are interested in exploring. The convening process helps the parties decide whether and how to proceed and clarifies who needs to be involved for an implementable agreement to be reached. In identifying who are the appropriate parties to bring to the table, the ADR practitioner will often work hard to achieve a balanced representation of parties and views.

In a first session, the facilitator performs introductions, establishes a common vision for the process, and clarifies understanding of the mandate for mediation. She or he elicits or sets out guidelines for behavior, explains the consensus decision-making process, and helps the parties articulate the major issues for discussion. Parties may also begin to identify their interests and what they would need for a mutually satisfactory solution to be reached. Some facilitators or mediators also include a brief training module during the first session to introduce parties to interest-based negotiation principles and procedures, such as those described in Fisher and Ury's (1981) *Getting to Yes*.

Because public interest mediations are so unique to their time, place, and issues, it is not possible to generalize about the focus or process for subsequent sessions or how long any one objective might require to complete. However, we can point to certain phases in public disputes that often follow one another. For instance, in typical latter phases, there will be deeper exploration of issues, the development of a mutually acceptable problem-solving agenda, an information development and exchange process, an option generation effort, and an initiative to reach agreement and package solutions.

What sets apart the successful public interest facilitations? Chris believes, "Parties often must have reached an actual or potential hurting stalemate, that is, the disputants must be aware that they are stuck, be willing to ask for help, and be motivated to change their situation. There must also be some overlapping of interests and some resources or benefits parties are willing to trade. In addition, disputants must be able to inform their constituents as negotiations proceed, persuade them of the desirability of the agreements they have reached, and have the ability to implement the jointly developed terms." As these success factors suggest, there are considerable challenges involved in achieving public consensus.

As mentioned earlier, some public interest disputes involve working across cultures, where differences in values, problem-solving approaches, and communication styles affect the dialogue. Different ethnic, organizational, professional, or regional cultures, or even systems differences among U.S. states, may radically influence both the procedures and solutions preferred by stakeholders. Even if the parties and the mediator share the same culture, parties may want or expect different approaches from the intermediary, anywhere from a very directive (dealmaker) to a very nondirective (orchestrator) intermediary approach.

Opinions About ADR Issues

The major change in this field that Chris sees is its growth. There are more practitioners every year, with a consequent trend toward specialization and regionalization of service provision. Chris attributes this situation to an increased willingness of public agencies at national, state, and local levels to use and fund ADR. Expansion of the field has been encouraged by both the Bush and Clinton administrations through executive orders and national legislation. Also, a number of agencies, such as the U.S. Environmental Protection Agency, have helped to develop solutions to barriers to participation, such as the lack of funding for public interest and environmental justice groups.

There are several debates among those who practice public interest ADR. The first has to do with the extent to which an intermediary must know the subject matter of the dispute. In Chris's opinion, "No one could possibly be expert at all the issues raised in complex disputes. It's more important that the intermediary be a quick study. However, as the field develops, it may well be that there will be more specialization among intermediaries."

Another interesting debate in this area is raised by the question of whether or not ADR interventions should be "transformational." That is, should the goal of participation in a facilitated dialogue include, or specifically focus on, personal change of participants or their relationships, regardless of their goals for substantive outcomes? In Chris's view, "The dichotomy between whether an intervention should focus on individual or interpersonal transformation or problem solving is a false one. In real life, there are few cases which have an exclusive orientation toward one of these ends. In most public interest disputes, intermediaries are striving both to find good substantive solutions and to improve parties' relationships and should help them to reach a depth of agreement or change that is mutually acceptable."

Professional Profile: John Schumaker
Natural Resource ADR Program Leader for BLM

Disputes We All Pay for: The Federal Government and ADR

Both facilitation and mediation are more cost-effective than litigation for resolving family and organizational conflicts. As the disputes become more complex and the number of stakeholders grows, so do expenses. Although the use of more cost-effective approaches seems sensible when someone else pays the bill, ADR is even more appealing when we, as taxpayers, are footing the cost of federal disputes. In large conflicts concerning public rights and public property, it is not unusual for court cases to drag on for years. Multiple attorney fees drain public resources that might be employed more productively. The use of ADR by federal agencies benefits them and benefits us.

Land use is a typical federal conflict that involves large sums, attracts multiple stakeholders, and usually drags on for years in the courts. The Bureau of Land Management (BLM) finds its policies disputed by many sources, from snowmobilers to Sierra Club members, from ranchers to Earth First. Along the way, many units of city, county, and state government may become involved. Litigation tends to polarize the already distrustful factions and drag out the disputes longer than most would desire. Judges and juries do not always appreciate the fine points of the science involved and may come to decisions that do not result in sound land use.

Introduction to the Practitioner

John Schumaker is a BLM employee who sees the application of ADR to land use conflicts and advocates the use of ADR for both internal and external conflicts. John became involved with dispute resolution in 1986 in Idaho as a mediator in a community mediation program and an arbitrator for the Better Business Bureau. As he learned about ADR from those sources, it soon became obvious to him that there was a great opportunity to apply collaborative conflict management to public land disputes. John is a national consultant to BLM managers, BLM solicitors, Justice Department attorneys, and those who want to know how to begin and organize an environmental dispute resolution activity.

John acquired his basic ADR skills through a community mediation program and notes how prevalent such programs are. These trainings acquaint the learner with what mediation is and how it works. According to John, "Good listening skills and getting other people to listen to each other is what facilitation is all about. After that, the beginner can acquire specialized skills such as facilitation and arbitration, if those are required." John also stresses the importance of experience, preferably as understudy to an experienced mediator. University and private programs are often helpful in providing both training and the opportunity to work under an experienced facilitator.

The ability to listen, to want to be part of the solution, and not to be egotistical are strengths that John brings to his work. Facilitators must know when to fade into the background. In his words, "If you are someone who always has to be stroked and be in the limelight, you're not going to do a good job at this because that's not what your role is."

The key to preparation is conducting a solid assessment. How much assessment is necessary depends on the nature of the activity, how detailed it is, how irritated the parties are, how extensive the issue is, and how much science is involved. In John's view, "Assessment includes who the players are, as well as what the issues are. Sometimes, assessments may be done quickly, but at other times, they can be lengthy and expensive. Long or short, the assessment is the critical piece. The greatest mistake a mediator can make is to skimp on the assessment phase." Ensuing difficulties include going down the wrong path and getting the wrong people at the table.

Work of the Practitioner

The typical public land dispute involves how best to use a piece of land, such as the request by the U.S. Air Force for a training range. These cases involve many people with a wide range of backgrounds, some sophisticated in the use of ADR, others not. The mediator works to make sure that all interests are recognized and addressed somehow in the process.

Assuming that an adequate assessment has been done, John says, "The most significant success factor for a federal dispute is perseverance. Mediators must work to listen to everyone, keeping the meetings inclusive and people well informed about what they are doing. In public land disputes, perseverance and hard work promote success."

John's toughest challenge comes before the mediation ever begins. That is, in convincing federal officials that it is in their best interests to use ADR instead of continuing on the litigation track. John is convinced that "the hardest work is getting people to the table, getting them to believe that their interests will be met in a collaborative decision-making process. Once at the table, they are usually satisfied."

Opinions About ADR Issues

Fortunately, John notes progress in this area. When asked about changes, he replies, "Changes are primarily in attitude, as evidenced by the federal attorneys who now call me on a regular basis. Federal managers don't necessarily understand how the ADR processes work, but they are tired of the old system and open to new ideas." Another challenge to ADR is the fact that virtually anyone who has the time and money can haul someone into court over an environmental dispute that will take years to litigate. A change John predicts is that the judiciary at the federal level will require disputants to at least attempt to work out a settlement before coming to court.

Disagreements arise in the federal sector about the nature of neutrality. John recommends that federal agencies use private and university facilitators, but there are those who could accept the neutrality of a federal intermediary. John also speaks about the credentialing debate among ADR practitioners. His opinion is that, "The reality is that the qualifications for someone to serve as a neutral is in the acceptance of the parties at the table. It's as simple as that."

Finally, John labels himself a "persistent optimist." As more people become aware of and participate in ADR, they will recognize the value of these processes. "Someday, citizens will demand that their government adopt such approaches; when this happens, federal agencies will regain the trust of the people they serve." In the meantime, John Schumaker will continue to preach and practice facilitated problem solving in BLM disputes.

Professional Profile: Michael Spangle
Director of Applied Communication at the University of Denver

---

Facilitation: Surfacing the Underlying Issues

Introduction to the Practitioner

Mike Spangle has been facilitating large groups (20-200 people) for many years. Mike brings an eclectic background with experience in ministry, counseling, consulting, teaching, and university administration. He has served as facilitator for disputes in settings that involved health care, environmental organizations, churches, military, corporations, and schools.

Mike credits his beginning as a facilitator to 5 years of facilitating church youth groups. While practicing in this format, he focused on group communication processes during his work on a master's degree in guidance and counseling. The two segments, practice and study, fused together into a deep understanding about how groups work under the guidance of a facilitator. For these reasons, Mike recommends that beginning facilitators take courses in group processes and conflict management to understand the dynamics that produce consensus or enable people to work together.

In addition, he believes that there needs to be training in negotiation, "because you are reframing what is being said and helping others to negotiate their perceptions as well as problems." Finally, if practitioners do not already have a counseling degree or similar training, they should have a class that teaches them to listen for issues that are not being expressed openly. Mike argues, "Listening in facilitation is different from interpersonal listening. It's listening for what their authentic self is saying. I ask, 'What are the organizational problems that nobody's hearing? Where are they stuck?' You're listening for issues that are not spoken, but you sense they underlie the surface problems."

The ability to listen for metacommunication (communication about communication) is one of the factors that Mike believes accounts for much of his success as a facilitator. In his words, "I have the ability to decenter and listen to what is not being said, as well as to what is." In addition, Mike is a warm facilitator, one who has the ability to encourage people to cooperate in a constructive manner toward a goal they deem important. Mike has their best interests in mind and cares about them. Members of groups with whom he works understand this and trust him. Finally, his counseling background with people problems allows him to tap into an understanding of group dynamics. The skills and abilities honed in counseling have shaped his reputation as an exceptional facilitator.

Work of the Practitioner

Mike prepares for a facilitation by "visiting with whomever I can get my hands on. Often, it's the leader, but in some cases, it would be someone else who has worked with that group." Ideally, he will interview a sampling of members before facilitating a group. "Prefacilitation assessment and planning can be as important as the time actually spent facilitating the group." He is concerned with knowing the group's history of working with outsiders. He states, "If it's a bad history, I would want to know that coming in, because I would be more sensitive to their attitudes. It's not about me, it's about the process. If they have a good history of working with outsiders, then I know we can probably go farther and faster."

Mike believes that identifying underlying issues is central in his personal agenda for the facilitation. Most groups have developed "smokescreen issues that hide the deeper problems that keep them apart." Often, the underlying issues are hard to determine. Mike finds that when he can get people to the underlying issues and address them, participants will feel that the facilitation has been successful. However, if all that members do is rehearse the issues and whine, then the facilitation is not successful in his mind. His standard is, "If we can get a commitment during the meeting or afterwards from management to address the underlying issues that create the frustration and the 'stuckness,' then it's a successful meeting."

Mike's toughest challenge is a group that is stuck on blaming and will not move into the realm of identifying common problems or engage in innovative problem solving. The members are stuck on "It's the supervisor's fault"; "The organization has always been this way and they'll never change"; or "We'll never get anything done as long as our problem people are with us." They seem to resist moving off of stuck. "I'm finding that the longer I'm in the business of facilitation, the more important I believe it is to identify potential problem members or the naysayers and visit with them on the side. If I can get them on board, I can solve some of the deeper issues dividing a group."

A second challenge occurs when he feels that he is leading groups in discussion about issues that leaders have no intention of changing. "I wonder why are we doing this? Is there something I could have done differently to alter the course of inaction?"

Mike mentions several mistakes from which he has learned. First, he occasionally may focus on problems that are not particularly significant to group members. He has learned that "just because you address a few highly visible problems doesn't mean that you've addressed the problems that keep the group stuck. One of the mistakes facilitators make is listening to the wrong things." Mike also has made mistakes with structuring the facilitation to achieve maximum use of the time. He recalls, "There have been times when I have not given enough time to devising action plans. Or we've spent too little time and gone right to action and addressed the wrong problems."

Mistakes are often associated with too little information about the group before the facilitation begins. Mike sees problems when neither he nor the participants know enough about their situation. He summarizes, "Lots of groups don't know what their problems are. They don't know they need a vision statement. They don't know they don't have a common goal. They don't know they don't have communication skills. I should have a sense of the group, before we begin." In response to lack of information, Mike has learned to structure facilitations so that there is more work in small groups and so that leadership is elicited from the participants.

Finally, Mike admits that he has not often followed groups after facilitations. Although not all facilitators would agree that their obligations extend beyond the meeting, Mike argues that "we can do harm if we open up a lot of problems in a facilitation, identify a few action items, but then fail to provide a process to monitor that the actions have been carried out. Group members will say, 'See, we tried again and nothing is any different.' I feel partly responsible because I was not firm enough about the importance of finishing what we've started."

Opinions About ADR Issues

Mike sees changes in the field of facilitation. He believes that there are growing numbers of more experienced practitioners versus those who are just dabbling. In addition, people with experience in facilitation are going back to school to find out what works and what does not, thereby raising the quality of facilitation practiced.

When facilitating groups, Mike sees a growing number of people who are aware that complex issues must be negotiated and that cooperation will achieve more than forcing. "Now, when I facilitate a group, they've heard or read about collaboration, teams, and win/win negotiation. They didn't know that 20 years ago. They sense that these concepts are important, and that makes it easier for me to talk about them."

There is more emphasis on dealing with change. Mike explains, "Dealing with change in a fast-changing culture is what people need to be more expert on—dealing with stress and change in groups is significant." Finally, the field of facilitation pays better. When Mike began facilitating groups two decades ago, he was expected to volunteer his time. Today, he believes that "it's a nice career now. Opportunities are growing, and there will be more, since the conflict management field is on top of the tidal wave for our organizations."

Facilitators disagree about how much training is required. Should people be allowed to facilitate just because they have an MBA or law degree, or should they be required to have facilitation training? Accreditation is probably in the future for facilitators, although practitioners differ about timing and content. What will be included in the list of appropriate credentials for facilitators? What skills are vital to successful facilitation? Mike Spangle's words and work make a strong case for training that involves greater understanding in group processes and greater ability in identifying the underlying issues that fuel disputes.

Chapter 6

Hybrids: Arbitration

Four things belong to a judge: To hear courteously, to answer wisely, to consider soberly, and to decide impartially. (Socrates, 400 BCE)

There are a variety of options at the formal end of the conflict management continuum. These options use elements of both collaborative and adversarial processes. For example, in voluntary arbitration, an arbitrator, who may eventually recommend a settlement, first encourages cooperative discussion and negotiation of issues. In many cases, parties settle prior to the arbitrator's decision. The arbitrator promotes cooperation within a structure that limits escalation of hostile behaviors. Another set of hybrids, discussed in Chapter 7, is grouped under a heading of judicial processes. Fact finding, neutral evaluation, dispute review boards, and mini-trials serve to promote constructive discussion within a more formal structure. In the end, if parties cannot cooperate to a level of mutual satisfaction, others will make recommendations about an equitable settlement of the dispute. Although arbitration and judicial processes contain a high degree of formality, they are a long way from the more elaborate legal proceedings, costs, and lengthy court battles involved in litigation.

Arbitration

Arbitration has one of the longest histories in both Eastern and Western cultures. Box 6.1 provides a quote from Emperor Kang-Hsi from the Manchu Dynasty. In Western culture, English merchants began using arbitration as early as the 13th century. Early American colonists, especially in New York, used arbitration to resolve business disputes. The field has grown so much that during 1997 alone, 60,000 cases were filed with the American Arbitration Association (AAA). Currently, arbitration is the ADR option favored for conflict involving

> **BOX 6.1**
> Quote From Emperor Kang-Hsi, Manchu Dynasty
>
> "The Emperor, considering the immense population of the empire, the great division of territorial property and the notoriously litigious character of the Chinese, is of the opinion that lawsuits would tend to increase to a frightful extent if people were not afraid of the tribunals and if they felt confident of always finding in them ready and perfect justice. . . . I desire therefore, that those who have recourse to the courts should be treated without any pity and in such a manner that they shall be disgusted with law and tremble to appear before a magistrate. In this manner . . . the good citizens who may have difficulties among themselves will settle them like brothers by referring them to the arbitration of some old man."

construction contracts, securities transactions, lemon laws, insurance claims, and labor disputes.

The London-based Advisory Conciliation and Arbitration Service (ACAS) describes arbitration as the "last peaceful resort" for resolving disputes. U.S. Supreme Court Chief Justice Warren Burger (1985) advises,

> I cannot emphasize too strongly to those in business and industry—parties ought to be treated as a "candidate" for binding private arbitration. If the courts are to retain public confidence, they cannot let disputes wait two, three and five years or more to be disposed of. (p. 6)

Arbitration Is . . .

Many cases are more complex and involve parties who do not value the relationship enough to cooperate. Mediation may not be the best choice. In these situations, disputants need a third party, an arbitrator, to hear their dispute and make the decision for them (see Table 6.1). By preagreement, the parties choose to make the decision binding or nonbinding. Arbitration differs from more formal court proceedings, such as adjudication. Benson (1996) explains, "The dominant characteristic of arbitration is that it is contractual and not statutory. Parties can define the arbitration process to be whatever they want and thereby tailor the dispute resolution process to their particular circumstances and dispute" (p. 55). Arbitration is informal, the rules of evidence are not strictly applied, the arbitrator may or may not provide reasons for the award, and the disputing parties may select the person who will serve as arbitrator.

Table 6.1 Mediation Compared to Arbitration

Mediation	*Arbitration*
Private sessions	Private sessions
Parties select mediator	Parties select arbitrator
Process addresses underlying issues	Process addresses issues that are presented to arbitrator
Parties control decision	Arbitrator makes decision
Mediators are active participants	Arbitrators are passive participants
Participation is voluntary	Parties can be compelled to participate
Continuing relationship important	Continuing relationship not important
Power may be imbalanced	Power imbalances equalized
May or may not produce finality on issues	Generally produces finality on issues

Best Conditions for Arbitration

Under ideal conditions, arbitration should not occur until parties have attempted negotiation and mediation. But there are circumstances where arbitration may be the best alternative for resolving disputes. Cooley and Lubert (1997) describe some of the conditions that make arbitration the preferred choice for resolving a dispute:

❏ Parties are deadlocked after an attempted negotiation or mediation.

❏ Parties will not have to maintain a relationship after the dispute is resolved.

❏ Legal issues predominate over factual issues.

❏ Parties have dramatically differing appraisals of the case's facts and how the law might apply.

❏ Parties have a history of acting in bad faith in negotiations.

❏ An immediate decision by a third party neutral is needed to protect the interests of a disputant. (pp. 35-36)

The British ACAS advises that

> arbitration is suitable for disputes where the issues are clear cut or concern an interpretation of an agreement. Good examples of arbitrable issues are disputes over pay or job gradings, dismissals and disciplinary matters, and demarcation of work. Issues of principle or complicated many-sided disputes are regarded as less suitable. (Crawley, 1995, p. 237)

The 1998 case between the United Auto Workers and General Motors (Box 6.2) provides an example where the process of arbitration can pressure disputants into mediated settlements before the arbitrator's final award is reached.

BOX 6.2
An Example of Labor Arbitration

In early June 1998, the United Auto Workers (UAW) from two Flint, Michigan, General Motors plants went on strike. At issue were production quotas, work rules, and GM's reluctance to invest in the plants. GM management argued that the company could not be globally competitive without restructuring its North American manufacturing operations and making them more cost-effective. In support of the strike, about 200,000 GM employees from other plants joined the strike, virtually shutting down GM production for 54 days. The estimated cost to GM was $2 million, the most expensive labor dispute in history.

The settlement called for major concessions by both UAW and GM, and a commitment to change how they will deal with future disputes. The end to the arbitration occurred on the eve of the final day of the 4-day hearing, "leading to speculation that both sides feared the potential of an unfavorable ruling and were rushing to end the strike before the arbitrator issued her decision" ("GM, Union Reach Agreement," 1998, p. 4B).

Phases of Arbitration

Arbitration involves a series of phases that includes the following:

1. Disputing parties initiate a case through the American Arbitration Association (AAA). An administrator schedules a conference between the parties to establish meeting times and to exchange information.

2. From a list of qualified arbitrators provided by AAA, the parties agree on an arbitrator. In some cases, a tripartite (three-party) panel may be selected.

3. During the preparation phase, documents are submitted to the arbitrator for review. All communication between the arbitrator and parties, except at hearings, must be submitted through AAA.

4. In large or complex cases, the arbitrator may require a prehearing to exchange documents, identify witnesses, and clarify issues of the case.

5. Although the disputing parties may ask that a decision be made based solely on written documents, generally, they will next engage in a hearing to present their cases. During the hearing, the claimant produces his or her case first. During presentations, the arbitrator may ask questions to clarify issues. Witnesses may be cross-examined. The arbitrator may disqualify irrelevant or repetitive evidence.

6. Decisions by the arbitrator are normally made within 30 days from the close of the hearing. The decision, or the award, is normally short and specific to all issues that have been discussed. No explanation for the award is required. The award may be presented to parties personally or by registered mail.

If the agreement was nonbinding and either party rejects the decision, the dissenting party may proceed to a trial. If agreement called for a binding award, the decision will be judicially enforceable. Grounds for overturning an arbitrator's decision are limited and include (a) arbitrator misconduct, (b) arbitrator exceeded his or her authority, or (c) failure to meet statutory requirements of due process (Coulson, 1980, p. 31).

Advantages of Arbitration

The private, informal, and expeditious process of arbitration makes it an appealing option for cost- and time-conscious industry. A half-day arbitration hearing costs between $500-$1,000 per day per party. Most clients and lawyers who express satisfaction with arbitration cite fairness and equitable procedures as reasons for their satisfaction. The confidential nature of the process prevents public disclosure of trade secrets and, in some cases, bad public relations.

In litigation, parties cannot select their judge. In arbitration, they can select an arbitrator with expertise and credentials that they believe will provide a fair process. Dunlop and Zack (1997) identify the ability to select the arbitrator as a significant reason for the commitment to solutions and low number of appeals.

In terms of judicial processes, a significant advantage that saves both time and money is the limitations placed on discovery for disputing parties. In his address to the American Bar Association, the late Chief Justice Burger (1985) asserted, "My own experience persuades me that in terms of cost, time and human wear and tear, arbitration is vastly better than conventional litigation for many kinds of cases" (p. 6). The American Arbitration Association estimates that the average time from filing a case until its conclusion is 110 days. In terms of the U.S. justice system, arbitration plays a significant role in reducing crowded court calendars.

An arbitrator may not give reasons for the decision but may explain considerations that have been taken into account for the decision. Some believe that providing reasons may exacerbate differences between the parties and create a new conflict centered on the arbitrator's reasoning.

Disadvantages of Arbitration

Because parties select an arbitrator and create an agreement about procedures they will follow, there may be a quality control problem. For example, arbitrators may be familiar with labor laws but lack expertise about current statutes and regulations involving employment and discrimination disputes. Because of fairness concerns, the National Association of Securities Dealers no longer requires discrimination cases to go to arbitration.

Quality control may be difficult to manage because arbitrators are not accountable to any supervisory authority. There are no norms, precedents, or safeguards for due process that must be followed. Many arbitrators have been accused of deciding issues based on compromise or splitting the difference rather than judging the issues based on the merits of the case. Arbitration is dependent on arbitrators with good training and good judgment.

Some have pointed out that nonbinding arbitration differs little in outcome from mediation. In neither process must the parties abide by the decisions or agreements. Both processes must rely on settlements that are mutually beneficial to all parties. The case of Rodney Cook (Box 6.3) illustrates how both recovery of damages and principle may serve as reasons for seeking arbitration. Arbitration always involves the risk that the arbitrator will not agree with your principles and that you may lose more than you might have had you gone to court.

There has been a steady decline in cases that go to arbitration. For example, from 1991-1992, cases involving construction disputes declined from 5,189 to 4,387, down 15%, while during the same period, requests for mediation increased by 15% at its competitor, Judicial Arbitration & Mediation Services ("Arbitrator Finds Role Dwindling," 1998, p. B1). In California, it takes an average of 2 years for HMO members to get arbitration dates ("California High Court," 1997, p. B8). Singer (1994) explains the trend away from arbitration: "Complaints that arbitration is expensive, unpredictable and laden with rules abound and have caused an increasing number of people to switch from arbitration to mediation or various hybrid forms of dispute resolution" (p. 28).

Voluntary or Mandatory Arbitration?

During the past 5 years, a debate has emerged about whether arbitration should be voluntary or mandatory. The construction and securities industries and the employment contracts of many corporations include arbitration clauses. The American Arbitration Association provides an example of one of these clauses:

> Any controversy or claim arising out of or relating to this contract, or the breach thereof, shall be settled by arbitration in accordance with the [applicable] rules of the American Arbitration Association and judgment upon the award rendered by the arbitrator may be entered in any court having jurisdiction thereof.

Some contracts include a provision that creates a graduated approach to the dispute, such as, "If the dispute cannot be settled through direct discussions or mediation, then unresolved issues will be solved through arbitration." In addition, parties may predetermine the number of arbitrators, from one to three; the qualifications of arbitrators; or rules for arbitration. Professionals debate the im-

---

BOX 6.3
Example of Securities Arbitration

The wife of Rodney Cook, a 19-year-old Marine sergeant, died in a car accident. Her life insurance policy left Rodney $85,000. He invested the money with a young, rookie broker who worked with Dean Witter Reynolds. Rodney's goal was to create a college fund for his child and a retirement fund for himself. Through a series of 100 high-risk trades over 2 years, the investor lost most of the money. Because arbitration is required for security industry disputes, Rodney agreed to arbitration with lawyers from the brokerage firm before a panel of three arbiters.

On the eve of the arbitration, Rodney turned down a settlement offer by the firm. During the 2-day hearing, two former Dean Witter Reynolds brokers testified on Rodney's behalf. In the end, the arbitrators awarded no money to Rodney. Of the 6,000 similar cases filed for arbitration each year, 53% of the time there is an award, but the award is 42% less than the median award investors would have received in court ("Investors Fare Poorly," 1998, p. A1).

---

pact of these agreements in cases where they prevent the use of other options or deny legal rights.

The Smith Barney and ICN Pharmaceutical cases described in Box 6.4 illustrate the judicial system's firm commitment to mandatory arbitration.

From January 1988 to June 1989, the University of Colorado Conflict Resolution Consortium compared 800 cases that were required to go to nonbinding arbitration with 800 cases that went directly to civil litigation. Burton and McIver (1991) report that 81% of the arbitrators, 68% of the attorneys, and 52% of the litigants said that they were either highly or somewhat satisfied with their arbitrations. On the down side, 32% of the litigants and 12% of the attorneys were highly dissatisfied. With modifications to the process, more than 75% of the participants favored continuation of the practice. Nevertheless, Colorado's state legislature ended this pilot mandatory arbitration program in July 1989.

Zinsser (1996) looked at the impact of mandatory arbitration agreements on an in-house dispute resolution system in a 25,000-employee corporation. He found that preemployment arbitration commitments had a negative influence on the system's resolution of disputes. He believes that the system would be stronger by offering arbitration to disputants as an option after a claim, rather than requiring it as a stage in the process.

Both the Equal Employment Opportunities Commission and the National Labor Relations Board advise against commitments to arbitration as preconditions for employment. The California Supreme Court ruled against Kaiser Permanente, which required arbitration for the claims of its members ("California High Court," 1997, p. B8). The National Association of Securities Dealers re-

---

BOX 6.4
Examples of Mandatory Arbitration

In 1994, Smith Barney fired Nicholas Prassas from its San Francisco office. Prassas explained the reasoning for his firing as "refusing to lie about campaign contributions that might have disqualified the firm from getting lucrative bid business from the state of Hawaii." In Prassas's complaint, he alleges that he was told by his boss to lie to the company's national manager about the contributions. He refused and was fired. By industry policy, the case went to arbitration. In 1997, Prassas asked a California Federal District Court to overturn the arbitration requirement and allow the case to go to litigation. The judge ruled that the case would remain in arbitration.

In 1997, Jerome Min moved to China to begin a job as general manager for ICN Pharmaceutical Inc. During his first few months in China, he noticed some significant irregularities in the firm's work practices. The directors were using substandard raw materials to produce the company's drugs for sale in China. In addition, the firm was selling large quantities of drugs that were beyond their expiration date. Min asked his senior executives to report the violations to the Chinese government. After several months and no action by his company, he reported the violations. He was promptly fired. Min preferred litigation, but a California appeals court ruled that, because of industry policy, he must go to arbitration. San Francisco lawyer Gay Mathiason explains, "Whistle-blower claims are the nastiest form of litigation we engage in. They take an incredible emotional toll on both employees and employers. Nothing can serve both sides better than resolving these claims quickly and with finality" ("Arbitration Policies," 1998, p. B1).

---

cently relaxed its requirement that all employment disputes be handled by industry-sponsored arbitration. San Francisco lawyer Cliff Palefsky suggests,

> If the NASD no longer requires arbitration of discrimination claims, there will be an immediate and beneficial effect on employees in the industry. It will help open doors and diversify an industry that has lagged 20 years behind the rest of the nation. ("NASD Set to End Practice," 1997, p. B4)

A number of variations to basic arbitration have grown popular during the past decade. Peek-a-boo arbitration and med/arb combine elements of arbitration with mediation. Final award arbitration combines elements of negotiation with arbitration. Finally, private trial combines arbitration with traditional judicial processes.

Med-Arb

Impartiality, which is one of the greatest strengths of mediation, may also be one of its weaknesses if "best agreement" is the goal. Mediators, by virtue of their role and ethical standards, rarely pressure parties to accept particular options or propose the best course of action for disputing parties. Mediation's goal is to help parties achieve a settlement that they believe best meets their interests. Med-arb provides a process wherein the third-party neutral can be more involved in the shaping of the final agreement. The parties agree that if they cannot settle the dispute, the mediator will assume the role of arbitrator and solve it for them. Consequently, med-arbiters have a greater ability to influence parties in directions that would promote greater agreement or settlement. Bush and Folger (1994) explain, "Having the ultimate power gives mediators an extra tool to help parties overcome bargaining pitfalls like posturing, overreaching and overreacting . . . [such as] encourage disputants to address issues [or] steer parties away from poorly reasoned choices" (p. 43).

The med-arb process occurs in phases:

1. Prehearing conference, where parties agree on meeting times and dates and submit documents for review
2. Hearing, where each party tells its story
3. Confidential meeting between each party and the med-arbiter, where interests and goals are discussed and where the med-arbiter attempts to find common ground on which final agreements might be based
4. Arbitration, if mediation has not produced a satisfactory agreement thus far
5. Agreement, which may be converted to court order (not possible in normal mediation unless pursuant to court action)

The strength of this process is the persuasive power held by the med-arbiter. Parties know they need to cooperate or they will lose the power to influence the outcomes. Additionally, if the mediation fails, the parties begin the arbitration phase with someone with whom they have already established a working relationship. Situations in which the greatest success has occurred with med-arb are chronic postdecree divorce cases and business disputes in which contracts contain critical time lines (Amadei, 1995). In an analysis of 1,500 labor disputes that went to med-arb, 85% were resolved before reaching the arbitration phase (Goldberg, 1989).

There are many weaknesses in the med-arb option. Parties who are dependent on the med-arbiter for a settlement may treat the med-arbiter like a judge and spend more time trying to persuade the med-arbiter than trying to formulate an agreement. They may withhold information during the mediation phase if they believe it would be more powerful during the arbitration phase. Additionally, some have expressed concern for the med-arbiter's ability to prevent information learned in the mediation phase from influencing judgments made during the arbitration phase. Singer (1994) points out that community dispute centers have essentially eliminated med-arb as an option because they regard it as too coercive a process.

The United Airlines-Allied Pilots labor dispute (Box 6.5) demonstrates how med-arb can work effectively to promote a settlement.

BOX 6.5
Example of Med-Arb

During 1997, the Allied Pilots Association agreed to mediation for a contract dispute with American Airlines. Five days of mediation failed to produce a settlement, and the APA's 9,300 pilots went on strike. Four weeks later, both parties began a med-arb, led by longtime labor arbitrator Robert Harris, chairman of the Presidential Emergency Board. If Harris could not mediate an agreement, he and the board would make a recommendation to the president. Historically, emergency boards encourage compromise by convincing both parties that the board is leaning to their opponent's side.

An airlines labor expert says, "Everybody stretches toward compromise because they're afraid of what the board might publish" ("American Talks With Pilots," 1997, p. A4). During the final days of the med-arb, it became apparent that the Emergency Board might recommend to Congress a settlement that favored industry. There was increased effort to compromise. Harris concluded, "Among the bad alternatives they were left with, getting an agreement was the best" ("Firestorm Is Brewing," 1997, p. A4).

Final Award Arbitration

Frequently called "baseball arbitration" because of its use in the sports industry, final award arbitration asks each party to submit in writing its last and best offer. Based on the case presented by parties, the arbitrator, within 24 hours, will choose one of the two proposals. The decision is final and binding with no compromise permitted. The arbitrator need not provide explanation for the decision. Theoretically, because no compromise is allowed, the process creates incentive for parties to resolve their differences before the arbitrator makes the final decision.

Private Trial

Some disputes are taken to a relatively new form of arbitration that combines elements of traditional court trials with arbitration. Occasionally, this ADR alternative is called Rent-a-Judge, a name given to it by the *Wall Street Journal*. This form of arbitration has been popularized by the television courtrooms of Judge Wapner on *People's Court* or *Judge Judy*.

Through legislation, six states currently authorize the use of the private trial to resolve disputes. Typically, private trial cases occur in states where the local docket is crowded, the money in dispute is large, and privacy is a high priority. The arbitrators are usually retired judges who charge significant fees. Their judgments are considered to be binding, although in California, these private decisions may be appealed through the appellate system. There are a few advantages of this option that do not occur with basic arbitration. Parties feel that they get their day in court. They get to hear a judge decide who is right and who is wrong. They receive a quick decision, based on the merits of their case, at a lower cost than going through formal court proceedings.

Professional Profile: Marshall Snider
Colorado Administrative Law Judge

From Lawyer to Arbitrator, Learning to Shut Up

Introduction to the Practitioner

To hear Marshall Snider describe how he decides labor and commercial disputes is to hear a textbook case of critical thinking at work. Undoubtedly, his law practice of 13 years prepared him well for the analytical approach that is fundamental to effective arbitration. He feels that legal experience, especially that gained through trying cases, is a great benefit to arbitrators. An arbitrator basically acts as a judge, and it is an advantage to know all the rules. However, he notes that not all successful arbitrators are attorneys.

Marshall's arbitration skills were further developed by training through the American Arbitration Association (AAA). Although once training more broadly, the AAA now trains only those who are on their list. Without prior experience in an industry or service sector, it is unlikely that the AAA would list someone. In the past, many new arbitrators went through a mentoring process with an established professional.

Work of the Practitioner

The amount of preparation for arbitration depends on whether it is a labor or commercial dispute. In the typical labor dispute, the arbitrator has no idea what the case is about before arriving at the hearing. In contrast, the arbitrator reviews written claims and responses for commercial disputes. These written materials tend to provide little detail but do give a general idea of issues. Even when they are detailed, arbitrators tend not to pay a great deal of attention, because documents are not evidence, and the claimants may not be able to prove their claims. At AAA, there will be a prehearing conference in which the neutral explains the nature of the proceeding to the parties. Marshall says that for this form of ADR, the "heavy duty job comes after the hearing, not before."

At a typical arbitration hearing, introductions are made and procedures clarified, with parties and witnesses all seated in the same room. There are opening statements from each side, and then evidence is presented, first by the claimant. Witnesses are cross-examined by the other side, and parties make closing arguments. In Marshall's practice, sessions last from 3 hours to 5 days.

Success at arbitrating is basically the employment of critical thinking skills. First, Marshall notes the ability to identify and consider both sides of a dispute. The temptation in considering both sides of a dispute is to judge one right and to stop listening to the other. Both sides need to be heard and acknowledged.

Second, cases are not always presented by the advocates in as logical and precise a manner as they might be. Presenters are not always trained advocates, and sometimes, much of the information offered is not relevant. A good arbitrator is attentive to detail, looks beneath the surface, and sorts out what is important. A logical analysis must be constructed from information not always presented logically.

Third, a sense of fairness flows from establishing processes and procedures and following them scrupulously. People need to know how the hearing will be conducted and that there will be no surprises. Regardless of the outcome, participants must come away with a sense of satisfaction that they were heard and understood, and that their arguments were considered.

Fourth, when he has come to a conclusion, Marshall asks himself certain test questions. "When the losing side receives this decision, what will they be critical of?" He then takes their issues one by one, asking himself if his rationale is valid. Does he feel comfortable with it? If he does, he writes it up. If he does not, he revisits the issue and thinks about it more.

Fifth, good decisional writing is an absolute key to a good work product and participant satisfaction. For commercial arbitrations, writing decisions is rare, but for labor arbitration, the arbitrator must clearly express the rationale so that the decision will be accepted. Understanding how the neutral reached a conclusion also supports that sense of fairness mentioned above. Marshall writes four and five drafts in order to express his decision in the clearest form.

Finally, in addition to these critical thinking skills that Marshall practices, he has found that there are others necessary for professional success. "One must not only be fair, one must generate the perception that he is fair. Not only must he have expertise in the subject area being presented, but he must convince potential clients that he is knowledgeable and understands the issues like an insider." Also necessary is the promptness in moving cases to hearings and deciding them in a timely fashion.

The toughest challenge in arbitration echoes that mentioned so often by practitioners in other areas: people who are difficult to deal with. When an advocate is causing a hearing to proceed in an inefficient fashion, it is frustrating to all concerned. When the neutral gets into heated exchanges with one side but not the other, the process is weakened. The arbitrator who loses his temper has lost the perception of fairness battle.

The second challenge mentioned is also related to people involved. Sometimes, the fair decision produces a bad result for a party who may be very sympathetic. The arbitrator must resist the temptation to favor the "good" party over the less likable but in-the-right party. Personal responses to participants are sometimes challenging to overcome.

One of the most difficult challenges goes to the heart of judging: Who is telling the truth? Two people come in with very different versions of the same event. As people get further from an event, their recollection becomes consistent with what is in their best interest. This behavior is less often outright lies than presenting the version that is most favorable to them. Marshall uses several tests to discern where the truth lies: "What do people who have no interest in the outcome say? What makes sense? What's my gut feeling about this person's sincerity?"

Determining truth is a serious matter to Marshall. He is aided by the recollection of two facts. First, he is being paid to make a decision; he cannot dodge the issue of credibility. Second, he was not there, and he will never know with certainty what happened—even the people who were there cannot agree! As noted above, he has test questions to help him be as thorough as possible.

Marshall appears to be a self-directed learner. That is, he is well aware of mistakes he has made and what he has learned from them. First, he has learned not to be as structured in his thinking, by which he means less directed by legal precedent. He is more open to what makes sense, what is reasonable, what is a good solution. He considers case authority but is less wedded to it than he was as a beginning arbitrator.

Second, Marshall also communicates less like a lawyer. In his words, "I've learned to keep my mouth shut. I used to be very active in hearings, asking lots of questions and directing the course of the proceedings. I think I did that because I've been a lawyer a long time and it was what I was used to doing. That got me into trouble a few times, and I've learned to be a bit more passive and interject myself only when it's absolutely necessary."

Written communication mistakes and their correction were similar. He used to write more than was necessary to describe the case adequately. Not every esoteric little issue has to be included. His time and client funds are thereby conserved.

From a business standpoint, Marshall feels he has learned to be more aggressive in protecting himself from demands that made his life unbearable. In other words, he is learning to say "no" to requests that, although reasonable from the other's perspective, were not practical for him. He has also learned to ask for more money than he used to. People will pay more if they believe the services are worth it.

Opinions About ADR Issues

Marshall does not note significant disagreements about arbitration among practitioners, nor does he see substantive changes occurring. He does mention administrative changes, such as the growth of providers of services (it used to be only the AAA). This has caused the AAA to change their procedures in order to compete. There are increases in the number of full-time arbitrators. In the past, conducting arbitration used to be something lawyers did on the side. Today, there are more professional arbitrators like Marshall; let us hope they are all so thorough and committed to fairness!

Professional Profile: Dan Kruger
Professor, Michigan State University School of Labor
and Industrial Relations

Every Employment Contract Contains the Seeds of Conflict

Introduction to the Practitioner

Dr. Dan Kruger, Professor of Industrial Relations at Michigan State University, expounds on the inevitability of conflict in the workplace. He sees the reasons for conflict arising from multiple sources. First, most of us want more benefits (money, privileges, time off, etc.) than most employers are willing or able to grant. Second, organizational changes occur in the realms of technology, structure, and processes, pressuring us to change our methods when most of us prefer the status quo—the devil we know being more welcome than the devil we do not know. Third, whatever else supervisors do, they must pass down instructions about the work to be done. Often, we assume that we are using language in concrete ways when the receiver has several ways of interpreting our message. Misunderstandings frequently result in unfulfilled expectations, which, in turn, result in conflict between the sender and receiver of the message.

Conflicts in values are likely to arise when an individual and the organization for which he or she works hold different values. Dan uses the example of doctors who hold patient care in highest esteem, conflicting with organizations such as HMOs, which may be primarily valuing a bottom line with maximum return for the stockholders. This type of value conflict is so intense in health care organizations today that Dan predicts that physicians may form medical unions to gain more bargaining power against administrators.

A fifth source of conflict relates to fundamental differences among us. The workplace of the 1990s is much more heterogeneous than the one it followed. Differences of gender, temperament, assumptions based on cultural and subcultural histories, and age quartiles (just get a supervisor going on directing Generation Xers!) all contribute to a rich mix of members who do not intuitively understand each other and, therefore, are more likely to conflict. Finally, if the workplace has a union representation, there will be explicit differences between labor and management in organizational goals.

Work of the Practitioner

This area of labor/management is the focus of Dan's arbitration work. Over the past 35 years, he has arbitrated roughly 800 cases involving grievances. Other work evolves out of two Michigan laws; the first law requires that when parties reach an impasse, a state agency appoints a fact finder. In this role, Dan hears the case and makes recommendations. The second law mandates arbitration for four occupations: police or sheriff's deputies, firefighters, emergency medical technicians, and 911 operators. When negotiators for one of these groups reach an impasse in collective bargaining, the Michigan Employment Relations Commission appoints an impartial chair who hears the case and renders a final, binding decision. Dan considers grievance arbitration, fact-finding in the public sector, and compulsory arbitration to be his areas of expertise. Of course, all these activities are in addition to his full-time job as faculty member at the university.

Dan's own training is both academic and experience-based. He has studied, published, and taught labor/management conflict for 40 years at Michigan State University. Therefore, it should come as no surprise that he is a strong advocate of formal training at the university level. There, courses in collective bargaining, mediation, fact-finding, communication, organization behavioral, and other areas prepare students to work effectively in organizational settings. Dan has been active in a number of professional organizations over the years and notes their value in continuing education for practitioners.

Dan attributes his success to three things: first and foremost, to his personal philosophy. He believes that his job as conflict resolver is to protect the integrity of the process. His arbitration work is extremely sensitive, because someone's job is on the line. It is vitally important that all parties believe not only in the integrity of the process, but also in the fact that the arbitrator has no hidden agenda. Dan is careful to communicate the fairness of the arbitration hearing as well as his own neutrality.

Second, Dan believes that his success is related to having served a community for many years and having built important networks during that period of service. He speaks of the value of attending meetings of personnel administrators, coming to know them and their issues well.

Finally, Dan says, "I am a self-directed learner. After a hearing, I reflect on what went well and what might have been improved on." These reflections help him to develop as a practitioner and also benefit his students, because the material shows up in later lectures.

Dan does not usually have much background before conducting a grievance hearing under a collective bargaining agreement, but he can assume that, typically, it will be a discharge case and that the employee wants his or her job back. Dan structures the hearing so that the grievant feels comfortable, because that person has never been through such a hearing. Whereas attorneys for management are usually familiar with him and with arbitration hearings, Dan understands the need of the grievant to feel at ease with him, so he spends time before the formal hearing begins, telling about his background, his role at the university, and generally telling stories. Then, when the hearing begins, Dan has communicated that he is genuinely concerned with their problem and needs their cooperation and trust to be most effective.

Dan spends the first 10 minutes of the hearing getting the parties to talk, telling him what the company and the union are all about. He also inquires about the factors that led to the hearing. He listens, asks questions, and adjourns. Finally, he makes a decision and writes an award. This is an extremely important part of the labor/management arbitration. In contrast to mediation, where the neutral's objective is to reach an agreement with little concern as to the content of that agreement, the arbitrator's reputation is at stake when he or she signs it. The quality of the award reflects directly on the reputation of the arbitrator.

The respect for quality predicts Dan's notion of what is essential for success: honesty, integrity, and knowing how to write well. He believes in "clean hands." For example, he has a standing rule that he will not accept gifts from either employers or unions. If either sends him a gift, he returns it with a note saying, "Thanks for your thoughtfulness, but I want to maintain my third-party neutrality. I appreciate your good will, but I cannot accept your gift." Such behavior has enhanced his credibility in the community.

Even with such strengths, Dan has encountered significant challenges. His toughest one was a case involving the City of Detroit and the Police Officers Association, which was a long, bitter dispute lasting more than 2 years. The issues were tough, involving several disputes. One was a salary increase, and the other was a residence requirement for police officers. The award ran more than 500 pages, finding for the city's zero increase and upholding the residency requirement. This has been criticized widely by civil libertarians, but Dan still feels his decisions were correct. Although it was indeed difficult, it was also one of the more satisfying cases.

There have been other difficult cases where, on reflection, Dan would now rule differently. For instance, he notes a case where he ruled that a certain behavior was past practice, but the employer argued that it was a contract violation. On appeal to the Circuit Court in Cincinnati, Dan's finding was reversed. The union attempted to take the case to the U.S. Supreme Court, but they declined to hear it. Dan now considers that he made an error, and the fact that one of his awards could end up in front of the U.S. Supreme Court taught him to write with their review in mind.

Opinions About ADR Issues

Dan identifies the increasing use of arbitration as the significant change in his field. Arbitration is used now by large companies in a nonunion setting with white-collar workers in an effort to minimize litigation. "Arbitration is an exciting field that tests one's imagination and creativity. More neutrals will be drawn into the practice as the use of it increases."

Despite this increase in the number of practitioners, there is no guarantee that neutrals will understand the dynamics of employment disputes. Understanding is particularly important because the whole nature of the employment relationship is changing. We have contingent workers, part-time workers, and contract workers; these conditions mean that organizational loyalty is greatly diminished. There are economic changes, technological changes, and social and legislative changes. The workplace and the workforce respond to these four components in the system of change.

"What worked 10 years ago may not work today, and because of the dynamic nature of organizational change, the solution to today's problem may be the seeds of tomorrow's difficulties. There are no final answers. That's the way life is, so let's get on with it!"

Of course, Dan is correct; there are no final answers to any question, especially those questions related to a dynamic subject such as conflict. However, listening to Dan Kruger speak about his 40-year involvement with labor/management arbitration is gaining a thoughtful, clear assessment from a skillful practitioner. Although the seeds of disputes may be distributed broadly, his crop of awards is impressive.

Chapter 7

Hybrids: Judicial Processes

For many claims, our system is too costly, too painful, too destructive, too ineffi-
cient for a truly civilized people. To rely on the adversarial process as the princi-
ple means of resolving conflicting claims is a mistake that must be corrected.
(Burger, 1985, pp. 3-4)

In 1850, Abraham Lincoln recommended, "Discourage litigation. Persuade your neighbors to compromise whenever you can. Point out to them how the nominal winner is often a real loser—in fees, expenses and waste of time" (Stern, 1961, p. 15). Knebel and Clay (1987) point out that it took a century and a half for sufficient reforms to occur in the judicial system to make nonlitigated settlements, as suggested by Lincoln, readily available. Many in ADR envision the courthouse of the future as a "multidoor courthouse" that offers a whole selection of options from which people will select the most appropriate way to resolve a conflict.

ADR is a cultural movement that is driven by innovative and transforming approaches to conflict. This includes judicial processes that blend public and private formats, legal and nonlegal procedures, and socially sanctioned norms with case law and legal statutes. This chapter looks at many of these innovative blends, including fact-finding, early neutral evaluation, dispute resolution boards, mini-trial, and summary jury trial. A few of the principles that distinguish these options from other forms of ADR that were previously discussed are the following:

- ❏ Parties lose greater control over processes and outcomes
- ❏ Shift is from mutually acceptable solutions to determining who is right and who is wrong
- ❏ Dispute moves from privacy of information and proceedings to wider disclosure
- ❏ Integration of formal court proceedings integrated with principles of mediation or arbitration

Judicial Methods

Fact-Finding

Fact-finding involves an impartial third party who is appointed by the court to investigate a complaint. The fact finder requires unlimited access to information and the ability to interview witnesses. Following the investigation, the fact finder issues a written report that goes to both the court and the disputing parties. The written report does not draw legal conclusions or include recommendations about resolving the conflict. In sensitive cases, such as those that involve sexual harassment, co-fact finders, a man and a woman, may be appointed to provide a balanced perspective. Depending on the findings, the disputants may come to an immediate agreement or select among their options of mediation, arbitration, or litigation to resolve the dispute.

Following grievances by two employees filed with Human Resources, a corporate CEO asked one of the authors to engage in fact-finding. The employees' manager, who also served as a vice president, has been the subject of numerous complaints over the past 4 years. The CEO wanted to know the depth of the complaints, both within the company and with agencies that work with the company.

The author conducted interviews with employees from the vice president's staff, employees from other departments, and people who served in agencies who worked with the organization. The CEO wanted to prevent escalation of the employees' complaints and believed that fact-finding would provide support for potential choice of action. Box 7.1 summarizes some of the findings of the interviews. Although not specifically linked to judicial fact-finding, the example illustrates how information might be gathered for use by an arbitrator to make a more informed decision about a dispute.

Early Neutral Evaluation (ENE)

In some cases that involve issues such as personal injury or employment discrimination, the court appoints a third-party neutral, who is usually a lawyer and knowledgeable about the subject matter. This third party listens to the facts and arguments of the case and then provides the parties with a legal opinion, which is not legally binding, about the range of outcomes that they might expect if they litigated the case in court. The phases of early neutral evaluation are as follows:

1. Written descriptions of positions and particular discovery necessary for case preparation are presented to the neutral evaluator prior to the ENE session.
2. In the ENE session, each party and its counsel present its positions. To focus and limit the areas of dispute, the evaluator discourages extraneous arguments and identifies areas where parties currently agree.

BOX 7.1
An Example of a CEO's Use of Fact-Finding for a Dispute

Public Relations International manages public relations for 600 businesses. The 60-employee firm works regionally, nationally, and internationally shaping the public image and visibility of the businesses it serves. Based on interviews by the author, the following comments summarize how people see Ken's effectiveness in the organization.

Colleagues describe Ken, one of the firm's four vice presidents, as abrasive and offensive at times. One staff member says, "He's uncooperative. He'll skip meetings even when we plan them around his schedule." Two of Ken's four staff members quit this year. When asked why, employees explain, "Ken doesn't support his staff publicly or privately. He is insensitive to their needs and defensive if they disagree with anything he does." The senior vice president adds, "We've quit having weekly senior management meetings because he personalizes everything."

Some staff members avoid meetings that he will be attending. One of the members on the community advisory board says, "Many people don't want to serve on the board with Ken. He's too cynical." Recently, several organizations threatened to take their business elsewhere. Several community advisory board members began withdrawing their support.

When asked how the problems created by Ken could be fixed, one of the firm's managers lamented, "It's too late, the damage has been done. Ken has lost credibility with the staff and in the community." Staff within and outside the organization agreed, "Ken's in over his head in this job. We've tried to help but he refuses it. We're tired of trying."

---

3. The neutral assesses the strengths and weaknesses of each party's case.
4. The neutral counsels the parties about what they might expect if they went to court and about their potential liabilities.
5. Based on the neutral's appraisal, the parties can discuss plans for motions or discovery, a deposition schedule, or further settlement talks.

The strength of this option is its ability to prevent unnecessary planning for litigation of a case with low potential for success. Disputants receive a realistic appraisal of the benefits and costs of litigation as an option and are provided an opportunity for resolving the case before it goes to court.

Dispute Review Board

For large civil infrastructure projects that involve high risk and liability contracts, dispute review boards (DRBs) have become the preferred ADR process for managing disputes. The DRB is composed of a panel of experts and is led by an ADR professional, all chosen jointly by the client and contractor. As a project develops, the board issues nonbinding rulings on contract issues. The presence of experts is expected to reduce the potential for litigation.

The DRB meets quarterly for full-day sessions, during which they receive briefings about the physical conditions of the site, the progress and development of the project, and the fulfillment of contractual obligations. Early in these discussions, risk and liabilities are specifically identified in the contract, along with steps for accommodating them.

An example of a successful DRB occurred in the building of the Channel Tunnel Project (the Chunnel), the underwater thoroughfare between England and France. Two French and two British engineers formed the core of the board. A French law professor served as the third party neutral who chaired the meetings. The contract stipulated that the board would hear disputes as they occurred and return decisions within 90 days. By preagreement, unanimous decisions by the board were fully enforceable unless overturned by arbitration.

The board based its decisions on the merits of arguments that were presented to it. During the 7 years of the project, the panel ruled on 20 issues. In addition, one decision required negotiation between the parties, and several involved partial decisions by the board before going to arbitration.

The success of the Chunnel DRB involved many factors, such as the following:

- Development of a carefully prepared contract before the project began
- Creation of a common set of data that served as a baseline for project decisions
- Agreed-upon criteria by which issues were assessed
- The ability to secure the services of highly qualified experts
- The ability of the experts to weigh decisions based on provisions of the contract and merits of the arguments.

The client, Eurotunnel, the contractor, and the owner agreed that the DRB's work was successful because of its ability to prevent unreasonable delays and to manage disputes as they emerged. The board provided the opportunity to proactively manage the communication among parties at each step of the project.

Mini-Trial

Initially called "information exchange," mini-trial enables disputants to engage in a nonbinding, voluntary, and structured hearing (normally 2-3 days) to resolve disputes over issues such as product liability, antitrust, contracts, patent infringement, and employee grievances. Sander (1993) cautions that a mini-trial is not suitable in cases that require an interpretation of a statute or a binding precedent, because these cases are better suited for court.

The first mini-trial occurred in 1977. Telecredit sued TRW for $6 million for patent infringement. The case involved 2 years of research that included more than 100 employee interviews and the preparation of more than 200,000 documents. The session was held at the Century Plaza in Los Angeles. Following the mini-trial, the parties took only half an hour to reach a settlement. The lawyers completed the final written agreement within 90 days. The success of the information exchange caught the eye of the *Wall Street Journal*, which coined the name *mini-trial* for the process.

Although this option is more expensive than either mediation or arbitration, it is far less expensive than litigation. In the TRW case, the parties estimate that they saved more than a million dollars in litigation costs. The U.S. Army Corps of Engineers has resolved claims of tens of millions of dollars through this process. The mini-trial agreement creates most of these savings. It establishes time limits for the different phases of the case, such as 60 days for discovery. Additionally, there may be a limit to the volume of documents that may be exchanged before and during the mini-trial. During the hearing phase, each party is given 2 hours to present its best case, followed by questions and rebuttal.

A well-respected attorney or retired judge is frequently chosen to hear the dispute. In some cases, the parties may select a three-person panel. This panel consists of one member sensitive to each of the sides and one who is perceived as impartial. Whether a panel, attorney, or judge, the presider's role is to make sure that the hearing proceeds according to agreement and that only relevant witnesses and documents are used. Decision makers and lawyers from both sides are required to be present during the proceedings.

Following the hearing, the parties may request that a panel of professionals engage in negotiations aimed at settlement. If the parties agree, the panel may serve as arbitrators and decide issues that they cannot resolve. Cooley and Lubert (1997) believe that mini-trials reach settlement a high percentage of the time and "have substantial future potential for reducing the amount of complex business litigation burdening our court systems" (p. 226).

MIT professor Lawrence Susskind (1993) describes the goals for mini-trial processes:

- ❑ Narrow the disputes to each party's assessment of critical issues
- ❑ Promote face-to-face dialogue that focuses solely on the merits of the case
- ❑ Encourage an exchange of information
- ❑ Through the use of more informal courtroom behaviors, prevent a business dispute from escalating into a lawyers' dispute.

Cost may prevent many people from being able to choose the mini-trial as an ADR option. Typically, a 1- to 2-day mini-trial can cost as much as $10,000 per side. Still, for major corporations, this is substantially cheaper than litigation.

Summary Jury Trial (SJT)

The summary jury trial involves a nonbinding trial (normally completed in one day) that follows the discovery phase of case preparation and occurs prior to actually going to full trial. In Colorado, "parties can stipulate that the discussions are settlement discussions and therefore are not admissible at trial and that neither party will call the evaluator as a witness at trial" (Izbiky & Savage, 1988, p. 851).

The usual time-consuming tasks of jury trial are eliminated in favor of a highly abbreviated format. Prior to the SJT, the parties file trial memoranda and proposed questions, and, if ordered by the judge, exchange lists of exhibits and witnesses. Jurors, selected from the normal jury pool, are not told that their decision is advisory. During the trial phase, parties are allowed 15-minute opening statements, 1 hour to present their case, and one-half hour for rebuttals. To save time during the trial, evidentiary objections are resolved prior to the trial's beginning, and no witnesses are called during the trial (although some judges permit videotapes of expert or critical fact witnesses to be played).

The jury then holds brief deliberations to arrive at a verdict (either unanimous or individual). The final phase occurs over the next several weeks, during which parties engage in posttrial settlement conferences. If these final discussions do not resolve differences, then the case may go to a full trial. This format enables disputants and lawyers to see how a potential jury might react to their arguments and case and how the presiding judge might rule on their issues.

Professional Profile: Edward Dauer
Professsor of Law and Dean Emeritus, University of Denver

Alternatives to the Latin Mass

Introduction to the Practitioner

Blending ADR elements appeals to law professor and dean emeritus Edward Dauer. A graduate of Yale Law School, he is licensed to practice in Connecticut, Colorado, and federal courts, including the U.S. Supreme Court. Rather than use the term "hybrid" to describe innovative judicial processes, Ed prefers the term "advisory process." He hopes to encourage practitioners to view this area not as a list of sanctioned procedures, but as the challenge to create techniques to overcome whatever is blocking agreement.

As president of the National Center for Preventive Law, Ed draws the analogy between the practice of law and the Latin Mass. In both, laypeople are separated from an important process (the lawsuit/the Eucharist) by an intermediary whose special language and rituals intervene in mysterious ways. Deeming this intervention disruptive in terms of conflict management, Ed was active with the Center for Public Resources Institute for Dispute Resolution since its inception in the late 1970s through its work in health care in 1993.

Ed's work involves him in research, particularly the application of ADR to health care. He is especially involved in improving the resolution of medical practice conflicts. His research has resulted in a number of publications, including a two-volume *Manual of Dispute Resolution*. He practices as an arbitrator and mediator in large commercial cases, and he teaches at the University of Denver Law School.

In terms of skills or training, Ed holds that a neutral should understand the substance of a conflict. In addition to process skills, the ADR professional obtains credibility with the parties by knowing their language and practices. The more nonbinding the process, the more critical the substance factor becomes. Although nonattorneys may practice some advisory processes, the issues usually arise out of lawsuits, and there is some advantage in using a neutral who can operate in both the court and the advisory process. However, it is well to remember that neutral evaluations are valuable because of the technical (typically nonlegal) skills that evaluators bring to a dispute.

In addition to substantive familiarity, the competent neutral in advisory processes frames the relationship between the parties as negotiation. He or she anticipates that the parties will be constantly attempting to persuade the neutral to the "rightness" of their view. The best neutrals will be able to shift between these frames of reference—aided by a long memory!

Work of the Practitioner

Ed prepares by obtaining copies of all important documents and asking himself, "What's it about, really? Not just on the surface." For instance, in his medical malpractice mediations, the surface position is typically about money; the underlying interest is often obtaining an adequate explanation and, if appropriate, an apology. Hostile workplace disputes may also be associated with monetary and other demands, whereas in reality, they may be political vendettas.

Using the example of a mini-trial, Ed stresses the importance of the executive as decision maker. Wise attorney-neutrals couch their arguments according to this important shift of roles. Ed finds that the caucus is a very useful tool in these settings, because separating the parties allows them to speak with more candor and less rancor.

Ed mentioned several challenges. Some are related to cases involving large numbers of claimants. Others involve what he terms "external linkages," that is, when a group not represented among decision makers has the power to influence their decision. The mistakes he has made appear to involve an excess of zeal on the part of the neutral. He says he has learned not to talk when parties are engaging in useful interaction, and not to float substantive ideas when he is not sure just how the parties would react. These can backfire.

Opinions About ADR Issues

Changes in advisory procedures reflect enhanced quality over the past decade. The AAA panelists now have more ADR training than previously. In the courts, there are higher standards for court-annexed procedures. As mentioned above, there is disagreement on whether courts have the authority to require advisory processes (the 6th and 7th U.S. Circuit Courts of Appeal have ruled against). Other than this, there is little debate about advisory processes. Their continued growth, both in new blending of ADR elements and in volume, should ensure that fewer Latin masses will be held in the courtrooms of this country. That will make Ed Dauer very happy!

Professional Profile: Cynthia Savage
Director, Colorado Office of Dispute Resolution

The Search for a Better Way

Introduction to the Practitioner

Lawyers whose focus is on problem solving sometimes regard the legal system as inefficient and/or inhumane. Cynthia Savage, Director of the Colorado Office of Dispute Resolution, had that reaction as a Harvard Law School student and as a young attorney at the attorney general's office. Searching for a better way to problem solve, she discovered ADR generally, and mediation specifically. Cynthia directs the statewide program that assists the courts in setting up and administrating court-referred mediation for civil and domestic cases. She also consults with other agencies of state government and works with the governor's office on task forces that relate to ADR. The study of her involvement will illustrate the typical function of state dispute resolution offices across the country. By 1999, 18 states had offices of dispute resolution, some of them with more than one location.

   The Office of Dispute Resolution (ODR) receives a small stipend from state government but is basically funded by clients who are referred by the courts. In this case, there are 37 independent contractors who conduct the civil cases (currently 14%) and the domestic ones (86%). Attorneys comprise approximately half of the contractor groups; there are also mental health professionals and a few from education and business.

In terms of qualifications, Cynthia is looking for experienced mediators who have had at least 40 hours of mediation training, have completed between 20 and 100 cases, and have some exposure to the court system. She cautions, "There is no roster to which new names of mediators may be added. ODR contracts with a limited number of mediators statewide. Applicants are screened through interviews and role-plays, following which recommendations are made to the chief judge for the district."

Clearly, working for an ODR program is not likely for a newly trained mediator. Cynthia stresses the importance of experience, as well as communication skills. She especially notes the importance of "listening between the lines." The ODR may require an internship for new contractors that may well include mediating under supervision for a period, the length of which varies with the individual contractor.

Work of the Practitioner

Preparation for mediation varies according to whether the case is civil or domestic. In the former, parties are usually represented, so contractors have confidential statements that they can review ahead of time. If they need to brush up on the basic law involved, they do so. In domestic cases, there is little prior contact, so there is little preparation. The intake procedure will inform the mediator whether or not there has been domestic violence. In this instance, parties may choose to "wave out" of mediation, or they may pursue it if they choose.

The typical ODR session lasts 2-3 hours; the average court order calls for one session, although more may be added. The mediator's work is typical of those in other settings: the "mediator monologue," which describes the process and the ground rules; information gathering; problem solving; solution selection; and, finally, a memorandum of understanding. Parties are encouraged to have agreements reviewed by their attorneys before signing.

The ODR has a high success rate. Cynthia explains, "Success depends on several factors: above all, if parties come in good faith and if the mediator is skilled. At my office, 76% of the cases come to full or partial settlement, and 7% settle after the ODR session." This is especially impressive when one considers that the agreements occur not where parties have volunteered to try, but in court-ordered mediation. Timing is also critical to success. There must be a balance between having enough information to enter into mediation, and not being so polarized that there is no further hope for settlement.

There are other challenges, Cynthia points out. As mentioned above, when parties do not come in good faith or are opposed to settling out of court, mediation is most difficult. At other times, it is the attorneys advising clients that lead to the difficulties. There are some lawyers who do not understand or respect mediation. Lack of resources may be a significant challenge in different ways. Difficulties may occur when there is a significant imbalance of resources between the parties. In addition, an absolute lack of resources may make entering into mediation impossible, although the ODR office offers free mediations to indigent parties.

In addition to these challenges, Cynthia notes some mistakes that she sees, especially among new mediators. First, they may be too attached to reaching an agreement and overlook the possibility that in a particular case, the parties' best option is no agreement. Other inexperienced mediators may give up too soon, judging that a mediator has "no power." Cynthia reminds us, "Don't underestimate the power of the mediator, simply because it may be present in more subtle forms than the usual judicial processes."

Experienced mediators may make mistakes by failing to balance between the two extreme ends of the spectrum of neutrality. As Cynthia sees it, "Some are too goal-oriented, rushing to solve the problem for the parties. Others are too process-oriented and fail to provide enough structure to reach agreement. ODR contractors strive to perform somewhere in between the two extremes."

Opinions About ADR Issues

Changes in court-mandated mediation are widespread because of increasing awareness of ADR. Cynthia reports, "There is growing judicial support for ADR. Judges see positive outcomes in cost savings, in the efficiency of ADR, and in the decrease in adversarial relationships among family members. More courts have adopted the multidoor courthouse approach, offering a variety of alternatives to litigation while retaining access to trial. There are more court orders mandating mediation or other forms of ADR." Through this judicial understanding, application, and support for ADR, attorneys have become more knowledgeable and accepting of the processes.

Courthouse debates around ADR have shifted from "Should we?" to "How do we?" Cynthia explains, "Administrators and contractors have differences of opinion about how best to conduct mediation, particularly along the spectrum from evaluative to facilitative." Another "how" question involves the qualifications of mediators and how formally these should be regulated. And how should services be provided? Should they be delivered by public or private entities? There are other definitional questions related to the ODR's courthouse context, such as whether a settlement conference constitutes mediation. These debates about how best to apply ADR in court-mandated mediations highlight how Cynthia's "better way" may be found.

Professional Profile: Jack Lemley CEO of English Chunnel Project

---

If You're in Construction, You're in Disputes

No industry is free from disputes. However, those in construction nominate it for industry front-runner in the number of disputes per day and per dollar. Even the wisest and most experienced contractors and owners cannot anticipate exactly how the unexpected will manifest itself, but they are certain that it will erupt in some form. Even the best written contracts are still dynamic documents designed to serve aggressive and sometimes volatile personalities in a high-pressure environment where the driving force is getting the work done according to specification, schedule, and budget. The larger the project, the more complex the ownership picture, or the more dollars involved, the more likely there will be adversarial relationships between owner(s) and contractors.

Introduction to the Practitioner

Megaconstruction has been the workplace of Jack Lemley through his 38-year career. Originally trained as an architect/engineer, he has worked as a contractor, owner, panelist on dispute review boards, and consultant. Jack manages and organizes the construction of multibillion-dollar infrastructure projects worldwide. For instance, he directed the construction of the water tunnel that connects Manhattan, the Bronx, and Queens. Later, he was CEO of the English Channel Tunnel (Chunnel) project and recently served as dispute review panelist for the new Hong Kong airport. He also served as management consultant for the entire Boston Central Artery and Tunnel (CAT) project, including a new tunnel connecting Logan Airport and the City of Boston.

Until the 1970s, the construction industry relied heavily on litigation and arbitration to resolve large disputes. Construction disputes might take years to reach the court, during which time projects were stalled, and those involved had assets that stood idle. When such disputes did finally reach the court, the complexities of multibillion-dollar construction were difficult to communicate to both judges and juries. For contractors, this situation was worsened by the fact that profit margins were shrinking and competition was growing. Some of the major owners of construction projects and construction companies decided that there had to be a better way.

Work of the Practitioner

Jack's first experience with a better way came when he was directing the construction of the Tennessee Tom Bigbee Waterway (a navigable canal that connects the Tennessee and Tom Bigbee river systems). As senior vice president of Morrison/Knudson Company, Jack had completed the $200 million project, but the company had been paid $50 million less than it anticipated. After the corporate counsel had filed suit, the General Counsel of the U.S. Army Corps of Engineers suggested that they attempt a mini-trial. Morrison/Knudson agreed, and each side appointed one panelist. A third person, selected and agreed to by both parties, acted as chairman. The trial was held, and the construction company was awarded $30 million of the $50 million it had demanded. Although some middle managers in the Corps of Engineers were not happy with the mini-trial approach, those at the executive levels on both sides were satisfied. The process was a great deal less expensive and time-consuming than going to court, and the decision was perceived as fair.

Even more than mini-trials, dispute review boards (DRBs) are widely used in construction today. Developed as an alternative to arbitration and the formal legal process, the DRB has become the preferred option to other ADR processes. DRBs provide for early resolution on the merits of disputes by experts in their fields. Each side names an expert of its choice, and those two agree upon a third. These panelists inspect the construction at least once a quarter, so that they are up to speed on progress and problems. In addition, either party may submit a dispute to them at any time.

Serving on such panels is not a job for beginners. Drawn from the construction industry, panelists must be expert in the class of work they will be judging. They must possess a fundamental understanding of contract law and procurement regulations. Most panelists range in age from 50-80 years. When they sign the contract to participate, they must agree to make panel obligations their first priority. For instance, as a member of the Hong Kong airport panel, Jack has flown there and back to his office in Idaho multiple times.

Jack has served as a panelist on DRBs, and he has directed projects in which DRBs were used, including the Channel Tunnel. He explains the advantages this way: "There is greater flexibility in resolving disputes. Issues are investigated by acknowledged experts in the field through the application of prevailing industry standards. This process allows the work to progress and avoids unreasonable delays. Though decisions are usually nonbinding, they focus the parties on the dispute early in the process, where the information and issues are best understood." He estimates that fewer than 2% of disputes addressed by DRBs are taken to court.

"Lots of scar tissue!" is Jack's response to what makes him good at what he does. He feels that his long experience in megaprojects, particularly in international construction and with tunnels, provides the knowledge base required to be an expert panelist. Obviously, he would not have been chosen for any of this work unless he was an enormously skilled executive.

Jack prepares for a DRB by reviewing all technical and contractual data. In line with the requirements of panelists, "I update myself quarterly on progress of the project. I keep good records. I pay attention to relationships." In addition to technical data, Jack thinks it important to gauge the respect, or lack thereof, between contractors and owners. He pays attention to body language and communication nuances to assess whether personal animosity has developed.

The English Channel Tunnel project provides one example of DRBs. Because of the large sums involved ($12 billion of private money), the owner, the multiple banks, and the two governments involved, "the contract documents provided for a permanent five-member disputes review panel to whom all disputes were referred. The president of the panel was a French law professor. The other members were two English and two French engineers of high repute. As a dispute occurred, the president selected two panel members from these four to form a three-member panel. His choice was based on selecting individuals who were most experienced in the disputed issue."

A unanimous decision by the panel was to be fully enforceable until and unless overturned by binding arbitration requested by either party—the owner (Eurotunnel) or the contractor (TransManche-Link). Jack reports, "This procedure worked quite well; there were 16 referrals to the panel, of which 13 were agreed to and enforced. Of the three others which went to arbitration, two were resolved through negotiation before reaching the final stage of judgment." Considering the number of dollars and players involved; the two countries with their separate legal systems, languages, and currencies; the use of divisive issues by politicians on both sides; and the turbulent history of British-French relations, this is an amazing success story.

Opinions About ADR Issues

What accounts for success in this and other applications of DRBs? Jack explains, "For such a process to work most efficiently for the benefit of all, a climate of trust is essential. Such a climate must be fostered and maintained through the establishment of a proactive, continuously reinforced communication environment." Jack also notes that panelists must have a sense of fairness and expend the energy necessary to reach settlement. He is clearly a person who is willing to work long and hard to help himself and others achieve fair settlements. In his words, "The harder I work, the luckier I get." Finally, "No procedure will be effective unless both parties are fully informed and really want to settle." The panelists, no matter how expert or hard-working, are ultimately dependent on the willingness of the parties to achieve settlement.

Jack acknowledges that he has made mistakes in his career. In assessing himself, he muses, "I'm less impetuous than I used to be. More consultative. Not quite as autocratic." He also names mistakes that he has seen panelists make. Chief among them is a lack of objectivity and impartiality. Mistakes may also occur in the selection of panelists, or in a poorly prepared contract. He advises, "A concerted effort should be made to establish a set of criteria by which review will be conducted and issue assessment will be done."

Changes in DRBs reflect growing use of the procedure. Jack sees "more education about the process and a cadre of people who are becoming expert in its use. This is true worldwide." Formal leadership of this effort is promoted by the construction industry, which promotes panels, establishes pro forma rules, and offers training. The resort to arbitration for construction disputes has declined as the use of DRBs has grown.

There is some disagreement among those who are familiar with DRBs as to whether or not one panelist should be a lawyer with a background in contract law. Jack says, "In my opinion, there should be, but I'm in the minority." As an early adopter of ADR in the large construction industry, Jack's opinion about DRBs is taken seriously by colleagues and clients. He has spoken about DRBs at American Bar Association forums and at construction industry conferences. His speeches, his practice, and his articles have helped to establish ADR in an industry where disputes are endemic.

Chapter 8

Designing Systems for Conflict Management

A quiet revolution is taking place in the methods Americans have available for dealing with conflict. Innovations, almost all of them fewer than 15 years old, are being developed not only to settle disputes out of court, but to supplement or replace the processes used by legislatures to budget funds, by businesses to manage employees, by therapists to treat families, and by diplomats to respond to crisis. (Singer, 1994, p. 1)

Apple founder Steve Jobs once summarized the goal of his organization as, "Ship it." Get the product to market in the most efficient, cost-effective manner possible. In concert with this goal, most organizations measure the effectiveness of their employees by their level of output. Conflict becomes a serious issue when it impedes productivity. It frequently lowers employee morale and contributes to absenteeism. In the past few years, we have noted an annual turnover rate of 30% in organizations where dysfunctional conflict is high. To prevent many of the above problems, a growing number of organizations have instituted procedures for managing grievances and disputes.

Dispute Systems Design Is . . .

Dispute systems design is an institutional, programmatic attempt to create collaborative processes through which individuals can address complaints or receive help in managing disputes. An understanding of systems concepts, such as open or closed to external information, interdependence of system members, and equilibrium (discussed in Chapter 1) are essential for designing effective organizational processes. Changes in one area cause changes in others. The goals for systems design may be to (a) resolve current problems, (b) contain the problems before they escalate, or (c) prevent the occurrence of similar problems in the future (see Figure 8.1). In families or organizations, managing the immediate dispute may serve people best. In sales organizations or sports, where conflict may actually benefit the group, containment may serve people best. For example, Apple Computer chairman John Scully once said, "We thrive on crisis." The third goal may be best suited in international relations or community groups. Kolb and Silbey (1991) caution that the goal of prevention may be problematic if it means eliminating dissension and conflict solely for the purpose of preserving the status quo. The Peaceful Valley Hospital case study (see Box 8.1) illustrates how managing current problems and prevention may both be achieved in systems design.

Ury (1995) proposes that organizational procedures for managing complaints and conflict should perform the following six functions:

- ❏ Heal emotional wounds
- ❏ Reconcile divergent interests
- ❏ Determine rights
- ❏ Test the relative power of parties
- ❏ Contain any unresolved disputes that threaten to escalate into violence
- ❏ Prevent disputes from occurring when possible (p. 380)

In the case of Peaceful Valley Hospital, the consultant enabled the nurses to reach many agreements. Through discussion, the nurses healed the emotional wounds from previous encounters, reconciled their diverging interests around scheduling, determined their rights based on their job roles, tested their personal power through negotiation of new procedures, and created a regular monitoring system through uninterrupted staff meetings to contain and prevent conflict from occurring. They were able to develop a system for monitoring and dealing with staff conflict.

Although having to contain potential violence was not a probable outcome at Peaceful Valley Hospital, there is potential in other settings. A 1999 Gallup poll of 1,000 workers found that 25% claimed that they were angry at work. Dealing with staff conflict, especially if it involves your supervisor, is challenging for most workers. In a study that surveyed 1,400 workers, University of North Carolina researchers found that 78% said that incivility (disrespect and rudeness) has worsened over the past 10 years. ("It's a Ruder and Angrier Workplace," 1999, p. 2G). During the 1990s, the phrase "going postal" emerged based on the high incidence of violence that occurred in U.S. post offices. Although the Bureau of Labor Statistics cited a drop in workplace violence in 1997, the need for constructive conflict management processes nevertheless remains essential.

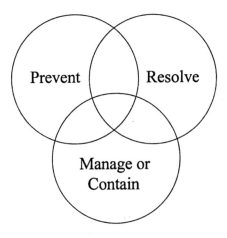

Figure 8.1. Goals for Systems Design

The case of the unhappy employee described in Box 8.2 demonstrates how situations can escalate quickly.

Design Principles

Based on Ury, Brett, and Goldberg (1988), we suggest the following six principles to guide the design of dispute resolution systems for organizations.

1. *Preparation and closure.* Build in consultation prior to design that explains to parties and seeks input about design processes that are to come. Past conflict management interventions will influence the impact of any current attempts. The organization's history with consultants should be discussed and every effort made to prevent a repeat of past mistakes.

After the design is implemented, provide for postdispute analysis and feedback. In essence, create a learning system that can respond to changing needs that have distressed the system.

2. *Collaborative focus.* At the very foundation of systems design is an emphasis on interest-based negotiations. The current system may support a power or rights approach, and parties will need to be taught and coached about more collaborative ways to approach the issues.

3. *Encourage loopback options.* Build in information sources that provide realistic appraisal of long-term costs of arbitration and litigation. Emphasize the financial, career, and energy alternatives to a problem. Ury et al. (1988) explain, "The designer can also build in ways to encourage disputants to turn back from power contests and to engage in negotiations instead" (p. 54).

BOX 8.1
Illustration of Dispute Design: Peaceful Valley Hospital

Eight nurses at Peaceful Valley Hospital manage the cases of 60 diabetic patients. The nurses' responsibilities include nutritional counseling, blood tests, physical examinations, diabetes instruction, and compilation of data for national research. The normal routine begins at 7:30 am, when patients begin arriving. They will move from station to station, where they undergo the various procedures. To be effective, the nurses must work as a team, moving the patients through the 1-hour processes.

Conflict began to emerge in the group about 3 months ago. On many days, patients were waiting at the doors when nurses arrived at 7:45 am, and some patients were still moving between stations at 5:30 pm, when nurses were due to go home. Some nurses would leave early before the work was completed. One nurse complained that others were sabotaging her by not sending her patients in a timely manner. Information about patients was not being shared between stations, and patients became annoyed by the same questions asked several times. Staff meeting time was consistently interrupted by patient needs. The conflict escalated dramatically when one nurse announced timing for a maternity leave, and the managing nurse announced that there might be no replacement. Senior executives of the hospital had begun getting complaints from nurses in the department.

Through discussion, a facilitator helped the group identify issues and design a system to manage immediate problems and reduce the probability of further problems. The senior nurse agreed that on alternate Fridays, for 2 hours, no patients would be scheduled so that the group could have uninterrupted staff meetings. Nurses agreed to stagger work hours so that those with young children could come in later and stay later. Nurses put a centrally located white board on which scheduling requests or messages could be placed. Others would be there for the early clients. One of the nurses explained that her slow behavior was related to problems she had with one of the other nurses. The two agreed to discuss their disputes one-to-one or, as needed, in the presence of the managing nurse before taking anything to higher levels. All parties agreed that there would be no more complaining to the hospital's leadership. Problems would first be addressed in staff meetings.

---

4. *Provide a menu of options.* These options should allow parties to loop back to solutions that are more collaborative. Arrange the options sequentially, from low cost to high cost, high control over outcomes to low control, and informal to highly formal. The following continuum of choices illustrates one form of menu.

Looking back at the Peaceful Valley Hospital illustration, the goal was to encourage collaborative discussion between nurses before involving the managing nurse as a mediator or hospital administrators as arbitrators. In Chapter 4, both teachers and administrators were aware that conflict could be escalated to school board officials, but chose first to loop back to facilitated discussion.

BOX 8.2
Example of Conflict Escalation

Recently, a regional manager for a chain of department stores located in malls encountered problems with a store employee. When the manager of a store left for another job, the employee believed that he would be promoted to store manager. This did not occur. The regional manager brought in a manager from another store.

The unhappy employee's response began with angry outbursts when the general manager entered the store. This escalated with letters and complaints to the national manager. Eventually, the employee made death threats against the regional manager. Both the police and the FBI entered the conflict. Eventually, the store's national leadership managed the situation by demoting the regional manager. The reason given: "inability to manage employees." The regional manager had no idea this conflict would escalate to such levels, especially because she believed that she was doing what was best for the store.

---

5. *Decide whether to serve in the role of an expert or a facilitator.* An early and important decision is deciding whether to approach the organization as an expert who, following assessment, recommends the best course of action for the organization, or as a facilitator who leads an organizational committee in development of a design.

The advantages of approaching the issue as an expert include the ability to direct a group on a productive path based on the experience of similar groups, and the saving of a great deal of meeting time that is required for using design groups. The advantages of using a group of people selected from the organization for evaluating, if not creating, elements of the design are (a) greater potential for buy-in by organizational members; (b) identification of potential problems for implementation; (c) networking with organizational champions necessary to make a new system work; and (d) organizational members who can implement, assess, and modify the system as it develops. The decision about how much to involve an organization's members in designing a system depends in part on the willingness of parties to engage in a time-consuming design discussion.

6. *Education and training.* Provide a network of organizational sources to educate parties about the advantages of using the dispute resolution system. Those who prefer bargaining, power contests, and rights-based procedures will need to be coached about the high relationship, financial, and resource costs of noncollaborative approaches. The design must anticipate resistance from noncollaborative parties. To accomplish this task, there must be a champion or power person in the system to support the designed procedures, or the design has little chance of success.

Table 8.1 Levels of Intervention for Dispute Design

Informal discussion

Negotiation between disputing parties

Facilitated discussion

Mediation · More formal

Advisory arbitration (review committee)

Formal arbitration
(by leadership or review committee) · Higher cost

Formal, judicial grievance procedures

There are a variety of levels for designing a system for managing conflict (see Table 8.1). Discussion and negotiation between disputing parties involves the least cost, greatest level of informality, and least need for third-party assistance. Facilitation, mediation, or review boards can be low cost if the system can train its own staff. Costs and formality go up significantly as we look outside the system for third-party assistance. The factors that determine the level of intervention include budget, legal issues, willingness of disputants to negotiate, availability of third-party neutrals, and the kind of problem.

Box 8.3 provides an example of a successful use of design groups to solve corporate problems that were affecting morale, turnover, and production.

Factors That Influence Success

Building on the above design principles, we can add strategic choices with which to design a system's procedures—its architecture. Costantino and Merchant (1996) provide six principles for creating a system's architecture:

1. Develop guidelines for whether ADR is appropriate.
2. Tailor the ADR process to the particular problem.
3. Build in preventive methods of ADR.
4. Make sure that disputants have the necessary knowledge and skill to choose and use ADR.
5. Create ADR systems that are simple to use and easy to access and that resolve disputes early, at the lowest organizational level, with the least bureaucracy.
6. Allow disputants to retain maximum control over choice of ADR methods and selection of neutral whenever possible. (p. 121)

BOX 8.3
Example of a Design Team Creating System Architecture

International Research Institute (IRI) is a 250-worker petroleum firm that performs analytical and development services for major oil companies. IRI's 25-member Department of Analytical Services began experiencing low morale and high turnover during the past year. The Human Resource Department regularly heard complaints from and about the department. Individual and group assessment interviews produced many problems, including the following:

- Perceived isolation from the larger company. Some members believed that they were "dumped" into the department to get rid of them. Projects were delayed or slowed down because of frequent miscommunication with other departments.
- Perceived isolation from the wider petroleum community. Their work had become more technical tasks and less analytical services.
- Disconnected from company goals and decision-making processes. Workers found out about decisions through the rumor mill.
- Felt discriminated against in evaluations because of being members of the department. Two grievances were filed in the past 6 months.
- Growing distrust of management. There was no explanation for policy changes. Workers felt left out.
- A design team, with representatives from each of the department roles, met for four 90-minute sessions to create a list of recommendations for presentation to the larger department for refinement and later to management. Following a discussion of goals and realistic options, the team made the following suggestions:
  - Recognize employee accomplishments by having reports to the field offices include the names of employees who performed the work.
  - Boost department visibility by having members of the department make presentations about their role to the staffs of other departments.
  - Change perceptions about the department by changing its name to better reflect its current function and better fit industry practice.
  - Improve communication with management by scheduling regular times for the vice president to exchange information at department meetings.
  - Create a department subgroup whose tasks will be to discuss how policy changes can be successfully implemented and to institute a formal departmental decision-making process.
  - Improve communication, reduce isolation, and clarify professional roles by scheduling visits of department personnel at field locations.
  - Create greater perception of fairness on annual evaluations by including comments from customers and personnel from other departments.

The first principle fits situations where small personnel moves or procedure changes eliminate distress to the system. To illustrate, in a 60-member organization, employees were in continual conflict about not receiving information in a timely manner. After an hour of discussion, we found that the problem revolved around mailroom procedures. The group created a mailroom committee to monitor, help, and guide the dissemination of information. The group did not need the development of formal ADR processes for complaints. They needed a mailroom committee to eliminate the source of their frustrations.

When designing the architecture for a system, during the assessment phase, identify a specific list of problems that the design will address. The importance of this factor surfaced in ADR work with an organization where there were frequent complaints about favoritism and power imbalance when the leaders made decisions. In the discussions, it was discovered that the leaders informed everybody about every step of decision making through the e-mail system. Many workers complained that they either did not have access to e-mail or did not know how to use it. The design architecture needed to focus specifically on e-mail access and training. When they agreed to fix this problem, there was no more discussion of favoritism or power imbalances.

Strategies 3-5 of Costantino and Merchant's principles rely on access to ADR procedures and training. Knowledge about the ADR system and how to work with it cannot be taken for granted. Consider one organization where people challenged promotion policies and work rules. A few workers began filing formal grievances. When asked why the workers did not go to their Equal Opportunity Advisor in Human Resources and use the normal complaint processes, they said that they were not aware of the processes. A major component of their design involves the EEO advisor scheduling time with each department to build relationships and provide training. As Costantino and Merchant (1996) explain,

> If ADR becomes too complicated to use or too frustrating to access, disputants will default to the status quo, the current dispute resolution mechanism (usually litigation or another right-based method), although in some instances the default mechanism may be for the disputants to walk away and not deal with the conflict at all. (p. 119)

Disputants are more receptive to assistance by third-party neutrals if they have a choice about who the neutral is. They will have greater commitment to the processes if they are able to negotiate the timing, duration, and procedures with the mediator. Additionally, because 9 out of 10 corporate neutrals are chosen from within the company, neutrals who possess a negative history with any of the disputants should have the right to refer the request to other in-house professionals.

Dispute Design Models

In 1990, as many as one third of all nonunion employees in the United States had access to an in-house, company-run dispute resolution process. Singer (1994) describes a set of grievance procedures used by many organizations:

1. Formalized response from the employee's supervisor
2. Response from the next level of management

3. Response from the division chairperson
4. Response from the "right of review" committee (p. 97)

General Electric uses a similar approach with a strong emphasis on the fourth step, which they call a "peer review" committee. The committee members are volunteers, primarily nonmanagement, who use a majority vote to arbitrate disputes. The committee limits disputes to breaches of company policy with regard to pay, work rules, and employee evaluations.

The role of organizational ombudsperson involves problem solving, mediating, facilitating, and, in many cases, designing dispute resolution systems for the organization.

Ombudsperson

The ombudsperson is a professional role that is growing in prominence in a variety of settings, including education, hospitals, nursing homes, corporations, and government.

The role is based on the Scandinavian practice where respected, independent public officials investigate citizen complaints against the government. Currently, more than 200 American corporations use some form of in-house neutral to handle employee and customer complaints. Ballys in Las Vegas, which employs 4,000 workers, recently provided mediation training for 24 staff members about how to improve staff communications, handle employee disputes, and deal with interdepartmental and supervisor-employee disputes. Serving outside of the corporate chain of command, the ombudsperson provides confidential assistance to people with complaints, concerns, or conflicts. Rowe (1991b) identifies many of the roles frequently performed by ombudspeople: counselor, informal go-between and facilitator, formal mediator, informal fact finder, upward feedback mechanism, consultant, problem prevention device, and change agent (p. 353).

One of the requirements for ADR professionals in general is the ability to be impartial or perceived as neutral. It is even more important for ombudspeople. If the ombudsperson does not function independently of the organizational structure, his or her role will be limited by lack of trust. Consequently, there may be a conflict of interest any time the ombudsperson is required to participate in policy-making decisions, serve as a witness in formal judicial proceedings, maintain explicit case records that management might use against an employee, or perform in some capacity as a manager of staff. Perceived neutrality legitimizes the function of the ombudsperson. Gadlin and Pino (1997) describe three components of this neutrality:

1. Resists taking sides during a conflict

Table 8.2. Continuum of Ombudsperson Roles

Systems change agent
Mediator
Facilitator
Shuttle diplomat
Fact finder
Coach
Counselor for discussing options
Source of referrals
Listener

Deeper involvement by ombudsperson (alongside Fact finder)

2. Possesses no stake in the outcome of a dispute
3. Demonstrates fairness, objectivity, and evenhandedness in relationships.

Facilitators, mediators, and arbitrators have a reasonably narrow range of options when they approach their ADR responsibilities. Because the tasks differ, facilitators are not necessarily good mediators, nor are mediators always effective facilitators. The first deals more with large groups, complex issues, multiparty interests, and more often with a nondirective style. The latter most often deals with smaller groups, more clearly defined issues, a few disputing parties, and a bit more directive style. The ombudsperson must do both and more. Rowe (1995) explores the range of options and skills that ombudspeople perform frequently. Based on level of involvement, Table 8.2 summarizes the roles of the ombudsperson based on the level of involvement of disputing parties and ombudsperson.

Listening. Providing empathy and emotional support is the least amount of involvement that we might expect of an ombudsperson. Often, this is enough. When people feel heard and respected for what they feel, this often defuses the emotional components of a problem. Just to hear another person say that the feelings are not unusual or abnormal is often a powerful remedy for reducing the level of conflict.

Referring to others who can help. As organizational cultures get more complex, people know less about who to go to for information. Effective ombudspeople develop an effective organizational network for finding answers to problems. The network may stretch all the way from an off-the-record opinion from a lawyer to the help of an administrative assistant who knows how to work around barriers in a system.

Developing options. Helping clients evaluate their options is a primary role for the ombudsperson. Clients can choose to (a) do nothing, (b) resolve the problem with the coaching the ombudsperson provides, (c) use a third party to intervene, or (d) use formal organizational processes to resolve the issue. The discussion must weigh many factors, including the emotional, professional, or financial costs of the option; the time it might take to reach a settlement; the potential for success; and the choice that the organizational culture is most likely to support.

Coaching. Frequently, people lack knowledge or skill for knowing how to approach a problem. The ombudsperson can draw on past experience to teach people tactics that have worked in the past with their particular kind of problem.

Fact-finding. Occasionally, clients may not have enough information to know the level and extent of a problem. Is the problem unique to them, or does everyone in the system feel the same way? If a problem has surfaced and the initial information appears confusing, the ombudsperson can interview all parties to clarify and expand knowledge about the issue.

Shuttle diplomacy. When people or departments have difficulty talking to each other, the ombudsperson may shuttle between disputing parties. In this role, the ombudsperson will have to be sensitive to people who feel threatened by such discussions. Objectivity and fairness means not making judgments until all parties have been heard fully. Additionally, caution should be observed to prevent disciplinary action from being taken against the person with the complaint.

Facilitative discussion. Some of the most important work done by ombudspeople occurs in informal discussions where potential or current problems are identified and discussed briefly. The ombudsperson may raise awareness or help employees explore possibilities. This may occur formally when the ombudsperson serves as a guest at a staff meeting or leads a staff meeting in a discussion about how they might work together more effectively.

Mediation. Using the ombudsperson as a third-party neutral enables parties to resolve a conflict in a confidential, off-the-record, nondisciplinary process. The advantage of the ombudsperson is that he or she will be able to hear the problem with greater understanding about the organizational culture than might a mediator from outside the system.

Systems change agent. Working with managers, directors, and management, the ombudsperson attempts to eliminate processes that create employee conflict, poor morale, or conflict. Rowe (1995) suggests, "A practitioner might notice a problem new to the organization and surface it in a timely fashion, thus serving as an 'early warning' channel for new issues" (p. 110). This might occur in departmental problem-solving sessions or brainstorming sessions with managers. Some ombudspeople teach conflict, stress, or change management skills to groups of employees.

Professional Profile: Mary Rowe
Ombudsperson for MIT

The Ombudsperson Eats Lunch Alone

Organizations are composed of members with overlapping relationships who are engaged in extended conversations. The personal and the political are always elements in organizational life: who reports to whom, who collaborates with whom, who is a mentor, who competes with whom for the bigger budget and the larger authority, who plays golf with whom over the weekend, and so on. These elements imbue organizations in Silicon Valley, the halls of the IRS, and the Vatican. Organizational politics is a fact of life.

The ombudsperson brings a position of neutrality and impartiality to all of this partisanship. The power of the position partly derives from its independence; ombudspeople are outside the usual reporting structure. They keep no case records for the employer; they have no power to insist or enforce solutions, and the majority of their work is unknown to anyone except the people who use their services. In the United States, ombuds are most frequently found in state government offices, federal agencies, universities, and large corporations. However, some ombuds are independent practitioners. Some serve specialty populations, such as children or prisoners.

The benefits of having an organizational ombudsperson are that the people they serve have assistance with problem solving and fair solutions to problems. The organizational ombudsperson typically outlines an array of possible responses to a given problem and allows the person with a concern to decide for him- or herself which option to choose. A common outcome is that people are often able to solve problems themselves or at least at lower levels than they might otherwise. Situations that can be problematic for formal grievance procedures (e.g., those in which the only evidence is he said/she said) may be explored and resolved using the skills and confidentiality of the ombudsperson.

The effectiveness of the position depends on the ability of the professionals to demonstrate confidentiality and integrity, dispute resolution skills, and usually systems change skills. Of course, effectiveness also depends on the culture and wisdom of line and staff management.

Introduction to the Practitioner

Organizational ombudspeople work hard to be seen as truly impartial. For example, they might decide never to have lunch one on one in public with anyone in their organization (hence the title of this section, which originated in a conversation with Mary Rowe, ombudsperson for MIT and a cofounder of The Ombudsman Association).

The university hired Mary in 1973 with the title "Special Assistant for Women and Work," but from the first, she was visited by men as well as women. She formally became a general ombudsperson in 1980. In her view, there was a good fit between the high value she personally places on impartiality and neutrality and the emphasis on fair solutions prized by this university, with its strong focus on science and technology, design and planning, humanities and management. "Engineers, scientists, planners, and managers think in terms of finding faults in systems and finding solutions to problems. And because they also think in terms of systems, it was not a large leap to apply systems thinking to the organization itself, and to appreciate how an ombuds office might assist the organization to keep improving organizational operation."

Mary says, "One function of an organizational ombudsperson is helping people to help themselves, whenever that is appropriate." The organizational ombudsperson is a confidential and informal information resource, communications channel, and dispute resolver, as well as a person who helps an organization work for change. Relatively informal ombuds functions she cites are listening, providing relevant information, reframing issues and developing options, making referrals, doing informal third-party intervention, looking into the problem, and generating generic solutions and systems change. Occasionally, ombudspeople may engage in formal, classical mediation.

Mary makes a distinction between such organizational ombuds like herself and classical ombudspeople, whose positions are created by law and who are generally appointed by legislative bodies. Classical ombudspeople receive complaints about the administrative acts of governmental bodies. "Classical ombudspeople serve as formal investigators and fact finders with subpoena power and strong legal safeguards for their independence and the confidentiality of their records."

Interested beginners may sign up for Ombuds 101, a course offered by The Ombudsman Association (TOA), along with other professional ombuds associations. Ombuds 202 and other specialized courses are available thereafter. TOA includes practitioners in hundreds of corporations, academic institutions, and governmental entities. You may reach TOA by contacting its web page: www.igc.org/toa.

Mary lists several qualities as important for the practice of ombudsmanry. "Humor and patience are essential. Practitioners must enjoy problem solving and not be concerned with getting credit for successful performance. This can also be a very lonely job. Ombudspersons need good support!"

Work of the Practitioner

Advance preparation for each case is usually not an issue, because Mary rarely knows who will be requesting her services until the people arrive in her office. Once they arrive, a typical session lasts 15-20 minutes on "bad" days, and 30-60 minutes on "good" ones. Mary typically begins a conversation by explaining how the office works, stressing impartiality, confidentiality, and the absence of case records. Whether or not another meeting is necessary depends on the complexity of the problem. Mary explores the problem with her visitor, helps develop responsible options, and ends with a summary of the visit. Given the frequency of these contacts, it will be no surprise that Mary sees the toughest challenge of ombuds work as coping with exhaustion.

In addition to assisting individuals, organizational ombudspeople spend about one third of their working time on systems change. This occurs in collaboration with colleagues, such as line managers, and staff, such as human resource personnel. For instance, an ombudsperson may notice a problem new in an organization, thus sounding as an early warning signal. Or, ombudspeople may notice a pattern of problems, which suggests the need for policy or procedural change. They may be invited to highlight problems of concern as organizations undertake self-assessment or processes of continuing improvement.

Ombuds occasionally train groups or facilitate meetings that address recurrent problems in an organization. The question of success is highly contextual. In broad terms, it usually means minimizing loss for all and maximizing joint gains. Mary says, "I divide mistakes into those I know I've made and those I'm unaware of . . . the most troublesome ones." In attempting to learn from her mistakes, she finds that errors are often related to a failure to analyze adequately whose interests are at stake and what they are. Of course, there are times when one cannot or should not ask about interests, making this discovery even more difficult.

Opinions About ADR Issues

Changes in ombuds work relate to the fact that this profession is expanding rapidly. Also, terms of service may vary, depending on the practitioner. However, Mary celebrates the fact that the organizational ombudsperson profession began to set out standards of practice several years ago, clarifying ombuds work for new professionals. These standards may be partly responsible for the fact that there is broad substantive agreement about ombuds work among practitioners. She stretches for an exception to this agreement, "Occasionally, ombudspersons may disagree around the edges, e.g., 'How serious would an imminent threat of serious harm need to be before an ombuds would break confidentiality?' "

Mary concludes by saying, "Being an ombuds is the most interesting job in the world." She is proud of the fact that the job of the ombudsperson is one of the most thoroughly integrated positions, with perhaps half of practitioners being female, and one fifth or more being people of color. She finds her colleagues intensely interesting and well prepared. Their appreciation for her leadership is equally sincere. Through her writing, practicing, and training of new ombudspeople, Mary Rowe continues to develop and guide this burgeoning field of conflict management.

Professional Profile:
Christina Sickles Merchant
Federal and Commercial Consultant

Capacity Building for Organizations

Sooner or later, ADR practitioners who have worked in organizations have nightmares about repeated ongoing conflicts with the same work team, the same department, or the same organization. It becomes apparent that, although the names and faces may change, there are certain areas within organizations in which the crop of disputes is bountiful. None of us will live long enough to resolve such a series one dispute at a time. Sooner or later, it becomes obvious that there is something in that organizational science that makes it so fertile for disputes.

Thus, nightmares turn to dreams of how organizational interventions could reduce the number and severity of disputes. There could be changes in the way disputes are handled. For instance, employees trained in interest-based problem solving could engage in problem solving earlier and more informally than most current grievance systems allow. One ADR practitioner in particular has been active in bringing this dream to reality.

Introduction to the Practitioner

Her clients made her do it! Christina Sickles Merchant maintains that her labor/management clients became aware of interest-based negotiations in the 1980s and requested more frequent use of it in their dealings. Other clients were pushing her to become more involved in the operational aspects of their organizations. Christina had much practical experience in operations from her 17 years as a federal mediator, as well as a degree from Cornell's School of Industrial and Labor Relations. She obtained formal training in organizational development in the midst of this career with the attainment of a master's degree in human resources and organizational development from the joint degree program of the American University and the NTL Institute. In the middle of her term (1994-1995) as president of the Society of Professionals in Dispute Resolution (SPIDR), her responsibilities for large-scale change from adversarial to partnership for her labor/management clients accelerated when President Clinton signed an executive mandate to do so. In the face of hundreds of clients learning about ADR and assessing the manner in which disputes are identified and resolved, Christina saw her practice of building self-mediative capacity emerge.

Christina notes that dispute systems design (DSD) occurs in a variety of dispute resolution contexts—those specific to disputes, processes, or the system as a whole. She reports, "In dispute-specific design, I encourage the convenors to choose the right dispute resolution for the problem, get the appropriately representative people for the team, work with people to prepare them to use the new process on the dispute, and then coach or facilitate the actual process application."

In the introduction and design of a new dispute process, Christina encourages practitioners first to assess the *need* for a new process and then search for an appropriate process to fit the organizational practice and culture. Finally, systemwide design involves the multitude of shifts in the human resource and organizational policy in order to lastingly support a change in dispute resolution practice.

DSD is not necessarily an appropriate area for beginners to enter. First, they need skills and training in organizational development, mediation, and third-party facilitation. This needs to be followed by "practice, practice, practice." Then, in order to build knowledge for wise counsel and advice, the student needs experience with a variety of disputes. In the area of skills development for systems design, the SPIDR Organizational Conflict Management (OCM) sector, formerly the DSD/OD sector, has begun to examine the core skills requisite for optional conflict management systems design practice and performance.

Christina believes that she succeeds because "I am client-focused, with no particular interest in telling people what to do." She believes her style is much more elicitive in nature as a mediator or facilitator so that clients, it is hoped, walk away strengthened in the skills to resolve disputes and knowledge about their organizational culture and preferred practice with respect to resolving disputes. She offers ideas to the parties and links them to others who have experienced similar circumstances. In addition, Christina is a believer in the heuristic value of stories. Narratives are a powerful way to communicate meaning that both parties may share. She also notes an adventuresome spirit; that is, she enjoys the creativity and risk associated with plowing new ground, and less so the maintenance activity of staying with just one organization and one process or program. Finally, she notes, "There are some personal traits which contribute to my success. As a mature person, I am careful not to induce dependency in clients. I have made a choice to focus my efforts on building understanding; giving away my skills, tools, and techniques; and in mentoring 'lay people' to become skilled providers of dispute resolution services within their own systems.

"I spend more time in preparation than anyone I know!" The payoff is that when the mediation begins, the right people are in the room and ready to work. Christina mentions reading and conference calls, wherein she asks tough questions and tests for commitment. She prepares people for a very open process, then works with them during the design process so that they become aware of the basic elements and common sense that lead to success.

Work of the Practitioner

A typical case is the application of interest-based negotiations to a multi-million dollar case (which had already been in existence for 18 years) involving 2,000 grievances over the application of the Fair Labor Standards Act (FLSA) to workers' overtime status in the U.S. Naval shipyards. Christina worked to ensure top-level commitment by the highest Navy and union authorities to the bargaining team's consensus, if reached. Next, she foresaw the necessity of having outside contingency fee counsel involved directly in the negotiations, as well as counsel for the Navy and union. She then focused on facilitating the 13-member team's work to resolve the disputes on a wholehearted consensual basis. Such multiple-party, large-dollar disputes are typical of her caseload.

Given the complexity implied by this example, you will not be surprised that Christina defines her toughest challenge as "adapting to what is going on at any given moment. It is impossible to know at the outset of the dispute what a good job on my part will look like. No matter how careful my preparation, I may need to do a quick redesign at any moment in order to keep the group on a successful path."

Did Christina learn from any mistakes? "Always! The only reason I know the importance of preparation is by not prepping. The only reason I know about having the right people in the room is by having somebody missing." The fact that many of the cases she handles cover untried territory means that she is constantly gathering and learning from feedback as her conflict management practice proceeds.

Opinions About ADR Issues

Christina observes several changes occurring in the field of DSD. First, she notes "exponential applicability. There is a permeable boundary between actually mediating a dispute and designing the next step in how to proceed to implement the result of the mediation and/or how to prevent similar disputes from recurring."

Second, there is an explosion of voluntary dispute resolution methods, and Christina challenges dispute resolvers to consider the practice issues involved. She asks, "What happens when many start practicing what was once the province of a few? How can quality be controlled in a world where everyone mediates?" She applauds the spread of mediators, because "to me, dispute resolution is more a belief system than exclusively a professional domain."

Finally, Christina raises the issue of understanding and reflecting on practice. She concludes, "I am drawn to the example of Kurt Lewin, who is often called a practical theorist. There are other practices and practitioners who are more comfortable with predictability and most likely keep their roles as neutral confined." Instead, Christina enjoys the experience of uncertainty and experimentation, and the expansiveness of working in a pioneering mode with systems to apply alternative dispute resolution processes to nontraditional arenas and to build dispute resolution capacity within the organizational climate and population.

Professional Profile: Frank E. A. Sander
Professor, Harvard Law School

Blueprint for the Multidoor Courthouse

The year 1976 is memorable for being the 200th birthday of the United States. It also encompasses a significant landmark in the development of the field of dispute resolution. That is when the multidoor courthouse concept was first proposed at the Pound Conference, a meeting sponsored by the American Bar Association (ABA), the Judicial Conference of the United States, and the Conference of State Chief Justices. Seventy years prior, Roscoe Pound, a professor at Harvard Law School, had given a famous address on the topic of popular dissatisfaction with the administration of justice. Warren Burger, Chief Justice of the United States in 1976, proposed a similar agenda for the 1976 Pound Conference.

The multidoor model suggests that there are many modes of conflict management, not just litigation. An array of alternatives should be made available to disputants, rather than just the one process that involves attorneys, judges, and juries. Cases arriving at the courthouse should be screened for their inherent characteristics to determine which of the approaches is most suitable for a particular dispute. Although this may sound quite self-evident today, when many courts have adopted this approach, it was a new idea in 1976.

Introduction to the Practitioner

The speech at the Pound conference was given by Frank Sander, a Harvard Law School professor. Frank taught tax and family law; he also conducted labor arbitrations. Frank had spent the prior year on sabbatical in Sweden, pursuing an unrelated topic. However, during that time, he had a chance to reflect on the contrast between labor and family disputes. In arbitration cases, problems seemed to be resolved rather quickly and with good will. Unfortunately, family disputes often were worsened by contact with the legal system. This contrast absorbed him.

Frank began to think and write about how a system of conflict management might be instituted, with litigation still a possibility but not a necessity. He circulated a paper among some colleagues, and, unbeknownst to him, a copy was forwarded to Warren Burger, U.S. Supreme Court Chief Justice, who was planning the Pound Conference. Justice Burger invited Professor Sander to be a conference speaker, because dispute settlement was one of a dozen topics chosen. Modestly, Frank calls this part of the story "being in the right place at the right time." Not only did the American Bar Association "pick up the ball" and become active in the area of dispute resolution, but one of the attendees was in a position to pursue institutionalization at the national level.

As it happened, Judge Griffin Bell attended the Pound Conference and was attracted to the idea of the multidoor courthouse. A few months later, Bell found a direct application for his interest when he was appointed Attorney General by President Carter in the fall of 1976. During his tenure, he set up the Office for Improvement in the Administration of Justice. This office established the first neighborhood justice centers in the United States; these centers represent some of the earliest efforts to institutionalize alternative dispute resolution. Thus, models of Frank Sander's multidoor courthouse were constructed soon after he proposed it.

Work of the Practitioner

Frank continues to institutionalize dispute resolution, sometimes in an advisory capacity consulting with court systems. Currently, he is the vice-chair of a committee set up by the Supreme Judicial Court of Massachusetts, which is dealing with how to institutionalize ADR within the Massachusetts court system. The goal is to retain access to litigation but reconceptualize it as one step in the progression of a dispute. On this committee, he works in concert with others to actually build the multidoor courthouse.

Far beyond Massachusetts, Frank consults with judges and court administrators about how ADR could be woven into the fabric of their systems. He has consulted in Australia, New Zealand, South Africa, and Israel. Recently, he spoke at a conference in Ottawa, Canada to chief justices from countries around the world, laying out the options that might provide a more multifaceted dispute resolution system. These options would then be set up as part of the public dispute resolution process.

Frank challenges judges and court administrators to engage with the questions that are implicit in a multidoor courthouse system. He asks them, "Who will fund the screening of cases and decide on what method is appropriate for which case? Will alternatives to litigation be voluntary or optional? How will the alternatives be funded? Will those who use them incur additional costs, as is now the case in the United States? Does it make sense to charge extra for those who choose methods more likely to result in a more efficient settlement?"

There are many questions that arise in the institutionalization of ADR in addition to cost, such as, Who will provide the services? Will the providers include volunteers? If so, how will dispute resolution grow to become a professional field in which people can make an adequate living? Will there be a time when teachers can stop saying to students who are interested in working in ADR after graduation, "Don't give up your day job"?

Justices are not the only ones on the receiving end of Professor Sander's challenging questions. Frank has also engaged members of the American Bar Association in dialogue designed to bring the multidoor courthouse closer to completion. For instance, he asked, "Should attorneys have an ethical responsibility to inform clients about their alternatives before proceeding with litigation?" He felt this was similar to the responsibilities physicians have to advise patients about alternative treatments. He recommended it to the bar, not only because clients would be better informed, but also because attorneys would have to educate themselves about ADR before informing clients and responding to potential questions. The recommendation has since been adopted in a number of places.

In addition to helping to institutionalize dispute resolution within courts and the legal profession, Frank educates students, attorneys, judges, and nonattorney practitioners in a variety of settings. He continues to teach courses on dispute resolution at Harvard Law School. He trains attorney and nonattorney practitioners in continuing education programs. He has written many articles for law and dispute resolution journals. The classic in this field, "Fitting the Forum to the Fuss" (co-authored with Stephen Goldberg), details which dispute resolution approaches are available and suggests how to decide which one to apply to a given situation. The textbook *Dispute Resolution*, written with Goldberg and E. Green, was a first in the field. Students at the law school and in continuing education have spread the multidoor courthouse concept far and wide. Readers of his text and articles do the same.

There is no answer to the question of which skills he would recommend to a beginner, because beginners would be unlikely to succeed at institutionalization. In terms of why he has been a successful architect of ADR, Professor Sander explains, "My formal role at Harvard Law School provides the clout that compels judges and court administrators to give ADR a serious hearing, and, often, to apply the model. I am a strong believer in incremental change and in pilot projects. Modest programs which demonstrate their worth are more valuable than dramatic efforts which may not prove lasting." He approaches changing justice systems as a long-range project that requires patience and commitment in working toward the ultimate goal.

This "go slow to go fast" approach also applies to Frank's experience of successful attempts at institutionalization. Patience is required, as well as the willingness to work with others who start from different premises. Those involved must commit to a project that will require extensive time and resources. The maturity factor often associated with success with ADR techniques is especially important in institutionalizing new systems.

Opinions About ADR Issues

Such success factors predict the challenges Frank cited. He says, "It is difficult not to be discouraged by the lack of funding for ADR programs. It is discouraging to deal with judges who believe that truth may only be discovered through jury trials."

Despite some discouragement, Frank finds optimism in the expansion of ADR in a variety of areas. He notes a growing number of law schools that have at least one ADR course, and some with quite extensive offerings. He notes, "More law firms are institutionalizing ADR, offering a variety of options to their clients. Some firms have discovered ADR because a judge ordered one of the alternatives applied to a particular case. Individual attorneys are providing ADR services, partly due to client pressure. Lawyers around the world look to the U.S. for models of ADR." The legal system has definitely adopted the multidoor courthouse concept in a variety of instances.

In addition to legal applications, institutionalization has taken a number of forms. There are now consulting organizations that offer training, research, and practice to the public. The for-profit organizations have their own reasons for advancing practice and spreading the word about ADR. Nonprofit organizations concerned with ADR have also been formed.

One of the nonprofits, the Center for Public Resources (CPR), deserves special mention because its effects have been felt so widely. Begun in 1980 in an effort to institutionalize ADR among industries, CPR now has more than 250 corporate members and 250 law firm members. These members pledge to try to solve disputes at the lowest possible level, that is, negotiating, mediating, arbitrating, and going to court only as a last resort. At semiannual meetings, neutrals such as Frank train and update members on ADR developments. Frank believes this "puts ADR into the corporate bloodstream," so that customers and clients of the CPR members who have disputes with them over products or services may ask to pursue the same approach to dispute resolution. Companies that understand and practice ADR are more likely to employ the methods with their clients and customers. CPR exemplifies the work of new organizations that have institutionalized ADR and are working to persuade others to join them in that change.

Finally, Frank speaks of the increase in the number of federal agencies that have adopted a range of dispute resolution methods, largely because of the Administrative Dispute Resolution Act, passed in 1990 and reaffirmed in 1996. In essence, this legislation directs all federal agencies to develop policies on the use of ADR, appoint an ADR specialist, and provide ADR training where appropriate. Since that time, many federal agencies have developed programs that limit the usual resort to litigation. There have been executive orders along the same line.

As noted above, there are a number of issues on which those who institutionalize ADR disagree. Allocation of resources and qualifications of neutrals are two issues that Frank Sander highlights. His own preference is for courthouse systems in which the choice of method does not penalize ADR users. He also advocates the use of full-time professionals as neutrals, fearing that other approaches will not encourage the professional growth of the field. Whatever the resolution of these important issues, Frank Sander's multidoor courthouse has become the master plan for institutionalizing ADR.

Chapter 9

Training and Education

Tell me and I shall forget.
Show me and I may not understand.
Involve me and I shall always remember.
                    —Native American Saying

In most surveys of groups or organizations in conflict, people voice a common theme: "We have a failure to communicate." Parties want to talk about their issues, but they are not interested in listening to the issues of others. They want others to be flexible, while they maintain an inflexible position. A study cited by Walton (1991) concludes, "For every person who is fired for incompetence, two people are fired for personality factors. The major contributor: lack of communication skills" (p. 6).

It is easy to become a prisoner to tactics we learned long ago, tactics that may be ineffective in today's organizational environment. The need for conflict management training and education grows as the issues become more complex, diversity in organizations increases, workers' responsibilities grow with less time to accomplish them, and as more people resort to violence as the solution to their problems. In a culture with profound changes in organizations, families, and communities, people need to learn new ways to cope. In *Workplace 2000*, Boyett and Conn (1991) propose that in the next decade, American workers can expect a great deal more training in interpersonal, team, and problem-solving skills. "Workers of tomorrow need the skills to break mental sets, think creatively, and find innovative approaches to problem resolution" (p. 281).

Events of the past few years reflect the need for conflict management training in communities and their organizations.

❑ The inability to negotiate location of key operations and the selection of senior management torpedoed the $35 billion merger of American Home Products and Monsanto. Dean Witter analyst Paul Brook explained, "The breakup had nothing to do with business issues. It has everything to do with the ability of the senior management to get along" ("AHP-Monsanto Merger," 1998, p. B1).

❑ The National School Safety Center reports that 1 in 12 students who stay away from school do so out of fear. The National Crime Prevention Council finds that because of fear, 10% of students drop out of school activities, 11% stay home or cut classes, and 12% carry weapons to protect themselves ("School Harassment," 1998, p. 10D).

❑ In a survey of 100 diversified corporate organizations, Sherriton and Stern (1997) found that 95% had recently undergone significant changes, such as merger, acquisition, new alliances, or movement to team processes. Thirty-one percent of respondents believed that their organizations had the knowledge, skills, and ability to address the issues of change.

❑ A West Coast union reports that 500 employee grievances, most dealing with disciplinary actions, occurred during a single year (Cascio, 1998).

❑ Two people are murdered and 18,000 assaulted each year in the workplace ("OSHA Issues Guidelines," 1996).

❑ The EEOC receives more than 12,500 sexual harassment complaints a year (Fisher, 1993).

Conflict in Organizations Is . . .

Workplace and organizational conflicts are complex. Conflict may begin with a poor fit of an individual and assigned responsibilities, but it escalates at a fast pace if workers perceive unfair rules, ineffective management, unclear responsibilities, or too much work assigned. Workers may choose to avoid discussion about the building tension, but it does not reduce the negative impacts on department production. Reynolds (1998) points out that common to both managers and workers in most organizations is an aversion to addressing conflict until the conflict reaches a point of crisis.

Expressions of conflict in organizations occur in many forms. The following statements provide a sampling of comments frequently heard.

"Why can't they do their jobs right?"—Interdependence of workers, especially when one worker's efforts affect the success of another, creates a climate ripe for blaming, griping, and complaining.

"We've got to get our own share."—Limited resources and organizational politics create a climate of turf battles and perceptions of unfairness. Each unit believes that it deserves more than other units.

"Why bother? It's not worth the effort."—Apathy and cynicism pervade organizations where there are few promotion opportunities, small annual pay raises, and limited benefits. Because individuals see no reward in collaboration, they say things to others with less sensitivity and more negativism.

"If they weren't the way they are, we'd do better."—Many conflicts involve negative attributions of other workers. Individuals say things like, "Management people are like that" or "What would you expect from someone with their background?" People will behave in unkind ways toward someone to whom they attribute negative motives or do not respect for his or her skills or experience.

Ramsey (1997) summarizes a few of the common causes of workplace disputes:

- ❏ Misunderstandings based on age, race, or cultural differences
- ❏ Disagreement about performance ratings or allocation of organizational rewards
- ❏ Fear of job loss or being bypassed for a promotion
- ❏ Rumors or falsehoods spoken about an individual or group
- ❏ Sexual harassment
- ❏ Blaming for mistakes or mishaps

Scholars identify many of the issues that should be addressed in conflict management educational or training programs:

Good conflict management means accepting the inevitability of differences and making commitment to dialogue. (Eisenberg & Goodall, 1993)

The goals, opinions, attitudes, and feelings of all parties are recognized as legitimate and everyone takes a constructive role in solving the problems. The conflict must be depersonalized so that the energy can be channeled into solutions rather than into combat. (Harris, 1993, p. 413)

Conflict can bring to the surface issues that require resolution, relieve tensions, and lead to the development of new channels of communication. (Koehler, Anatol, & Applebaum, 1981)

Strategies for managing conflict may be organized in one of four approaches: Focus the group on superordinate goals; restructure or reframe current problems so that there is greater potential for mutually beneficial solutions; discuss changes to group structure or communication processes; or train parties in effective ways to confront, smooth situations, or bring conflict to resolution. (Daniels, Spiker, & Papa, 1997)

When workers are constantly pressured to produce more, faster, and with fewer resources, anger and frustration are natural by-products. Likewise, job uncertainty produces fear, insecurity, and anxiety. Whenever these elements exist in the organization, tensions become heightened and conflicts more frequent. Consequently, the organization's members demonstrate shorter patience with changes and more displays of defensiveness as they attempt to protect themselves from emotional or career harm.

The True Cost of Conflict

The cost of conflict occurs at several levels: individual, departmental, and organizational. According to a survey by New York City-based Accountemps, the world's largest temporary staffing service, executives spend 9 weeks each year—18% of their work time—resolving personality clashes between employees. That is nearly double the amount of time they spent on employee mediation 10 years ago (Jaffe & Scott, 1998).

Cascio (1998) says that a West Coast union reports that they spend about $600,000 and 4,580 labor hours annually on employee grievances. Each case that goes to arbitration costs about $6,700. The conclusion of a 1995 survey of public relations professionals reflects the irony of these statistics: Ninety-five percent of the conflict problems never should have made it past the immediate supervisor or manager (Reynolds, 1998).

However, the cost factor to resolve conflicts can go beyond judicial costs. Lost time, low morale, and increased absenteeism cost organizations in terms of productivity and profitability. Individuals who call in sick may actually be taking a "mental health day" to get away from the stress caused by unresolved conflict. For example, Imperial Oil Ltd. estimates that in one year, absenteeism, employee turnover, lost productivity, and legal expenses cost the company $8 million (Demirijian, 1997).

Box 9.1 illustrates a standoff between two departments of the Petroleum Institute who are unable to manage their conflict. They lacked the willingness to engage in problem solving and appeared more willing to tolerate the high costs of lost contracts, employee turnover, and antagonistic relationships. A committee composed of members from both the administration and research departments recommended the creation of staff linkages between the departments to remove delays and build a working relationship. The people who serve as linkages could return to their departments and inform or train staff about what was needed to get proposals completed on time. This was the solution recommended by the staff, but the senior administration did not adopt it. They chose instead to find a new administration manager.

Differences Between Education and Training

It is a mistake to assume that people who volunteer for a community group have the skills to work constructively with others. It is naive to believe that people selected for their technical expertise will work collaboratively with other experts. It is a trap to believe that professionals who agree on a common goal will be able to negotiate effectively issues of shared concern. The failure of the $35 billion AHP-Monsanto merger described earlier is a case in point. Training and education seek to bridge the gap between *want to* and *able to*.

Although the terms *education* and *training* are often used interchangeably, the two may be differentiated. Davis and Davis (1998) describe training as "the process through which skills are developed, information is provided, and attitudes are nurtured, in order to help individuals who work in organizations become more effective and efficient in their work" (p. 44). Training may focus on

---

BOX 9.1
High Costs of Failure to Get Along

Petroleum Institute, a firm with 900 employees, loses $1 million per year in contracts because of the failure to submit contract proposals to companies on time. Two departments, one that conducts the research and a second that does the administration of contracts, share responsibility for completing the proposals.

The research managers assess the problem as, "We submit proposals to administration according to the rules they give us. We get the proposals back with a note to change them according to the new rules. When our support staff calls administration to ask for guidance, it takes a week and our staff are talked to rudely."

The administration manager complains, "We're always short staffed and overworked. The research people are a bunch of prima donnas. They're not willing to follow the rules that govern proposals. They leave figuring out the rules to us and then complain because we're asking them to do the proposal right. They're rude to my staff and a big reason for our high turnover."

This is the third administration manager in 3 years. The research manager says that the problem centers in poor administrative leadership and recommends that the current administration manager be replaced.

---

competence in specific skills such as problem solving, communication, negotiation, and mediation. Training answers the question *how.*

In contrast, education answers the question *why* or under what conditions. Costantino and Merchant (1996) explain that "Education is a dynamic ongoing process of increasing awareness of conflict itself, about the typical and individual responses to it, and potential choices in conflict management" (p. 135). Frequently, educational programs include training as a component of the program. For example, the ADR program at the University of Denver integrates theory and practice with insights of both scholars who research and practitioners who use the skills daily.

The following examples illustrate the variety of education and training being offered by organizations:

AT&T Southwest managers hold workshops with the goal of identifying and discussing organizational values. The workshops promote awareness about how differences in values inhibit the effectiveness of teams, resolution of conflict, and the breakdown of communication.

At Ford Motor Company's Fairlane Training and Development Center, workers learn a problem-solving process called Global 8D. The model includes developing interim containment before discussion of long-term solutions, defining root causes, proposing methods for monitoring long-term results, and identifying how to prevent recurrence (Davis & Davis, 1998).

For several years, US West formed "Futuristic Teams," groups of employees drawn from branch offices in the states that the utility served. The representatives met for 3 days to discuss significant problems or challenges facing the company. During Day 1, they carefully defined issues and potential solutions. On Day 2, they established criteria for the best solutions and debated the pros and cons of solution paths. Day 3 involved presentations of portions of their debate to senior management, who were tasked with making decisions about the problems.

Employees at the Quaker Oats Company bring project or communication problems to a training program, where they learn and practice a five-step problem-solving process: problem definition, problem verification, solution brainstorming, implementation, and evaluation. Through structured exercises, employees learn to solve their own problems in systematic ways (Davis & Davis, 1998).

Sherriton and Stern (1997) point out that training should be "perceived as an intervention rather than just a means of informing or providing skills" (p. 174). They argue that training must be regarded as only one of many strategies that work together to achieve the desired outcome. Training will not resolve organizational conflict without decision-making processes, structural design, and leadership behavior that supports elements of the training.

Designing Training Programs

Costantino and Merchant (1996) list as the primary tasks for design of a conflict management training program as identifying the following:

- ❑ Purpose of training or education
- ❑ Target audience
- ❑ Subject matter
- ❑ Required expertise
- ❑ Program format
- ❑ Logistics.

The tasks begin with determining the purpose for the program. The choice of lecture, media, and role-plays depends upon whether the purpose is to raise awareness, resolve current problems, teach new behaviors, or influence the culture's managing of conflict. Each kind of audience for which training is planned brings to the program different skills, work experience, and needs.

For example, for a group of professionals from several industries, we proposed training in negotiation and conflict management. But we were not sure how to focus the content, so we called several of them together for a discussion.

They said, "We want our people to know how to use the most appropriate communication channel to communicate their messages, to have skill in delivering difficult messages without making others defensive, to demonstrate effective listening, and to know how to communicate constructively in groups." The topical areas we planned needed to be narrowed so that we could address specific needs and applications relevant to the organizations.

Logistical needs such as overhead projectors, flip charts, markers, and sufficient handouts should not rest on unchecked assumptions. Many trainers who have not planned these needs find that they will have times when they cannot use an overhead because the bulbs burned out, cannot use the flip chart because no one brought markers, or must do group discussion in a room with immovable chairs. If there will be small group discussions, are there break-out rooms?

Weave together presentations, interactive discussions, and experiential exercises. The experiential exercises provide opportunity for participants to find relevance in subject matter and insights that may not be achieved through presentations. Balance the time commitments of presentations with time needed for role-plays or panel discussions. It comes as a surprise to some trainers when a role-play or simulation goes longer than expected and there is no time left to cover planned content areas.

Additionally, trainers need to anticipate the presence of difficult participants. It is not unusual for students to come with private agendas to conflict management courses. Through continuous questions and examples, they use the group for personal therapy. The teacher should not expect the group to manage these people; it is the responsibility of the teacher. Keep a section of the board for tangential questions and say, "We'll try to deal with that later." Divide the class into small workgroups to weaken the control of problem members over the group. Face away from problem members during discussions so that they have difficulty catching your eye for questions. Without proper management, one difficult member in skills-oriented courses can seriously divert group energy.

Heitler (1990) views training as a form of coaching where coaches help people engage in cooperative behaviors instead of viewing others as rivals. She believes that two conditions will increase the likelihood of cooperation: participant confidence in their problem-solving skills and perception of others' willingness to solve problems. These two conditions may be facilitated through training. Heitler (1990) proposes several techniques to achieve these goals:

❑ Help participants reframe issues in a way that softens antagonism.

❑ Through verbal drills, promote awareness about the impact of provocative tones of voice.

❑ Teach participants to listen for what is right instead of what is wrong.

❑ As a teacher, demonstrate constructive responses to antagonistic or uncooperative statements.

❏ Give participants practice in answering "yes and . . ." instead of "yes but . . ." to statements they find argumentative.

❏ Use the prisoner's dilemma game to demonstrate the negative consequences for persistent antagonistic behavior.

Factors That Inhibit Success

National training and development consultant Nanett Miner, EEd, provides four reasons why training fails (personal communication, October 29, 1998).

1. Frequently, organizations select in-house trainers based on technical expertise, without regard to training education or experience. Often, these programs lack a logical sequence, balance between presentation and experiential activities, or the best choice of resources. After the training fails to accomplish the intended purpose, the organization becomes reluctant to attempt such training a second time. Training is like sky diving. You may do it well on your first jump, but it would be a whole lot easier with training and practice.

2. Miner laments, "If you have a hammer, everything looks like a nail." Some people believe that if you conduct training, it will solve the problem. "Not true," quips Miner. She describes her experience at General Electric. Engineers came to their jobs from college with no project management training. So, GE decided to provide project management training for its new graduates. GE found that after the training, only about 1 in 20 of the participants could do project management effectively. When Miner investigated the problem, she discovered that follow-up was as important as the training itself. The success rate went up considerably when the new managers worked with mentors on their first few projects following training.

3. Trainers need to adapt course content to the ages or skills of participants. Miner points out that most corporate training programs rely heavily on presentations that are not effective with adult learners. Adults require a program that includes interactive discussion, content with immediate applicability, responsiveness to questions, stories that link content to their experience, and experiential activities. For example, Box 9.2 provides an example of how an experiential component was integrated with complex content.

4. Be sure that the problem requires training. For example, at one company, customer service received an unusually high number of complaints about one department. Management decided that customer relations training for the department was the answer to the problem. The trainer wanted to prepare content based on need, so interviewed a few members of the department. The same problem kept coming up: With only one fax machine, it was difficult to send materials to a client in a timely manner. At times, representatives got tired of walking down to the fax machine and failed to send out the material at all. The answer was not more training, it was a second fax machine. Training may not solve

---

BOX 9.2

Example of an Experiential Component in an Adult Training Program

A Fortune 500 company made industrial modems for three industries: ATM machines, grocery store scanners, and airline systems. The company's management decided that it wanted its engineers to understand how the circuits of the three systems worked together. When they asked the designers of the systems, they discovered a very complex process.

The trainer identified 12 roles performed by workers that comprised the organizational circuit enabling the three systems. She gave each of the participants written instructions about his or her role. During a class simulation, students played their roles while they put Legos together in patterns that represented the operation of the system's circuit.

"The Legos enabled the engineers to reduce the complexity of the organization's complex circuit within and between the systems to something they could touch and feel." Adult learning requires the trainer to link the relevance of subject matter to the context of participant experience.

---

conflict problems in some organizations because the problem may be ineffective managers, a difficult employee, antagonistic clients, or the structure of the system that prevents responsive staff.

Conflict Management Skills Training

Norwest Banks of Colorado provide conflict management training that is required for managers and voluntary for the rest of the staff. The program focuses on facilitating proactive skills for preventing conflict before it escalates. The phases of the day-long training are as follows:

1. Participants discuss and practice nondefensive behavior through listening, empathy, and "I"-statement drills.
2. The group identifies cultural triggers that fuel defensive communication, such as value differences between Generation Xers and baby boomer managers, differences in nonverbal behaviors created by racial background, conflicts related to gender differences, or differences in communication styles.
3. The leader presents a problem-solving model that begins with agreeing on a definition of a problem, brainstorming options for solving the problem, selecting the best option for the current circumstances, and evaluating the impact of the potential solution.
4. The group analyzes and discusses case studies drawn from employee experiences within the organization.

5. The leader describes people who are difficult to work with. The group discusses strategies to work effectively and manage conflict with these difficult people.

Cross-Cultural Skills Training

Diamond and Fisher (1995) describe training workshops conducted in Cyprus during May and June 1993. The workshop participants were five Greek Cypriots and five Turkish Cypriots, all educators in their respective communities. The model for the workshop used small problem-solving groups that were led by skilled, impartial facilitators. The strategy for the program involved bringing together representatives from antagonistic groups to "share their perceptions and concerns, mutually analyze the conflict, and jointly develop creative ideas for directions toward resolution that might be fed back into the policy-making process" (p. 289). Program designers promoted dialogue through discussions, role-plays, simulations, and structured exercises. The workshop had four phases:

1. Program begins with a discussion of underlying fears and needs of the two communities.
2. Participants discuss the dual role of education: its ability to maintain the current state of conflict or its ability to deescalate conflict.
3. Small, bicommunal subgroups propose peace-building activities that might be used in their educational systems.
4. Participants conduct a force-field analysis that identifies the strengths of each of the proposals and the potential resistance that the proposals will receive.

Evaluation questionnaires given after the training indicated that the discussions accomplished several of their goals. The workshops created dialogue, a greater understanding of the cultural similarities, and greater awareness of the conflicts between the communities.

Prudential Intercultural provides a different format for understanding conflict across cultures. Three days of training for Prudential Insurance employees begin with presentations designed to provide depth of understanding about cultures. The presentations are followed by role-play exercises, where employees engage in a variety of behaviors associated with a culture, such as dining rituals and gift giving (Davis & Davis, 1998).

Clarke and Lipp (1998) describe an industry program for workers in U.S.-based Japanese subsidiaries. The program attempts to help U.S. and Japanese workers develop greater understanding about each other's intentions and perceptions so that they can work together effectively. The program uses a seven-step process.

Step 1: Problem identification. Each of the Japanese and American workers writes a brief description of a conflict incident or situation that occurred in his or her work setting. Still working individually, each person then develops an explanation, based on his or her culture's expectations, about how and why the problem occurred. Additionally, each participant identifies the typical approach within his or her culture for handling a problem like the one he or she described.

Step 2: Problem clarification. In order to clarify differences in understanding, the groups adjourn to separate rooms and discuss what they wrote down. Later, they reconvene, and each group explains how people from its culture approach this type of problem. The goal is to help both groups reach a mutual understanding (not necessarily acceptance) of each other's approaches. Additionally, this helps both groups understand that there are reasonable explanations for behaviors that group memebers see in people from other cultures.

Step 3: Cultural exploration—reversing roles. Each group discusses what it would be like for the group members to approach a problem from the perspective of the other group. To heighten cultural awareness, each group could role-play behaviors that it would expect from the other group in a specific situation. The goal of this step is to increase understanding and reduce perceptions such as "I wish they could be more like us" or "Why don't they do it our way?" For example, the Americans might become sensitized to the importance of the Japanese value of not "losing face" within their community. The Japanese might develop more respect for American independence and the drive for individual achievement.

Step 4: Organizational exploration. Group members discuss the differences between the corporate culture of headquarters in Japan and the U.S. subsidiary. Additionally, they discuss the impact of state or government laws that affect their business choices. Participants identify corporate culture issues such as quality standards, team expectations, or values that affect how people work together.

Step 5: Designing new approaches to conflict resolution. The trainer creates a chart that is composed of three columns. In the first column, the trainer lists a conflict. The second column lists the expectation or value that would be applied to resolution of the conflict. The third column lists innovative approaches that respect the values of both cultures.

Following the participants' discussion of the third column's innovative approaches, they focus their efforts on a shared goal. This phase frequently highlights cultural differences about goals. American workers become more focused on short-term goals, and Japanese workers prefer long-term goals. Shared goals will then be broken down into specific steps involving who, what, where, when, and how the goal will be achieved.

Steps 6 and 7: Integration of training into company culture. The final two steps of the cross-cultural training involve integration of insights back into the industry setting. Step 6 identifies the criteria that will measure the success of the training on behaviors in the workplace and how assessment of the level of success will take place. During a recent intervention, members of a troubled group agreed to conduct a departmentwide assessment in 6 months to determine the effectiveness of conflict management training. In another organization, Human Resources measured the effectiveness of department training by the number of complaints filed with Human Resources, the turnover of employees, and the number of sick days taken.

The last step involves reporting the successes of training throughout the organization. Workers need to know the benefits of training on the organization's culture. Success stories and changes can be discussed and publicized.

Roundtable Forum

The Canadian Forest Round Table on Sustainable Development illustrates an educational approach to building collaboration with a diverse group. The program promotes dialogue through information exchange, agreement on data, shared experience, and field trips. The National Round Table on the Environment and the Economy (NRTEE) defines *roundtable* as a collaborative process that brings conflicting stakeholders together to interact in a relatively apolitical forum using some form of consensus decision making. The conflicts that the forum addresses involve the rate of deforestation and the clear-cutting of forests in places where selective harvesting methods might be used.

Twenty-four stakeholders with a major interest in the forest environment engage in these discussions. The Forest Round Table represented the broadest range of interests ever brought together in the Canadian forest sector. Stakeholders come from industry, environmental groups, labor organizations, government forestry, parks and wilderness groups, churches, aboriginal peoples, universities, trappers, and wood lot owners.

The NRTEE did not want the biggest industry players at the table because of the potential power imbalances. Instead, industry representatives were chosen because they were "leading lights" in the association. Therefore, industry representatives did not completely reflect the current policy and practice throughout the Canadian forest industry.

During the first meeting of the group, participants formulated specific goals for the discussion process. The first goal was development of a shared vision and principles for sustainable development in forestry in Canada. The second goal was for each stakeholder organization to develop an action plan for their organization in accordance with these principles. The final goal was to make recommendations to policymakers. Nine sets of meetings were held over a 2-year period. Driscoll (1996) identifies several accomplishments of the forum's process: raising awareness, expanding perspectives, and developing relationships.

Raising Awareness

Through intensive discussion and, at times, debate, members raised their level of understanding about the issues. One of the environmentalists who participated saw argumentation as being essential to "rattling people out of complacency and ignorance" and "bringing out the superficiality and irrationality of some arguments." One particular debate took place deep inside an Alberta forest during the third set of meetings. Forum members exchanged perspectives, but no one moved for an hour. In one industry member's words, "Everyone took turns talking, and everyone took turns listening. Something emerged in that conversation in the woods. At the end, you could see both sides budging just a bit." Twenty-one of the members believed that the dialogues created a more positive attitude toward the conflicts.

Expanding Perspectives

Expanding perspectives became a benefit in a great deal of the discussions. Prior to the meeting, the industry representatives thought that all environmentalists were "wacky wing-nuts," and the environmentalists had seen most businesspeople as "criminals" and "unwilling to change." Through participation, members were able to interact with other stakeholders and, concurrently, reassess both their perceptions of these stakeholders and their own assumptions concerning sustainable development in forestry. Over time, members developed deeper understanding of the multiple and diverse values represented at the table. One member admitted that prior to the forum, he had never used words such as habitat, ecosystem, and biodiversity.

Developing Relationships Through Community Building

Sharing social experiences provided an important component in the roundtable experience. Members unanimously agreed that the informal activities (meals, coffee breaks, and evening socials) and field trips were essential to breaking down barriers and facilitating constructive conflict management among members.

Forum members viewed field trips as creating dialogue by developing shared experiences among group members. One member said, "Having industry members and environmentalists alike out in the bush wearing jeans helped bring people to the same level." During field trips, members discussed their love for nature, interest in bird watching, and families at the same time as discussing conflictual topics such as clear-cutting or pesticide usage. The field trips focused dialogue on specific issues and out of the realm of purely philosophical discussion.

Driscoll (1996) argues that consensus-based, collaborative initiatives are increasingly being chosen as an alternative to traditional confrontational approaches to conflict resolution and problem solving of complex social issues. The roundtable forum and the dialogue process can help stakeholders to change perceptions and reframe perspectives through interaction, integration of new insights, and development of shared experiences.

Conflict Management and Training in School Settings

The U.S. Department of Education reports that during 1997, nearly 6,300 students were expelled from American schools for carrying firearms. Fifty-eight percent of the expulsions were for handguns and 17% for shotguns. As evidenced in many of the recent reports about school violence, many students have chosen to express their anger in destructive ways. Renate Caine, former educational psychology professor at California State University at San Bernardino, states that when students feel threatened, their brains shift into primitive, instinctive states for defending themselves (Easterbrook, 1999).

The way some schools have responded to the threats for greater violence has been tighter security. A few of the violence prevention measures include spiked fences, motorized gates, bulletproof metal-covered doors, metal detectors, and security guards who search student desks and lockers. Some complain that this only makes prisons out of the schools. Other schools have hired more counselors and violence prevention coordinators.

Conflict resolution programs in the schools first emerged in the early 1970s, promoted by the increasing concern of educators and parents about violence in the schools. The Children's Project for Friends, a Quaker program that teaches nonviolence in the New York City schools, was the first to introduce conflict resolution discussions into U.S. schools. By the fall of 1995, the National Association for Mediation in Education estimated that there were more than 6,000 school-based conflict resolution programs operating in the United States, and that more than 300,000 had been trained in basic collaborative negotiation techniques (Girard & Koch, 1996). Judith Ladd, president of the American School Counselors Association, says,

> Nearly every school in the country recognizes that this [conflict in schools] is a more serious problem and is doing something about it. Most are adopting stricter codes of conduct, and many are integrating conflict resolution into school curricula. With coaching, kids can play a major role in making school a safer environment. ("School Harassment," 1998, p. 10D)

Elementary and Middle Schools

Another successful school program involves The Conflict Center in Denver, Colorado. This is a nonprofit organization, created through grants, corporate partners, and contributions, whose mission is to provide conflict management training in schools. Their goal is to reduce levels of physical, verbal, and emotional violence. Most of the Center's efforts are geared to the elementary school level, because the Center has found that this is the most effective time to make a difference in children's attitudes about conflict.

The fundamental assumption of the Center is that young people often lack conflict skills training and anger management. They know how to flee a conflict. They know how to ask an adult how to solve a problem. Or they may know how to fight for what they want. But many lack effective problem-solving skills.

The Conflict Center staff believes that the most lasting benefit comes when schools sign up for a full year's program. During the summer, before school starts, the Center staff provides 10 hours of training to all of the adults who work in the building, from principal to janitor. The training staff believes that the adults must model effective behavior if they expect the students to follow. The adults agree to teach conflict management skills to all of the students for a full year. The training involves a 3-week immersion cycle followed by lessons two to three times a week for the rest of the year.

The Center focuses their training on basic problem-solving skills and the win/win negotiation model. They put on a "Ten Tips" card the following list of principles:

- ❏ Respect everyone's ideas and needs.
- ❏ Turn problems into possibilities.
- ❏ Listen so people will talk, and talk so people will listen.
- ❏ Focus on the problem, not the person.
- ❏ Build "power with" not "power over" others.
- ❏ Express feelings without blaming others.
- ❏ Own your part of the conflict.
- ❏ Strategize to reach mutually agreeable solutions.
- ❏ Create options . . . one way always creates losers.
- ❏ Solve the problem and build the relationship.

The Conflict Center staff provides ongoing support by providing sample training for each of the classes and distributing materials that can be integrated into course lesson plans. If teachers have problems with specific children, they may request coaching and consulting help. The Center staff works directly with the "choice kids," those whom teachers identify as having made poor choices relative to conflict and anger management. Included in the program is a segment on playground management, where teachers instruct students in peer mediation techniques. In addition, the Conflict Center makes available to the school's staff a library of tapes, films, videos, books, magazines, and journals on conflict and anger management.

Outcomes are very encouraging. Typically, there is a 30%-50% reduction in referrals to the principal's office for playground fights. The youth enjoy taking responsibility as conflict managers on the playground and peer mediators for the school. Children look forward to coming to a learning environment in which they feel empowered and safe. Families benefit because the children apply the same set of skills at home with brothers and sisters. Those adults weary of managing youth conflict enjoy watching the children take responsibility for their own problems.

Los Alamitos School District

One such successful conflict resolution program is the Los Alamitos Unified School District in California. This district has approximately 8,000 students, comprising six elementary schools (K-5), two middle schools (6-8), and two high schools, including a high-risk school.

At one Los Alamitos school, 130 students begin each day participating in a highly successful 12-step conflict management program. Del Clark, trustee on the board of education for the Los Alamitos Unified School District, states,

> The schools and community take a very unified approach in implementing the conflict resolution programs in the schools. The schools have been very proactive in teaching kids the diversity of problems. There are also high expectations of parents getting involved in their children's education. The end result is that kids feel a personal safety in the school. And safety in the community equals safety in the schools. (S. Schleusner, interview, July 7, 1998)

Two of the Los Alamitos schools received the Blue Ribbon Award for excellence because of their conflict management student training programs. The schools attribute their success to training that begins in the elementary and middle schools. Program leaders select students who serve as "conflict managers." These managers, identified by specific colors of shirts, are trained to resolve conflict both in the classrooms and on the playgrounds.

The Los Alamitos high schools continue the work of the middle schools by providing formal mediation training for students. In a structured setting with all disputing parties present, the youth mediate sessions under the supervision of a faculty member.

University

During the 1998-1999 school year, the University of Denver instituted a peer mediation program for students. Two of the center's founders, Jennifer Williams and Christine Austin, describe the center's purpose as a way to provide

> an environment that promotes a civil, interactive campus community and to reduce traditional disciplinary actions. Participation in the center provides stu-

dents cooperative training in communication and conflict resolution in order to accept personal responsibility for their actions and to enhance understanding of social interdependence. (J. Williams & C. Austin, interview, November 1 & December 10, 1998)

The center provides volunteer services for students with problems such as student code violations, interpersonal conflict, grievances, problems involving alcohol or drugs, and disciplinary referral. The Director of Student Judicial Affairs, two graduate students, and two professional mediators from outside of the university provide oversight for the center. Students who mediate must first complete 21 hours of mediation training. Mediators are screened from cases where there is prior history with any of the students involved in a problem.

When the center receives a case, the Director of Judicial Affairs determines whether the case is appropriate for mediation. If it is, parties involved in the problem are matched with student mediators who have experience or expertise working with the kinds of problems presented. The students may strike from the list of mediators names of people with whom they may feel uncomfortable as mediators. If the case is not resolved successfully, it is referred to the Office of Student Judicial Affairs for adjudication.

The center leaders measure success through questionnaires given at the conclusion of the mediation sessions, a second questionnaire given 6 months following the mediation, and through interviews conducted by the University Ombuds officer. Citing the work of scholars who have worked with similar programs, Williams and Austin point out that "peer mediation can reduce the emotional and fiscal costs of handling disputes or grievances and produce more satisfying and durable results for the participants" (J. Williams & C. Austin, interview, November 1 & December 10, 1998).

Values Workshops

As organizations undergo changes, their core values, which frame goals or behavioral norms, become vague. Conflicts occur over "shoulds" in management-employee or employee-customer relations, formulation of strategic plans, or product quality.

In order to limit some of the conflicts that occur because of value differences, companies such as Levi Strauss, Nordstrom, Puget Sound Power, and AT&T conduct values workshops, where discussions seek to merge employees' personal values with those of their team or organization.

Levi Strauss management considers values to be a priority behind every business decision. Nordstrom asks employees to behave and make decisions with customer satisfaction as their core value. Puget Sound Power initiated a series of focus groups to explore personal and organizational values. After discussing the company's core and individual values, employees found ways to balance work and family responsibilities.

Jaffe and Scott (1998) propose a four-step process for conducting organizational values workshops:

> *Step 1: Define personal values.* Begin with personal values. Because people have different values, this helps participants to see how many different priorities can exist.
>
> *Step 2: Share values with the team.* After participants sort their values, it is time to share them with the team. The goal is for people to clarify together which values are central to their shared work.
>
> *Step 3: Create a team values credo.* Team members work together to define their shared values on how they want to work together, as well as the values for achieving organizational and team goals.
>
> *Step 4: Create a charter of team values.*

Conclusion

Training will not solve all organizational or community problems. Success requires highly motivated learners and content adapted to the learner's preferred learning styles. Conflict management training requires a blend of presentation, discussion, and application. Many trainers use the formula: one third presentation and two thirds discussion and application.

Learning specialists estimate that the factors that best predict adult learning involve the following:

- ❏ 50% based on having a learning mind-set (openness and motivation)
- ❏ 40% based on a learning relationship with instructor and co-learners
- ❏ 10% based on content (adults can learn just about anything if they need to)

Experienced trainers create a safe learning environment where participants are invited, not coerced, to learn new skills. Learners receive information where connections to current life experience are clear and where they are given a chance to discuss and practice what they learn.

Professional Profile: Nancy Rogers
Professor of Law and Associate Dean, Ohio State University

Why They Came to Law School

Lawyers play a vital role in the development of ADR. Some of them have been at the forefront of the field, chairing committees, speaking to colleagues or community leaders, and training other attorneys and members of the public in ADR skills. Some attorneys have opposed the involvement of nonattorney mediators, claiming that they are practicing law without a license. Still others are serving in university settings, educating and training future attorneys, and consulting and writing with regard to the development of public policy relative to ADR.

Introduction to the Practitioner

Nancy Rogers is one of the latter, a professor of law at Ohio State University College of Law. In addition to teaching courses in dispute resolution, Nancy oversees and coaches law students who are developing mediation skills in a court mediation program. She is one of the faculty members who recently revised the curriculum to include three ADR components:

1. Most law school students take required courses that include units on ADR.
2. Students may elect to take the survey course in ADR.
3. Students may elect to take a certificate in ADR, which requires 15 hours of ADR coursework and 112 hours of public service.

The courses cover the practice of mediation, law, and social systems, and a research and writing course requires work of publishable quality. Later, papers will be included in a manual to be published by the Ohio Supreme Court. Few law schools offer students such depth in research, writing, and skill development.

Work of the Practitioner

Nancy has been a contributor to the discussion on legal, policy, and ethical issues involved in ADR. She is the co-author of three books on dispute resolution, as well as numerous articles. She has received recognition from The Center for Public Resources Institute for Dispute Resolution, as well as President Clinton, who appointed her to the board of directors of the Legal Services Corporation. She states, "I see no reason why courts shouldn't help with negotiations as well as litigation."

Nancy believes that "it is early in the development of ADR to specify exactly what skills and training are most effective for beginning practitioners." However, despite this caveat, she suggests that the most important credential for mediation is experience and feedback about the way a person mediates. The description of the curricular reform she co-sponsored demonstrates that Ohio State law students are provided both theory and practice.

Nancy believes that her success is due, in part, to her professional surroundings. She says, "An academic setting provides the time and resources to research and write. Another important feature of a university environment is the presence of colleagues who stimulate and challenge the teacher's ideas. In a land grant institution such as Ohio State, there is also the opportunity to determine how the law school can assist the courts in furthering the development of ADR." Nancy believes that it is the opportunity to be located in an academic setting that permits her to make the contributions she does.

Further evidence of Nancy's success is evident in a typical classroom experience. She recounts, "In my experience, law students often have a particular interest in mediation and find that they feel as though this is why they came to law school. They often tell me that they came to law school wanting to help people work through their problems. As they learn to mediate, they realize that with these techniques, they can contribute in that way." Other students have attached no particular importance to the ADR course in the beginning but left it feeling that they want to spend a significant portion of their careers involved with ADR.

In teaching ADR skills, Nancy tells students to use everything they have learned about people in their life experiences. This causes them to focus on putting themselves in the shoes of others, to understand why others feel the way they do and what is important to them in order to move forward and find a solution to the issues facing them. She teaches students how to use their own experiences in helping others to resolve problems.

Opinions About ADR Issues

Faculty face several tough challenges in teaching ADR in law schools. Nancy explains, "It is possible for students to find a way to practice ADR as a portion of what they do and still make a decent living, even if in the early years, ADR doesn't provide their primary source of income. However, mediation skills may be one of their most valued life skills, even if they use it in only a limited way professionally, or even if they perform mediation only on a volunteer basis." She reminds her students of the words of Abraham Lincoln, "As a peacemaker, a lawyer has a superior opportunity of being a good [person]." She notes that our most valued life skills are not always the way we make our living.

Tough challenges should not imply that challenge is a bad thing; indeed, the challenges of a new field such as ADR were partly what drew Nancy to this area of teaching. She explains, "Innovation is always challenging. Incorporating improvements and keeping up with developments in ADR mean frequent revisions of one's writing and the curriculum. Of course, accommodating a growing field such as ADR without short-cutting the traditional academic law school content is difficult."

It is especially challenging for educators to discern how the university's public service role may be accomplished effectively. Such questions as "In what ways are universities a resource to the courts?" pose significant demands. Gathering and interpreting information about court-annexed mediation programs would be one example of how Nancy's university serves as a resource.

Law school educators do make mistakes and correct them. Nancy responds, "One error some have made is thinking of a new area of practice as a profession. Mediating may be a life skill and should be a separate career path for only a small portion of those who learn to do it." A second mistake some educators made was to ignore the field of ADR as it was emerging. Recently, great interest in both public and private sectors has sparked more interest by law schools.

Finally, the first courses in ADR at law schools were offered as electives to students who were especially interested. Now, most faculty reason that even if a student never intends to practice ADR processes, he or she should be somewhat knowledgeable, because most lawyers are involved at some point in their careers. This is the rationale for adding units on ADR to required courses.

The increased involvement of attorneys in ADR processes signifies that a major change for law schools is the expansion of courses in that area. Although few law schools have developed their curricula to the extent that Ohio State has, Nancy would be surprised "if all don't at least offer one ADR elective. Some offer more; for instance, the University of Missouri now offers a master's degree in ADR (LL.M)."

In a general sense, Nancy notes that mediation is now institutionalized. In her view, "Mediation is established within so many of our institutions that it has become part of the fabric of our country. The culture of disputing has changed! In turn, the way that courts and public agencies institutionalize mediation within their processes will leave major footprints." These decisions will drive more changes and influence the course of mediation greatly.

Naturally, there is and should be debate among attorney educators about the way in which courts and other public agencies structure their mediation programs. Nancy challenges, "For instance, who should pay for these programs?

Should mediation be provided as a part of the court process for no additional fee, just as the trial is now? What will be the consequences 10 years from now if the court becomes the major source of income for a large pool of private mediators? Will it affect the integrity of the court that so many people's livelihoods rest on its referrals? Will courts feel politically powerless to change their referral mechanisms because there are so many vested interests riding on those decisions?"

Currently, decisions on how to institutionalize ADR programs are being made differently among jurisdictions. Nancy advises, "Sometimes, decisions are not consistent within a jurisdiction, within different branches of the court, or among agencies. Law school educators (and others) need to study this diversity and decide which are the best and wisest systems." One of Nancy's national bar committees involves drafting a model mediation law in hopes of bringing the debate about structure closer to consensus.

Nancy offers a second example of how legal educators differ, this time in the classroom. Some professors teach their own views about ADR; others feel that students should be exposed to the full range of debate about law and ADR practice. As you might surmise from this profile by now, Nancy herself believes in exposing students to the various positions relative to ADR issues.

Finally, Nancy highlights the debate about credentials. Her concern is that "mediators will 'pull up the ladder,' trying to set up qualifications for other mediators that only people dedicated to full-time practice could reasonably meet. Such qualifications would narrow the pool of available mediators and eventually raise its costs." She encourages mediators to be quite thoughtful about this, and to realize that there are advantages to broadening the pool of mediators and that there is a role for mediation throughout society.

Law students who are trained and coached in Nancy's classes will come away with an appreciation for this and other important issues on which ADR practitioners are divided. They will develop both academic and practical approaches to ADR. Best of all, they will remember why they came to law school.

Professional Profile: Rosemary Romero
President and Executive Director, The Western Network

Teaching and Modeling Mediation Skills at School

Volunteers account for a significant proportion of conflict management work. Some people volunteer to support community efforts and do not intend to pursue consensus-building as a career. Others volunteer to enhance their ADR skills, hoping that they will be able to charge for similar services later. Public schools across the country have adopted conflict management programs, often staffed primarily by volunteers. Agencies such as the New Mexico Center for School Mediation in Santa Fe and the Conflict Center in Denver provide foundational programs that train principals and teachers, teach children peer mediation, provide curricula and other resources, and work with especially difficult situations. However, the continuation of this work depends to a large degree on the willingness of teachers and parents to build on these foundations.

Introduction to the Practitioner

Rosemary Romero, a professional mediator in environmental affairs, volunteered when her daughter's school asked her to assist there. The school had already instituted several programs typical of elementary schools. For instance, it had a playground conflict managers program. In these programs, students trained in peer mediation take turns being conflict managers on duty during recess. Research shows that the use of conflict managers results in dramatic drops in playground fights. Rosemary was aware of this program, but she could see that students could use these same skills on a wider basis.

Rosemary is also motivated by the need to honor her cultural roots. She wants Hispanic parents to bring their heritage of conflict management to children, lest youngsters imagine that ADR is "just an Anglo thing." She reminds children that "Hispanics in the Southwest have had mediators for centuries. They were called majordomos." These were highly respected older individuals who mediated water rights in an arid area where land ownership is often less important than control over water for irrigation. Rosemary also wanted her own child and others to better understand her work in consensus-building. In the elementary school, Rosemary helped children to understand the basics of conflict resolution and how Hispanics have contributed to the field.

When her daughter went to junior high, Rosemary's role changed. She went from being a teacher and role model to directly mediating student conflicts. She recalls, "The disputes of junior high students escalated from playground fights to gang activities, complete with weapons. Young girls were submitted to violent gang initiations, and some were already pregnant." In this setting, her role was to convince the young teens that "there's a different way than harm or death." Again, most of the students are Hispanic, and some of them are poor. Although Rosemary has the cultural tie with them, she has never had to struggle with poverty. In her view, "Lots of the kids need more than conflict management. They need therapy. Conflict management programs are Band-Aids over serious social problems."

Rosemary's opinion is that many people can qualify to be conflict management volunteers in public schools. Of course, a teaching background is an asset, as is being a parent or having some experience working with children. However, there are many ways to be involved and helpful. The main thing is to be willing to "get our hands dirty." As community members, we must ask ourselves, "What do I bring to conflict management?" and start from that point.

Rosemary attributes her success in working with youngsters to several factors, beginning with her Hispanic heritage. "I look like them, I speak their language (Spanish), I understand where these kids are coming from." She feels a need to support members of the Santa Fe community, where gentrification by wealthy non–New Mexicans has displaced many natives. This commitment is sincere, and the children feel it.

Rosemary's college education and professional success set her up as a role model for students whose families might not have encouraged them to seek higher education. Her own commitment to continuing education in her field is important to her and convincing to them. Finally, she understands and practices forgiveness. In her view, "Forgiveness is at the heart of conflict resolution." Students who meet with her learn about and experience forgiveness.

Work of the Practitioner

Preparation for school mediations is minimal. Typically, Rosemary is given a brief overview from teachers or the principal. Rosemary attempts to contact parents and involve them whenever possible, but they are seldom available. She explains, "A typical session is me sitting down with four to seven kids who have experienced a miscommunication. The dialogue often begins with, 'I heard . . .' Kids read a lot into body language, and misunderstandings are common. Kids talk to other kids about something that was said, and gossip may end up in the threat, 'Meet me after school.' "

Fights between New Mexico youngsters and Mexicanos (Mexican immigrants) also occur. In these sessions, there could be as many as 30 students. Most mediations are held immediately after school, but if there seems to be a serious threat of violence, students will be taken out of class and Rosemary called on the spur of the moment.

Rosemary attributes her success to several factors. Obviously, she brings her expertise as a professional mediator and her commitment as a mother-volunteer. However, she names some success factors particular to the school situation. She advises school mediators, "Don't reschedule. Kids are flighty. The element of surprise works in your favor. Mediating on the spur of the moment is often the best way to go." Likewise, she notes, "They don't like it. They don't want to be there. The key to success is to keep them in the room." Finally, she finds success in "being present." She tells the students, "I'm here. What will it take to solve this?"

Rosemary's greatest challenge resulted from a conflict in which physical harm had been done to a young girl. Her parents were so upset and outraged that despite her best efforts, they could not forgive and ended up moving out of the state. She laments, "They were in a place we couldn't reach."

Mistakes might be in the form of acting as the Lone Ranger. Rosemary recalls a gang mediation when she might have been more successful had she been paired with a man. Girls are treated poorly in gangs, and male members have very little respect for women generally. In preparing for a mediation, she reminds us to ask the question, "Who are the colleagues who can help us?"

Opinions About ADR Issues

One change that Rosemary notes is the increased receptiveness of schools to conflict management generally and to mediation specifically. She recounts, "Mediation has become part of the curricula at many schools. Teachers are more aware [of it]. More schools are teaming with parents to respond to student conflicts." Because she is a volunteer, Rosemary is not aware of what disagreements, if any, professional mediators in school settings might have.

Using her heritage, her skills, and her commitment, Rosemary has found a way to make her community's school a more peaceful place.

Professional Profile: Jo Anderson
Director of the Illinois Education Association-National Education Association's Center for Educational Innovation

The Reformation of an Artful Polarizer

Public education is an arena in which we all have an interest. At stake is the quality of education our children and grandchildren experience. Stakeholders include students, parents, teachers, administrators, support staff, and community members. Decisions that affect public educational systems need to reflect the views of all of these participants. Achieving consensus among such disparate groups is difficult. Add the traditional dynamics of teacher union versus school board, and deep conflicts are guaranteed. How can collaborative decision making evolve out of such a mix of interests and such a divisive tradition?

Introduction to the Practitioner

Jo Anderson is an employee of the Illinois Education Association-National Education Association (IEA-NEA), where he serves as Director of the Center for Educational Innovation. Jo has spent his career working toward school restructuring based on community consensus. The Center serves as a catalyst for positive changes in education, providing resources, expertise, and motivation to the Illinois Educational Association. Jo is a founder and facilitator of the Consortium for Educational Change (CEC), a network of 50 school districts throughout the Chicago suburbs that is working collaboratively to restructure and improve schools. Local universities are also members. Since the CEC was instituted, it has become the prototype for other networks; currently, there are 14 networks across the state of Illinois. These networks include stakeholders, such as the ones mentioned above, who represent schools within a district.

Jo Anderson studied political philosophy at the University of Chicago's graduate program called the Committee on Social Thought. He was trained as a community organizer at the Industrial Areas Foundation, Saul Alinsky's training institute. He thinks of himself as a "child of the '60s, dedicated to building a better world." He taught some courses at Loyola but focused his energies during the 1970s on the Illinois Education Association, representing teachers' unions in bargaining sessions with their local school boards. He describes his role at the time as "an artful polarizer."

After a time, Jo could see that teachers' unions and school boards were "trapped in a Kabuki dance." Traditions of hard bargaining and zero-sum negotiation went unexamined. Paradoxically, the better Jo did for teachers on bread-and-butter issues, the worse were the relationships between teachers and their administrators when the negotiators went home. In addition, he could see that there were a number of important issues that were not covered in contracts, particularly involving teachers' sense of how to undertake educational reform. Both sides were frustrated; neither could force the other side to do what was vital to improvement. The teachers could not make the school boards listen to their opinions; the school boards could not force the teachers to be motivated. Jo identified the need to develop totally new approaches.

A new form of unionism was called for. In the 1980s, the Carnegie and Rand reports addressed the vital need for collaboration between labor and management in school systems. In 1985, Jo and management representatives helped to facilitate a more collaborative approach to negotiations. This was the beginning of a vast change effort. As the bargaining culture in some suburban Chicago school districts shifted from adversarial to more collaborative, these districts began to search for ways to extend collaboration beyond bargaining to school change. In 1987, the CEC was founded to institutionalize the drive toward continuous improvement.

These organizational efforts did not lose sight of the personal changes demanded by such cultural shifts. Jo refers to a quote from Margaret Wheatley: "Change happens one conversation at a time." Jo believes that Stephen Covey's ideas are central to enduring change. First, participants must have the knowledge to participate wisely. Second, they must have the desire—what Covey calls "working from the inside out"—getting their personal lives in order so that they can then work with others to transform systems. The CEC delivers Covey programs to its participants so that they may acquire the 7 habits of highly effective people, which are so fundamental to becoming change agents. Finally, mastery of facilitation and organizational development is a critical skill for change agents. Team programs prepare participants to learn and use tools of organizational development such as diagnosis, communication, and problem solving.

Jo believes that the ability to listen to others and understand their perspective is the most important skill for a beginning practitioner. The quarterly forums for school district leaders that are sponsored by the CEC use a sharing strategy called "Deep Listening." Jo feels that this goes beyond skill to attitude. He says, "Effective organizational change agents have the ability to help others connect rather than conflict. They know how to step outside of their own frames and appreciate the point of view of different stakeholders."

Jo attributes his own success to several factors, chief among them being his community organizing skills. He also has a sense of vision. He can respond in a compelling way to the questions, "What kind of institution do we need to create to serve schools? What do we need out of collaboration beyond a good agreement?" Next, he has the ability to think strategically. After the vision has been developed, explained, and subscribed to, Jo is adept at seizing the opportunities that will bring it into existence. Finally, in working with various stakeholders, Jo has the capacity to synthesize different viewpoints, highlighting the interdependencies among diverse participants.

In preparing for large, complex contract negotiations, Jo finds it most helpful to "review, but don't get lost in the details. Be at peace with yourself. Center. Take time to read, but also to reflect." Jo thinks it is all too easy for the change agent to become immersed in the fray and lose sight of the big picture.

Work of the Practitioner

A typical attempt to develop conflict management systems takes place in the annual summer institute sponsored by the CEC. There, as many as 500 participants in 40 school district teams gain a national perspective by hearing from distinguished speakers on multiple-stakeholder change efforts. Participants engage in planning, learning, and sharing activities in a retreat setting. Many districts use this time to launch their work for the coming year or to reflect on the previous year. Jo helps to facilitate and coach at these meetings.

Jo's thoughts on what is essential for success begin with careful attention to detail. "Make sure there are no surprises connected with the changes you ask people to accept; God is in the details." Second, he stresses the virtue of patience, citing the example of a facilitator who dealt with conflict by emphasizing common ground and postponed a contentious issue until later. At the same time, such patience must be balanced by maintaining momentum. There must be some clear short-term results that motivate a group to keep working toward agreement. Finally, Jo notes that lasting success is dependent on "reculturing the school district. Movement toward systemic change requires all involved to subscribe to the new, more collaborative culture."

The ambitious nature of "reculturing" suggests the major challenge that Jo identifies: "We are constantly being pulled back into the past." The weight of traditional authority structures, the lack of practice with new ways of resolving conflicts, and the tendency of some participants to restrict themselves to single issues are all factors that pull school reform backward. Jo also sees a challenge in the potential estrangement of leaders from their constituents. When the leaders receive training and appreciate the benefits of interest-based bargaining, they are no longer in sync with the rank-and-file teachers, who may still be thinking that their leader's job is strictly bread-and-butter issues, best achieved in a competitive arena. Jo says, "The experience of the leaders has to be replicated for their constituents, or conflict systems will never truly take root in school systems."

Reflecting on his mistakes, Jo advises involvement of all vital stakeholders in organizational change. He remembers that he began in a bilateral form, working first with teachers and boards. Later, he could see that many more stakeholders should be involved and added families and community members. However, he notes that "having everyone at the table is a goal, not always a practical reality." He feels that the underdevelopment of informational systems is a mistake; in order to convince the public that systems change is productive, more outcome data must be collected, interpreted, and distributed. A third mistake is that the traditional training approach to systems change is not ideal. In Jo's view, "Training should rely more on just-in-time modules and teachable moments." Finally, Jo sees a mistake in piling up system change on top of already overscheduled school personnel. People begin with good intentions but end up in a "crash and burn." Sometimes, the best way to begin a systems change is to take time to think about what improvements might be made.

Opinions About ADR Issues

The question of "What is changing in your area?" is an ironic one to put to a change agent. The answer is, "Not enough!" Systems are slow to adopt conflict management. Some systems and some teachers go back into isolation, even after training.

What do practitioners disagree about? "Everything!" The most basic struggle in Jo's area is the tension about redefining what a teacher's union is. There is a long history of schizophrenia anyway; "teachers have never been quite sure whether they are a union or a profession. Now, the new conflict management system produces a role change for the teacher's union: not just protecting teachers, but protecting teaching." The tension around peer review is a current example. Everyone will have to struggle with the new role for the union, as well as his or her own role change. In the past two decades, Jo Anderson's role has shifted from "artful polarizer" to change agent for school systems.

Chapter 10

Summary of Practitioner Insights

Summarizing the views of 25 practitioners from a variety of collaborative conflict management modalities is a daunting task. There are some questions that elicited responses specific to a practice or to an area of conflict. However, most questions produced trends that suggest directions that ADR is taking or descriptions of best practice.

The authors of this book have tried hard to interview a diverse group of practitioners; not only do they represent differences in practice content, but they vary in age, background, and geographical location. However, we do not argue that the following generalizations would necessarily hold if one were to conduct a random sample of practitioners. We deliberately invited practitioners who are experienced, articulate in expressing their thoughts, and developers of the field. A list of the questions and commonalities of responses follows.

1. How did you become involved in the practice of ADR?
There's got to be a better way.

The largest group of interviewees is involved in one way or another at universities. Several, such as Daniel Kruger, Nancy Rogers, and Frank Sander, are members of full-time faculties and practice ADR on the side. Others, such as Myra Isenhart, Mike Jenkins, Joan Kelly, and Marshall Snider, reverse that balance. They spend the majority of their professional lives in practice and teach on a regular, but adjunct, basis.

Still others, such as Lenny Marcus, Mary Rowe, Mike Spangle, and Larry Susskind, are involved with institution-building within university settings. In the latter's words, "Thirty years ago, we knew that the more people in a community debate, the more problems there would be. There was no theory after that." They have spent their careers building the theories that guide practice. They have built the programs that deliver ADR, such as Rowe's groundbreaking work on ombuds at MIT and Marcus's trainings in conflict management for health care professionals, offered through the Harvard School of Public Health.

Until recently, Marjorie Corman Aaron was the director of the Program on Negotiation at Harvard Law School and taught courses there.

The work of university faculty involves more than teaching, practice, and institution-building. All of those mentioned above have published in journals and books. They speak to professional and community groups, explaining ADR and the advantages of collaborative conflict management. Many interviewees mentioned mentoring and coaching others who are more recent practitioners. Practitioners associated with universities develop better ways to manage conflict, make that information public, and help others to gain the requisite skills.

The second largest group of our interviewees was originally trained in the law. Members of this group became sensitized to the harms created by the use of litigation in inappropriate situations. As Aaron said, "Litigation is a terribly circuitous way to achieve settlement." She was not alone: Dissatisfaction with overuse of the court system to resolve disputes was expressed by attorneys Edward Dauer, Barbara Ashley Phillips, Rogers, Sander, and Cindy Savage.

Lawyers designed, sponsored, or joined alternatives to the courts. Some of them, such as Sander, proposed a totally new model of dispute resolution, such as the multidoor courthouse. Others taught, administered, and promoted these new ways, such as Savage in the Office of Dispute Resolution. Snider moved from litigation to arbitration. In Rogers's words, "There is real promise in court mediation programs. There is no reason why courts shouldn't help with legal expertise as a springboard toward a better way."

A third group of interviewees came to collaborative conflict management through work with multiparty disputes. Bill Drake, Jenkins, and Susskind came from graduate studies and work in urban planning, which also demanded consensus from stakeholders with quite differing interests. They came to consensus building because the methodologies of social change and planned development were in need of overhaul. As long as one stakeholder can veto a plan, and it takes all players to generate approval, a better way must involve satisfying interests on all sides.

Jo Anderson and Chris Moore were trained in community organizing and understood the difficulties of bringing many disparate groups to agreement. John Marks knew the multiparty conflict scene from his career in the foreign service, as well as his work as a Senate staffer. These men, coming of age in the 1960s, were drawn to large social and political issues because of their commitment to particular causes. As Marks explains, "After 10 years of activism, I got to the point in my own life where I wanted to build a new system rather than tear down the old system. . . . I saw that I wanted to change the world from an adversarial to a nonadversarial place." These interviewees describe their motivations for involvement in global, idealistic terms: "changing the world" "making the world a better place," "building a more democratic decision-making process." The better way is a remedy for flaws in the process of multiparty decision making, especially decisions that significantly affect public interests.

A related group of interviewees came from the ministry to consensual decision making. Spangle and Speed Leas hold religious values that are consonant with those of the community organizers who want to build a less adversarial world. Similarly, others, such as Isenhart, Jack Lemley, Chris Merchant, John Schumaker, and Mark Udall, found that the nature of their work and/or client demand motivated them toward involvement in ADR. Rosemary Romero applied her ADR skills in the local junior high because of her feelings around parenting and her Hispanic heritage.

2. What kind of work do you do?

Everything from mediating a divorce to international crisis intervention.

One way to describe the kind of conflict management work done by the interviewees is to focus on the number of disputants. Many practice with more than one size of group, but most of them specialize in one size.

For instance, the small group is represented by the work with couples, children, and families done by Joan Kelly as a family mediator. Jenkins holds meetings with potential businesspeople who want to establish a presence within the city of San Diego. Udall negotiates with other state legislators in committees of 8-12 members to produce a bill that has a reasonable chance of success when it goes to the larger body. As he points out, "It's vital to understand each committee member's interests. Carry, don't marry a bill."

Isenhart works primarily with workplace teams that range in size from 3 to 15. The civil arbitration practiced by Kruger and Snider usually involves small groups. Phillips and Aaron primarily mediate with individual disputants who hope to avoid litigation. Rogers oversees small groups of law school students learning to mediate. Medical malpractice mediation engages Dauer and Marcus with a patient, his or her family, a physician, and possibly a representative from the health care system.

Disputes that typify small group work with families are divorce, child custody, support, and property. In the workplace, disputes concern scarce resources, change adaptation, goal realignment, sexual harassment, partnerships, and labor-management. Civil disputes might be about personal injury, contract interpretation, medical malpractice, professional liability, or intellectual property. Negotiation, mediation, and arbitration are conflict management methods that are often used with small groups.

Larger groups usually require different processes. Lemley describes megascale construction projects that use dispute review panels to resolve conflicts. Schumaker applies facilitation in public meetings where citizens give feedback to Bureau of Land Management proposals. Spangle and Anderson facilitate public school disputes involving administrators, teachers, and parents. Merchant and Moore work in organizational systems and use dispute system design. Bill Drake has instituted forums in South Africa in which "the people who are killing each other at night are very civil in meetings." Marks has done substantial institution-building overseas, adding radio, television, and even sports events to the usual processes for discovering common ground.

Disputes in large groups encompass an array of social, economic, and political disputes. Disposal of environmental waste, siting of public facilities, land, and water quality are typical issues that demand that various levels of government make decisions with input from a variety of citizen stakeholders. Negotiated regulations (reg-negs) involve an ADR process that brings together government officials, corporate representatives, and citizen groups to work out the fine points of how a new piece of legislation will be implemented. Dialogues between pro-life and pro-choice advocates are held to establish common ground and decrease the level of hostility among participants. Labor-management negotiations are usually concerned with pay, benefits, and working conditions. International disputes may be about borders, ethnic and religious representation, state-sponsored repression of civil rights, or terrorism.

Whether small or large, the types and numbers of disputes are staggering. Fortunately, our interviewees have devised a variety of methods for dealing with them.

3. What skills or training would you recommend for a beginning practitioner?

A list of requisite skills, with listening at the top of everyone's list. Some training, some theory, but practice with coaching emphasized.

The question of which skills are required produced a list of requisite conflict management skills, with one that is paramount. Virtually all interviewees spoke of the importance of listening. Many of them emphasized that listening is the primary tool. Trained in communication, Isenhart and Spangle spoke about listening for the unspoken meanings. Moore and Savage agree: The latter calls this "listening between the lines." Often, what is not said is the key to breaking a deadlock.

Listening was also mentioned frequently by attorney-mediators. Several agreed with Phillips's assessment that "lawyers are trained to be advice-givers, and unless they unlearn this orientation, and listen more, they will not be helpful mediators." However, attorneys also spoke of the legal skills that they could use to advantage. Aaron's experience is that because she is an attorney, other lawyers representing clients in a mediation know that they cannot fool her with legal jargon or maneuvers. She also notes that most attorneys are adept at persuasion and legal analysis, both of which are helpful in ADR. On the other hand, Susskind terms the outcome of legal training for consensus-building skills "trained incapacity."

A number of communication skills in addition to listening were mentioned. Isenhart, Leas, and Spangle emphasize the importance of understanding group dynamics. Leas believes that third-party neutrals who deal with organizations should be expert at group process. They should possess both intellectual and political understandings of groups.

Marcus spoke of the importance of trust of the neutral by each of the parties, saying, "Everything you say and do is being scrutinized for whether or not they can trust you." Several interviewees mentioned the skill of creative thinking. Because parties would not bring disputes to a neutral unless they were stuck, it is important to be able to "think outside the box." Some referred to this ability as generating options, others as discovering common ground, and Phillips called it "creating a new story."

The topic of what training is recommended for beginners elicited contrasting responses with regard to formal training. Some, such as Moore and Susskind, think that understanding the theory and principles of conflict management is basic to good practice. Kelly advises new family mediators to take at least 60-100 hours of training that should include conflict theory and management. She advises practicing mediators to continue their education through internships and co-mediations.

Other interviewees differ. Drake and Marks believe that the theory is basically common sense, and little formal training is required. In Drake's words, "Conflict management has been overintellectualized. [Best practices] reflect common sense and intuition, honed by training." Udall does not believe that there is any way to prepare for negotiating in a legislature. He promotes on-the-job training, which, in his area, goes by the nickname "immersion dunking." Finally, some, such as Rogers, withhold judgment on the training issue, explaining, "It is too early to say which teachings or trainings are most effective."

A few interviewees explain that their practice is not accessible to beginners. Sander's education of judges, Merchant's dispute system design within federal agencies, and Anderson's networking of school districts are examples of work that would be open to a few with specialized expertise. For these activities, participation depends on years in the field and considerable credentials.

Practice with feedback is what virtually all practitioners agree is essential for conflict management training. Although recommending it highly, many lamented the lack of opportunities to apprentice in this field. The importance of mentoring for beginners was also noted by many interviewees. Again, very few formal mentoring networks exist.

4. What makes you good at what you do?

I practice the skills I recommend for beginners.
I have personal qualities which are congruent with the role of the neutral.

Many of the interviewees claimed for themselves the same communication skills they recommend for beginners. Shumaker, Drake, and Phillips emphasized their willingness to listen. In the words of the latter, "When I really listen, I'm the best I can be." The skills of critical thinking and clear writing were emphasized by Snider and Kruger, both of whom arbitrate. Aaron, Merchant, and Spangle focused on their ability to put disputants at ease and to build relationships and trust. As the former put it, "I'm a chit-chatter." Merchant is skilled at helping those who are stuck come up with new ideas.

Reasons other than communication skill were mentioned by several disputants. Many of these could be labeled personal qualities. Aaron and Moore were among those who label themselves "quick studies." Kelly mentions her eye for detail and her preference for sharp focus, which helps parties navigate complex legal and financial issues. Kruger accepts the qualities of honesty and integrity for himself. Udall explains that part of his success in the legislature depends on his ability to focus on issues and not overpersonalize conflicts. Snider notes that he is fair and able to convey the perception of fairness, which disputants need to experience. Isenhart believes that the feminine socialization process is congruent with values implicit in the collaborative approach to conflict management.

Drake, Merchant, Rowe, and Schumaker all stress the importance of being able to submerge one's ego. Rowe explains that an ombudsperson needs to "be able to give credit to others, to enjoy problem solving, to have humor and patience." Merchant expresses this quality as being client-focused and says, "I am not an egomaniac." Schumaker describes how he "fades into the background at the appropriate time." Drake responds to this question by saying, "The judges of that are the people I serve and my colleagues." He concludes that an effective neutral is modest and humble.

Many interviewees speak of their experience as neutrals as fundamental to their success. Lemley claims to have "scar tissue" from his 30+ years in the construction industry. Others speak of quality training and mentoring, of stimulating colleagues, and of learning from team members. Susskind stresses the value of reflective practice, submitting negotiation experiences to constructive criticism from team members, peers, and clients. Many interviewees believe that ongoing learning from past experience is closely related to future success.

5. How do you prepare for a session?

Whatever my practice requires or allows: From years of background study and prenegotiation to "Hello, I'm your mediator."

Some mediators place enormous emphasis on preparation. Drake believes that international conflict managers should not attempt to be effective in more than one country. There is too much to know about the history and the players; "I become immersed in the culture of South Africa. I've been there repeatedly, but when I'm not there, I keep up with the newspapers and e-mail my colleagues frequently." Schumaker is also a firm believer in "turning over every rock" before starting on land use facilitations. Merchant spends enormous amounts of time conducting meetings and conference calls in order to test commitment and plans.

Others reframe the formal preparation process in favor of what is actually learned by working with clients. Susskind and Moore speak of lengthy prenegotiation phases in the multiparty disputes they handle. Marks believes in learning through engagement, especially when the conflict is overseas. He describes how neither the issues nor the possible solutions are evident until one has struggled with the conflict for some time. Setting up the wrestling matches in Iran required 2 years of "preparation."

Some neutrals engage in more traditional preparation. Leas does a preliminary needs assessment for a congregation, then holds private interviews with central actors and group interviews with others. Aaron looks for key issues in an upcoming dispute by having conversations with the attorneys involved and reading relevant documents. Kelly asks each family who comes for mediation to complete an intake form, which prepares her for the nature of the conflict. Phillips interviews the disputants and then builds an agenda, making sure that at least one statement from each party appears on that agenda. Spangle asks questions about the group to be facilitated, including its history of working with outside consultants.

For still others, readiness may involve self-preparation. Both Dauer and Marcus speak about the importance of reflecting on "What's it about, really? Not just on the surface." Anderson's way is to be at peace with himself, to spend time centering before a session. His advice is, "Don't get lost in the details." Preparation of the neutral may be cognitive, spiritual, or both.

There are neutrals whose work allows them no preparation. At the Colorado Office of Dispute Resolution, neutrals may be assigned to cases without much, or any, background on the issues. Jenkins sometimes begins negotiations without previous information about the participants. In mediation centers, there are many walk-ins. The neutral's use of preparation is very context-dependent.

6. Describe a typical session.

There isn't any such thing.

"Typical" is a term whose meaning is contextual. For instance, there may be a typical session for family mediators or for trainers, but the two bear no resemblance to one another. For these practitioners, the number of people being served varies from 2 to 2,000. The time required to resolve the conflict ranges from one meeting to 12 years. The roles taken by neutrals vary from negotiator to judge. Those who mediate with small numbers use mostly "off the shelf" approaches, in the sense that they have developed a protocol that they follow regularly. Those who deal with larger groups and community issues have some regularities but spend more time in prenegotiation customizing their approach.

7. What is essential for success?

Mediator attributes, skills and experience.
The use of certain procedures.
Client characteristics, including timing.

A number of interviewees responded to this question by citing personal qualities that successful neutrals possess. If you believe, as Leas said, that "conflict management is an art, not a science," then it makes sense to start with the attributes of the "artist." Anderson, Sander, and Schumaker stressed the virtue of patience. Moore and Aaron noted the energy and stamina that neutrals need. Many interviewees mentioned the importance of communicating hopefulness to people who had tried other ways of solving conflict and failed. Several others called attention to the ability to read people and to use intuition. Still others spoke of the ability to discern the hidden or unspoken issues. Leas emphasized self-management in the face of others' anger; Aaron and Kelly said that successful mediators must be comfortable with conflict.

In a closely related category, many interviewees responded to the success question by naming conflict management skills and techniques. Many spoke of the importance of creating an environment of fairness. The neutrality of the practitioner must not be in doubt. Kelly sees the successful mediator as "fair, evenhanded." Moore thinks in terms of "no hidden agendas" and points out that the neutral must not only be fair, but must demonstrate fairness. The arbitrators, Kruger and Snider, are particularly strong on fairness, at their sessions and in their written reports. Kruger notes, "My job is to protect the integrity of the process."

There are other mediator skills that were frequently mentioned. Many of them may be labeled communication skills. As mentioned earlier, many interviewees attributed their own success to intense listening. The list also includes the skill of decentering to best understand what each party is feeling and saying. This involves acuity with both verbal and nonverbal communication, or in Spangle's words, "listening between the lines." Several neutrals stressed the importance of communicating that understanding to each of the parties.

Another important communication skill is the use of reflection questions to assist parties to see the conflict in a new light or to help them discover common ground. Skill in generating options that disputants may not have known of or considered before is important. Phillips offers, "Success is when you've delivered the most credible process you're capable of and opened people's eyes to options." Skill in cutting through volumes of material and isolating key points is critical to success, especially with complex issues. Being able to summarize the points to the satisfaction of both parties rounds out the list of communication skills.

Mediator experience is also mentioned as critical to success. A number of interviewees spoke about the high quality of the training they have had. Mentoring was noted as formative, as was continuing education and networking. Isenhart believes that in addition to helpful mentors and colleagues, experience with students and clients provides learning opportunities. Finally, several practitioners speak of themselves as self-directed learners, using past work as feedback. In Marks's words, "We look in the morning, we revise at lunch. Feedback is embedded in our approach. The key is to look at what's working and to build on that."

Many interviewees cited procedures as a source of success. Susskind, Marks, Drake, Moore, Shumaker, Udall, and Anderson describe the prenegotiation period they use with complex disputes. Issues such as who will be at the table, how communication among the parties will be handled, to what extent the press will be kept informed, as well as other prenegotiation issues, may well be deal-breakers if not carefully handled at this point.

Others stress the importance of orienting parties to the ADR process once it begins. Careful explanation of responsibilities and setting of reasonable expectations are cited as success factors, especially where parties are new to the process. Spangle and Anderson speak of the importance of follow-up once client work is completed. In Anderson's words, "We are constantly being pulled back into the past." The remedy he sees for this is "reculturing," meaning continuing work in building more collaborative systems. What comes before, during, and after conflict management all bear on its success.

Clients are an important variable in success. Moore notes that there are some minimal requirements for success: "Clients must have some overlapping interests and sufficient resources to pursue mediation." Savage agrees and adds that resources may mean time, money, and commitment. Jenkins, Spangle, and Savage all note that clients must "come in good faith." In addition to willingness to engage, several practitioners said that clients must possess basic levels of cognitive and psychological ability for an ADR process to work.

Leas and Phillips point out that clients must have some reason to hope for a better outcome than they have been able to achieve alone. Moore and Isenhart note that success is more likely when clients feel some pain; in the former's words, that there be a "hurting stalemate." Marks feels that timing in international affairs is important. In his experience, success is more likely either before a conflict has erupted, or after it has gone on so long that people are weary of it. In war as in love, timing is all.

8. What are challenges in your work?

The type of work I do has significant challenges built into it.
Clients can present difficult challenges.
There are some challenges I feel personally.

Sometimes, the greatest challenges are present before negotiations begin. That is, several interviewees believe that persuading disputants to try ADR is the most significant challenge. Sometimes, the parties are not familiar with the processes suggested; sometimes, they have other reasons for not coming to the table. Convincing people to forego litigation is often a significant challenge. Dauer notes a related challenge that he labels "external linkages." Where external linkages are present, a group not represented at the table has the power to undermine agreements made by the stakeholders who are present. Like prenegotiation difficulties, this dynamic happens away from the actual problem-solving session.

Certain contexts present inherent difficulties. Certainly, international conflict management has all the issues of complex, multiparty disputes with intercultural differences layered over all. As Drake points out, differences in interaction norms affect the problem solving: "Where people are used to hearing each other out, conflict management requires a considerably longer time period." Moore explains that differences in values as well as communication styles have compounded his work overseas. Others point to the challenge for conflict managers to continually adapt to unfolding developments.

Some neutrals are involved in work that has high levels of negative emotions. Aaron says that employment cases "cry out for mediation. [Work-related disputes] are difficult because people have so much invested in their work emotionally." Kruger agrees, citing a long, bitter dispute around workplace issues as his most challenging assignment.

Other types of conflicts also exhibit high degrees of negative emotion. Kelly speaks of the difficulty that family mediation clients have in keeping the "heat of battle from clouding their thinking." Udall describes negotiation in the legislature as "a very tough process. Even the most powerful people 'get rolled' sometimes." Leas reminds us that problem solving in church settings means sometimes dealing with people who feel they have been told the truth by God, so they must keep fighting in order to be faithful to that revealed truth. This type of unwavering conviction, combined with negative emotions, leads Marks to say that dealing with the pro-choice/pro-life dialogues is harder than the work he does overseas in warring countries.

Many interviewees name client characteristics as responsible for their greatest challenges. Snider and Spangle explain that parties who are hostile to the neutral or who are not open to discussion present difficulty. Susskind speaks of the challenges of working with parties whose paradigm is the zero-sum game, who bring no background with consensus-building, or who possess inadequate problem-solving skills. Phillips experiences the most challenge in working with those who lack motivation or feel they are gaining from continuing a conflict. Isenhart and Merchant note the frustration of working within organizations whose culture is not compatible with consensus decision making.

Sometimes, it is client behavior that is challenging. Occasionally, mediators will be surprised to hear parties disavowing statements they made earlier in private caucus. As mediation develops, parties may become overly dependent on the mediator to tell them what to do. They may come with a history of violence or exhibit violent behavior in the session. These are examples of client behavior that our interviewees find professionally challenging.

Finally, there are some personal challenges noted. Rogers and Sander regret that ADR has not developed to such an extent that more practitioners can make a career of it. One interviewee finds it challenging to be fair in situations in which his own personal response to one party is strong. Several others spoke about the challenge of self-management when they are verbally attacked. One cited overcommitment as the major challenge; another finds exhaustion the enemy. Challenges may be inherent in the work, attributed to clients, or reflective of internal struggles.

9. Have you made mistakes, and if so, what have you learned from them?

> *Yes, that's how I learn.*

Responses to this question were positive; almost all interviewees could easily name mistakes they had made or errors to which they are especially prone. However, with several exceptions, the mistakes named are varied. Among this group, there are few "typical" mistakes.

Performance errors rang from the beginning of a conflict management effort to its end. Prenegotiation errors are among the few that were named by more than one neutral person. Four spoke of the lack of thorough preparation and solid assessment. Three emphasized the problems to follow when not all of the necessary participants are at the table.

One of the few ways to find trends is to look at mistakes named by attorneys. Several respondents supervise beginning attorney mediators. One of the supervisors said, "Lack of balance is the most common mistake. Some will be too goal-oriented and push too hard. Others will be too process-oriented and fail to achieve a final agreement." Three attorney mediators spoke about the need to listen and demonstrate understanding. As one put it, "Don't assume you understand the parties' needs until you've really listened well. Don't be a smarty-pants lawyer."

Once into the ADR process, there are no clusters of answers. One interviewee warned about the importance of gaining an agreement in principle before attaching prices to anything. Another emphasized the communication breakdowns that are possible in working through organizational levels. Two respondents admitted that they had "lost it" when personally attacked in public and had subsequently spent time perfecting self-management in such situations. Conflicting advice about concluding the session probably reflects personal tendencies toward error. For instance, one said, "Don't hang in too long in tough cases; know when to quit." Another countered with, "Don't give up too soon."

Finally, several interviewees cited errors made after the disputing parties have reached agreement. Both arbitrators felt that writing up their judgments is a critical step. If the written rationale is not thorough and convincing, problems will follow. One facilitator admitted that had he followed up with a group, the members would have been more likely to have kept their agreement. An overseas conflict manager stressed the importance of maintaining links with disputants through e-mail and phone.

10. What changes in this field do you notice?

> *Growth in numbers and the development of an ADR infrastructure.*
> *One must guard against the illusion of progress.*

Virtually all interviewees spoke of growth in one form or another. Some spoke about the increasing numbers of the public who understand and ask for

ADR processes. The U.S. government has increased its use of ADR substantially over the past decade. Public agencies are more willing to use ADR, and some even offer funds so that citizen groups may sit at the table with corporations that have greater resources. State offices of dispute resolution are becoming commonplace. Internationally, there are at least 50 countries that are engaged in the application of ADR within and across borders.

Some interviewees cited the dollars associated with growth. Others described the growing number of practitioners in their field. This growth is also accompanied by regionalization and specialization of practitioners. Udall notes, "Consensus values have infiltrated most organizations, even legislatures."

Many respondents spoke about the development of an infrastructure. Academicians tended to notice the growth of theoretical underpinnings. Colleges and universities are offering courses, certificates, and sometimes even degrees in conflict management. These offerings are likely to show up in the liberal arts curriculum, in schools of social work, and in international relations programs. Most law schools have added at least one ADR course, and some have instituted programs. Savage says, "The debate has shifted from 'Should we?' to 'How do we?' "

Many respondents called attention to the growth of nonprofit organizations that offer practice, training, and research. There is also growth in the number of for-profit firms that seldom conduct research but do offer practice and training. A number of law firms have added ADR options for their clients. As Leas puts it, "We have gone from the practice of techniques to a field of practice."

A number of respondents balanced their assessment of growth with caveats about resistance. Despite all the growth noted above, Jenkins experiences the persistence of the hard bargainer. Sander points to the lack of funding for ADR projects and the number of judges who are "wedded to the old ways." Anderson warns that school personnel and school systems are slow to adopt consensus-building techniques and sometimes revert to the old ways after they do. Marks advises that the field draws solo practitioners performing fee-for-service work. This makes any systematic progress very difficult. Leas asks the fundamental question: "To what extent are systems transformable?" Conflict managers must be realistic about what changes are possible.

11. Are there topics about which practitioners in your field disagree?

Yes: What should the role of the courts be?
Yes: What should the qualifications of neutrals be?
Yes: How activist should a neutral be?
Yes: How do we evaluate outcomes?

These disagreements engaged our interviewees (no one answered 'no' to this question). Rogers, Savage, and Sander noted that the role of the courts in establishing ADR is hotly debated. Questions being addressed include the following: How will cases be screened for allocation to the appropriate ADR process? Will alternatives be mandated or voluntary? How should services be provided? How will costs be allocated? Currently, these important questions are being answered in different ways in different districts. There is no consensus about these issues among legal professionals. The way the questions are addressed by attorneys will affect the entire ADR system. Research is needed to assess outcomes of these various approaches.

The qualifications that a neutral should possess was often mentioned as a subject of disagreement. Sometimes, the question took the form of "To what extent should a neutral be an expert in the subject matter of the dispute?" Kelly maintains that in the area of family disputes, a neutral must know family law, not to give advice but to inform. Dauer finds that his credibility as a mediator in health care disputes is partly dependent on his informed understanding of medical language and practice. In the field of environmental disputes, Moore holds that there is no way any one person can be expert on all issues, so the most important credential a neutral brings is being a quick study.

There are additional questions around qualifications. Sander worries that if volunteers practice ADR on a part-time basis, the field may never develop as a professional practice. Kelly is concerned that in their haste to build boundaries around the fast-growing field, some states have decreed that only attorneys may perform family mediation. Associations of professional conflict managers in many states are grappling with the licensure question: whether to, when to, how to.

The debate around activism also may take several forms. There is the old question of how active a neutral should be. Susskind is noted for his espousal of the activist position, believing that when neutrals can take actions to move negotiations forward, they should do so. Aaron asks disputants if they want to know what she would recommend, and if they do, she tells them. Others are less comfortable with an activist approach and opt for a mediation style that assumes that both option generation and decision are the disputants' responsibility.

Another form of debate around the role of the neutral concerns the goal of conflict management. Is it dealmaking, is it transformation of the disputants, is it something in between? Those who address violent confrontations tend to lean toward transformation. Marks and Drake see themselves in the business of creating an environment in which peaceful dialogue may take place. Anderson uses the term "reculturation" to describe his work in transforming school systems to value and adopt consensus-building.

Opposition to transformation appears when the object is no longer systems, but individuals. Susskind is "bothered by the idea that people should walk away from the table 'better people.' " He sees this as paternalistic and manipulative; he feels that a transformational perspective on disputants creates unreasonable expectations. Other neutrals see that involvement with ADR can be a learning experience wherein disputants expand their ideas about and techniques for how to manage subsequent conflicts. Moore believes that there is a false dichotomy in dividing neutrals into transformers and deal makers. He says, "In real life, there are few clean cases. Most intermediaries do both."

Evaluation is a topic of debate among professionals. In terms of the substance of dispute, Phillips feels that a mediator should not take on the role of evaluator within the same case. This is currently being done by some mediators. Several mediators addressed the difficult question of evaluating success after working with clients. At the present time, the achievement of settlement itself is being used as a 'success' outcome by many court systems. Some neutrals are being asked to list their rates of settlement. This puts pressure on neutrals to negotiate settlement, even though that may not be in the disputants' best interests. Parties should know that their best remedy may not be ADR. The Consensus Institute has built an approach to evaluation that is more complex and more defensible than just settlement rates.

The question of how to evaluate international work is especially difficult. So many other factors besides the peacemakers' efforts contribute to further violence or the reduction thereof. When the goal is creating an environment where peaceful dialogue is possible, how can anyone isolate the resources and the efforts of one overseas organization? When the engagement of the organization stretches over years, when does one look for results? It is impossible to prove a negative, so no one can tell whether conflicts would have been worse without the presence of intermediaries. As Marks says, "To my knowledge, no soldier ever put down his machine gun immediately after one of our radio broadcasts."

Leas raises the issue of how applicable the current model of ADR may be to all segments of society. He identifies the model currently being taught as patently white and middle class. Finally, he sums up the debates among professionals by reminding, "Consensus building is an art, not a science." Disagreements on any of these questions may be related to professional training, to the area of practice, or to personal style. Taken together, they illuminate the important questions in this field of practice.

References

Adler, A. (1927). *The practice and theory of individual psychology*. New York: Harcourt, Brace and World.

AHP-Monsanto merger dies from culture clash. (1998, October 14). *USA Today*, p. B1.

Alberts, J. K., & Driscoll, G. (1992). Containment versus escalation: The trajectory of couples' communication complaints. *Western Journal of Communication, 56*, 394-412.

Amadei, R. (1995). Mediation/arbitration: An ADR tool. *The Colorado Lawyer, 24*, 554-556.

American talks with pilots to resume with Emergency Board as mediator (1997, March 12). *Wall Street Journal*, p. A4.

Amy, D. (1987). *The politics of environmental mediation*. New York: Columbia University Press.

Arbitration policies are muting whistle blower claims. (1998, August 6). *Wall Street Journal*, p. B1.

Arbitrator finds role dwindling as rivals grow. (1998, 28 April). *Wall Street Journal*, pp. B1, B10.

Argyris, C., & Schön, D. A. (1974). *Organizational learning: A theory of action perspective*. Reading, MA: Addison-Wesley.

Bazerman, M., & Neale, M. (1992). *Negotiating rationally*. New York: Free Press.

Benson, R. E. (1996). The power of arbitrators and courts to order discovery in arbitration—Part 1. *The Colorado Lawyer, 25*(2), 55-60.

Blake, R., & Mouton, J. (1964). *The managerial grid*. Houston: Gulf.

Blau, P. (1964). *Exchange and power in social life*. New York: Wiley.

Bok, D. C. (1983). What are America's law schools doing wrong? A lot. *Student Lawyer, 46*, 12.

Borisoff, D., & Victor, D. A. (1989). *Conflict management: A communication skills approach*. Englewood Cliffs, NJ: Prentice Hall.

Boyett, J. H., & Conn, H. P. (1991). *Workplace 2000*. New York: Plume.

Bradley, G. W. (1978). Self-serving biases in the attribution process: A reexamination of the fact or fiction question. *Journal of Personality and Social Psychology, 36*, 56-76.

Brett, J. M., Bargness, Z. I., & Goldberg, S. B. (1996). The effectiveness of mediation: An independent analysis of cases handled by four major service providers. *Negotiation, 12*, 239-269.

Burger, W. E. (1985). Using arbitration to achieve justice. *Arbitration Journal, 40*(4), 3-6.

Burton, L., & McIver, J. (1991). A summary of the court annexed arbitration evaluation program. *The Colorado Lawyer, 20*, 1595-1598.

Bush, R. A., & Folger, J. P. (1994). *The promise of mediation*. San Francisco: Jossey-Bass.

California high court says HMO members opt out of arbitration. (1997, July 21). *Wall Street Journal*, p. B8.

Carpenter, S., & Kennedy, W. J. D. (1988). *Managing public disputes*. San Francisco: Jossey-Bass.

Carroll, J. (1987). Indefinite terminating points and the iterated prisoner's dilemma. *Theory and Decision, 22*, 247-256.

Carver, T. B., & Vondra, A. A. (1994, May-June). Alternate dispute resolution—Why it doesn't work and why it does. *Harvard Business Review*, pp. 120-130.

Cascio, W. F. (1998). *Managing human resources*. Boston: McGraw-Hill.

Chrislip, D., & Larson, C. (1994). *Collaborative leadership*. San Francisco: Jossey-Bass.

Clarke, C. C., & Lipp, D. G. (1998, February). Conflict resolution for contrasting cultures. *Training and Development*, pp. 20-33.

Conrad, L. A. (1983). Supervisors' choice of models of managing conflict. *Western Journal of Nursing Research, 47*, 218-228.

Cooley, J. W., & Lubert, S. (1997). *Arbitration advocacy*. South Bend, IN: National Institute for Trial Advocacy.

Coser, L. A. (1957). Social conflict and the theory of social change. *British Journal of Sociology, 8*(3), 197-207.

Coser, L. A. (1967). *Continuities in the study of social conflict.* New York: Free Press.

Costantino, C. A., & Merchant, C. S. (1996). *Designing conflict management systems.* San Francisco: Jossey-Bass.

Coulson, R. (1980). *Business arbitration—What you need to know.* New York: American Arbitration Association.

Craig, J. H., & Craig, M. (1974). *Synergic power: Beyond domination and permissiveness.* Berkeley, CA: Proactive.

Crawley, J. (1995). *Constructive conflict: Managing to make a difference.* London: Nicholas Brealey.

Cupach, W. R., & Canary, D. J. (1997). *Competence in interpersonal conflict.* New York: McGraw-Hill.

Daniels, T. D., Spiker, B. K., & Papa, M. J. (1997). *Perspectives on organizational communication.* Madison, WI: Brown and Benchmark.

Davis, A. M., & Salem, R. A. (1984). Dealing with power imbalances in the mediation of interpersonal disputes. *Mediation Quarterly, 6,* 17-26.

Davis, J. R., & Davis, A. B. (1998). *Effective training strategies.* San Francisco: Berrett-Koehler.

Delbeq, A. L., van de Ven, A. H., & Gustafson, D. H. (1975). *Group techniques for program planning: A guide to nominal group and Delphi processes.* Glenview, IL: Scott, Foresman.

Demirijian, A. (1997). Conflict in the workplace: The impact on organizations. *Optimum, The Journal of Public Sector Management, 27,* 6-10.

Deutsch, M. (1973). *The resolution of conflict: Constructive and destructive processes.* New Haven, CT: Yale University Press.

Deutsch, M. (1991). Subjective features of conflict resolution: Psychological, social and cultural influences. In R. Vayrynen (Ed.), *New directions in conflict* (pp. 25-56). London: Sage.

Dewey, J. (1910). *How we think.* Boston: D. C. Heath.

Diamond, L., & Fisher, R. J. (1995). Integrating conflict resolution training and consultation: A Cyprus example. *Negotiation Journal, 11,* 287-301.

Donahue, W. A. (1991). *Communication, marital dispute and divorce mediation.* Hillsdale, NJ: Lawrence Erlbaum.

Driscoll, C. (1996, April). Fostering constructive conflict management in a multi-stakeholder context. The case of the Forest Round Table on sustainable development. *International Journal of Conflict Management,* pp. 156-172.

Drucker, P. (1995). *Managing in a time of great change.* New York: Truman Tolley.

Dunlop, J., & Zack, A. (1997). *Mediation and arbitration of employment disputes.* San Francisco: Jossey-Bass.

Easterbrook, M. (1999, August). Taking aim at violence. *Psychology Today,* pp. 53-56.

Edelman, J., & Crain, M. B. (1993). *The Tao of negotiation.* New York: Harper & Row.

Eisenberg, E. M., & Goodall, H. L. (1993). *Organizational communication: Balancing creativity and constraint.* New York: St. Martin's.

Ellinor, L., & Gerard, G. (1998). *Dialogue.* New York: Wiley.

Erickson, E. H. (1950). *Childhood and society.* New York: Norton.

Filley, A. C. (1975). *Interpersonal conflict resolution.* Glenview, IL: Scott, Foresman.

Fincham, F. D., Bradbury, T. N., & Scott, C. K. (1990). Cognition in marriage. In F. D. Fincham & T. N. Bradbury (Eds.), *The psychology of marriage: Basic issues and applications* (pp. 118-149). New York: Guilford.

Firestein, R. L. (1990). Effects of creative problem solving training on communication behavior in small groups. *Small Group Research, 21,* 507-521.

Firestorm is brewing among pilots over tentative terms of AMR contract. (1997, March 21). *Wall Street Journal,* pp. A2, A4.

Fisher, A. B. (1993, August 23). Sexual harassment: What to do. *Fortune,* pp. 84-88.

Fisher, R., Kopelman, E. K., & Schneider, A. K. (1994). *Beyond Machiavelli: Tools for coping with conflict.* Cambridge, MA: Harvard University Press.

Fisher, R., & Ury, W. (1981). *Getting to yes.* New York: Penguin.

Fisher, R., Ury, W., & Patton, B. (1993). Negotiation power: Ingredients in our ability to influence the other side. In L. Hall (Ed.), *Negotiation: Strategies for mutual gain* (pp. 3-13). Newbury Park, CA: Sage.

Folger, J. P., & Poole, M. S. (1984). *Working through conflict: A communication perspective.* Glenview, IL: Scott, Foresman.

Folger, J. P., Poole, M. S., & Stutman, R. K. (1993). *Working through conflict: Strategies for relationships, groups and organizations.* New York: HarperCollins.

French, J. (1941). The disruption and cohesion of groups. *Journal of Abnormal and Social Psychology, 36,* 361-377.

Frey, L. R. (1995). Applied communication research on group facilitation in natural settings. In L. Frey (Ed.), *Innovations in group facilitation* (pp. 1-23). Cresskill, NJ: Hampton.

Freud, S. (1925). *The unconscious* (J. Riviere, Trans.). London: Hogarth.

Gadlin, H., & Pino, E.W. (1997). Neutrality: A guide for the organizational ombudsperson. *Negotiation Journal, 13*(1), 27-37.

Girard, K., & Koch, S. J. (1996). *Conflict resolution in the schools: A manual for educators.* San Francisco: Jossey-Bass.

GM, union reach agreement. (1998, July 29). *Rocky Mountain News,* p. 4B.

Goldberg, S. B. (1989). Grievance mediations: A successful alternative to labor arbitration. *Negotiation Journal, 5,* 9.

Goldberg, S. B., Sander, F. E., & Rogers, N. H. (1992). *Dispute resolution: Negotiation, mediation and other processes.* Boston: Little, Brown.

Hall, C. S. (1979). *A primer of Freudian psychology.* New York: World.

Hargrove, R. (1998). *Mastering the art of creative collaboration.* New York: McGraw-Hill.

Harris, T. (1993). *Applied organizational communication.* Hillsdale, NJ: Lawrence Erlbaum.

Haynes, J. M. (1994). *The fundamentals of family mediation.* Albany: SUNY Press.

Heider, F. (1958). *The psychology of interpersonal relations.* New York: Wiley.

Heider, J. (1986). *The Tao of leadership.* Aldershot, UK: Wildwood House.

Heitler, S. M. (1990). *From conflict to resolution.* New York: Norton.

Hilgard, E., & Bower, G. (1966). *Theories of learning.* New York: Appleton-Century-Crofts.

Hocker, J. L., & Wilmot, W. W. (1991). *Interpersonal conflict.* Dubuque, IA: William C. Brown.

Hoff, B. (1982). *The Tao of Pooh.* New York: Dutton.

Hoffman, D. (1996). How to keep your company out of court—New methods of dispute resolution. *Directorship, 22*(2).

Homans, G. (1958). Social behavior as exchange. *American Journal of Sociology, 63,* 597-606.

Honeyman, C. (1988). Five elements of mediation. *Negotiation Journal, 4,* 149.

Investors fare poorly. (1998, February 8). *Wall Street Journal,* pp. A1, A8.

It's a ruder and angrier workplace these days. (1999, August 15). *Rocky Mountain News,* p. G2.

Izbiky, J., & Savage, C. (1988). ADR: Explanations, examples and effective use. *The Colorado Lawyer, 18,* 843-857.

Jaffe, D. T., & Scott, C. D. (1998, March). How to link personal values with team values. *Training and Development,* pp. 24-30.

Jandt, F. (1985). *Win-win negotiating: Turning conflict into agreement.* New York: Wiley.

Jarboe, S. (1988). A comparison of input-output, and input-process-output models of small group problem-solving effectiveness. *Communication Monographs, 55,* 121-142.

Jones, E. E., & Nesbitt, R. E. (1971). The actor and the observer: Divergent perceptions of the causes of behavior. In E. E. Jones, E. Kanouse, H. H. Kelley, R. E. Nesbitt, S. Valins, & B. Weiner (Eds.), *Attribution: Perceiving the causes of behavior* (pp. 79-94). Morristown, NJ: General Learning.

Kaner, S. (1996). *Facilitator's guide to participatory decision-making.* Philadelphia: New Society.

Karambayya, R., & Brett, J. M. (1989). Managers handling disputes: Third-party roles and perceptions of fairness. *Academy of Management Journal, 32,* 687-704.

Keltner, S. (1987). *Mediation: Toward a civilized system of dispute resolution.* Annandale, VA: Speech Communication Association.

Kimmel, M. G., Pruit, G., Magenau, J. M., Konar-Goldband, E., & Carnevale, P. J. (1980). Effects of trust aspiration and gender on negotiation tactics. *Journal of Personality and Social Psychology, 38,* 9-23.

Knebel, F., & Clay, G. S. (1987). *Before you sue.* New York: Morrow.

Koehler, J. W., Anatol, K. W. E., & Applebaum, R. L. (1981). *Organizational communication: Behavioral perspectives.* New York: Holt, Rinehart & Winston.

Kolb, D., & Associates. (1994). *When talk works: Profiles of mediators.* San Francisco: Jossey-Bass.

Kolb, D., & Silbey, S. S. (1991). Enhancing the capacity of organizations to deal with disputes. In J. W. Breslin & J. Rubin (Eds.), *Negotiation theory and practice* (pp. 315-322). Cambridge, MA: Program on Negotiation.

Komorita, S. S., & Lapworth, C. W. (1982). Cooperative choice among individuals vs. groups in n-person dilemma situations. *Journal of Personality and Social Psychology, 42,* 487-496.

Landsberger, H. (1956). Final report on a research project in mediation. *Labor Law Journal, 7*(8), 501-507.

Lawrence, P. R., & Lorsch, J. W. (1967). *Organization and environment.* Boston: Harvard Business School Press.

Lax, D., & Sebenius, J. K. (1986). *The manager as negotiator: Bargaining for cooperative and competitive gain.* New York: Free Press.

Levine, S. (1998). *Getting to resolution.* San Francisco: Berrett-Koehler.

Lewicki, R., & Litterer, J. (1985). *Negotiation.* Homewood, IL: Irwin.

Lewicki, R., Litterer, J., Mintan, J., & Saunders, D. (1994). *Negotiation.* Chicago: Irwin.

Lewin, K. (1951). *Field theory in social science.* New York: Harper.

Likert, R., & Likert, J. G. (1976). *New paths of managing conflict.* New York: McGraw-Hill.

Marwell, G., & Schmitt, D. (1967). Dimensions of compliance-gaining behavior: An empirical analysis. *Sociometry, 30,* 350-364.

McCallum, D. M., Harring, K., Gilmore, R., Drenan, S., Chase, J. P., Isko, C. A., & Thibaut, J. (1985). Competition and cooperation between groups and between individuals. *Journal of Experimental Social Psychology, 21,* 301-320.

Michelini, R. L. (1971). Effects of prior interaction, contact, strategy and expectations of meeting on gain behavior and sentiment. *Journal of Conflict Resolution, 15,* 97-103.

Miller, G., Boster, F., Roloff, M., & Seibold, D. (1977). Compliance-gaining message strategies: A typology and some findings concerning effects of situational differences. *Communication Monographs, 44,* 37-51.

Moore, C. W. (1996). *The mediation process.* San Francisco: Jossey-Bass.

Muldoon, B. (1996). *The heart of conflict.* New York: Putnam.

NASD set to end practice of submitting all employment disputes to arbitration. (1997, July 21). *Wall Street Journal,* p. A4.

Nelson, W., Petelle, J. L., & Monroe, C. (1974). A revised strategy for idea generation in small group decision making. *Speech Teacher, 23,* 191-196.

Newton, D. A., & Burgoon, J. K. (1990). Nonverbal conflict behaviors: Functions, strategies, and tactics. In D. D. Cahn (Ed.), *Intimates in conflict: A communication perspective* (pp. 77-104). Hillsdale, NJ: Lawrence Erlbaum.

No end for steel strike. (1998, October 3). *Rocky Mountain News,* p. 4B.

Northrup, T. A. (1989). The dynamic of identity in personal and social conflict. In L. Kriesberg, T. A. Northrup, & S. A. Thorson (Eds.), *Intractable conflicts and their transformation* (pp. 55-82). New York: Syracuse University Press.

OSHA issues guidelines in workplace violence. (1996, November/December). *Mountain States Employees Council Bulletin,* p. 3.

Osgood, C. E. (1962). *An alternative to war or surrender.* Urbana: University of Illinois Press.

Oskamp, S. (1970). Effects of programmed initial strategies in a prisoners dilemma game. *Psychometrics, 19,* 195-196.

Peace, N. E. (1994, March). Massachusetts schools redesign their collaborative bargaining. *Labor and Employment Law, Massachusetts Bar Association,* pp. 1-7.

Phillips, E., & Cheston, R. (1979). Conflict resolution: What works? *California Management Review, 21,* 76-83.

Poole, M. S. (1991). Procedures for managing meetings: Social and technological innovation. In R. A. Swanson & B. O. Knapp (Eds.), *Innovative meeting management* (pp. 53-110). Austin, TX: 3M Meeting Management Institute.

Poole, M. S., & DeSanctis, G. (1990). Understanding the use of group decision support systems: The theory of adaptive structuration. In J. Fulk & C. Steinfeld (Eds.), *Organizations and communication technology* (pp. 175-195). Newbury Park, CA: Sage.

The price of being green. (1998, June 28). *Rocky Mountain News,* p. 14G.

Pruitt, D. G., & Lewis, S. (1977). The psychology of integrative bargaining. In D. Druckman (Ed.), *Negotiation: A social psychological perspective* (pp. 161-192). Beverly Hills, CA: Sage.

Pruitt, D. G., & Rubin, J. (1986). *Social conflict: Escalation, stalemate, and settlement.* New York: Random House.

Putnam, L., & Poole, M. S. (1987). Conflict and negotiation. In F. Jablin, L. Putnam, K. Roberts, & L. Porter (Eds.), *Handbook of communication* (pp. 549-599). Newbury Park, CA: Sage.

Raiffa, H. (1982). *The art and science of negotiation*. Cambridge, MA: Belknap.

Ramsey, R. D. (1997, November). Peacekeeping in the workplace: How to handle personality clashes among employees. *Supervision*, pp. 6-8.

Raven, B. H., & Rubin, J. Z. (1983). *Social psychology*. New York: Wiley.

Reynolds, S. (1998, Winter). Managing conflict through a team intervention and training strategy. *Employment Relations Today*, pp. 57-72.

Roloff, M. E. (1976). Communication strategies, relationships, and relational changes. In G. Miller (Ed.), *Explorations in interpersonal communication* (pp. 173-196). Beverly Hills, CA: Sage.

Roloff, M. E. (1981). *Interpersonal communication: The social exchange approach*. Beverly Hills, CA: Sage.

Ross, L. (1977). The intuitive psychologist and his shortcomings: Distortions in the attribution process. In L. Berkowitz (Ed.), *Advances in experimental social psychology* (Vol. 10, pp. 173-220). New York: Academic Books.

Rowe, M. P. (1991a). The corporate ombudsman: An overview and analysis. In J. W. Breslin & J. Rubin (Eds.), *Negotiation theory and practice* (pp. 443-446). Cambridge, MA: Program on Negotiation.

Rowe, M. P. (1991b). The ombudsman's role in a dispute resolution system. *Negotiation Journal, 7*, 353-362.

Rowe, M. P. (1995). Options, functions, and skills: What an organizational ombudsman might want to know. *Negotiation Journal, 11*, 103-114.

Rubin, J. Z. (1983a). Conflict from a psychological perspective. In L. Hall (Ed.), *Negotiation: Strategies for mutual gain* (pp. 123-150). Beverly Hills, CA: Sage.

Rubin, J. Z. (1983b). Negotiation. *American Behavioral Scientist, 27*, 135-147.

Rubin, J. Z. (1991). Some wise and mistaken assumptions about conflict and negotiation. In J. W. Breslin & J. Z. Rubin (Eds.), *Negotiation theory and practice* (pp. 3-11). Cambridge, MA: Program on Negotiation.

Rubin, J. Z., & Brown, B. (1975). *The social psychology of bargaining and negotiation*. San Diego: Academic Books.

Rubin, J. Z., Pruitt, D. G., & Kim, S. H. (1994). *Social conflict: Escalation, stalemate, and settlement*. New York: McGraw-Hill.

Rummel, R. J. (1976). *Understanding conflict and war* (Vol. 2). Beverly Hills, CA: Sage.

Sander, F. (1993). The courthouse as alternative dispute resolution. In L. Hall (Ed.), *Negotiation: Strategies for mutual gain* (pp. 43-60). Newbury Park, CA: Sage.

Sander, F. E., & Goldberg, S. B. (1994). Fitting the forum to the fuss: A user friendly guide to selecting an ADR procedure. *Negotiation Journal, 10*, 49-68.

Saunders, H. (1985). We need a larger theory of negotiation: The importance of prenegotiating phases. *Negotiation Journal, 1*, 249-262.

School harassment has outgrown playground bullying. (1998, October 20). *USA Today*, p. 10D.

Schwarz, R. M. (1994). *The skilled facilitator*. San Francisco: Jossey-Bass.

Scott, G. G. (1990). *Resolving conflict*. Oakland, CA: New Harbinger.

Shapiro, D. L., Shepherd, B. H., & Cheraskin, L. (1982). Business and a handshake. *Negotiation Journal, 8*, 365-377.

Sherriton, J., & Stern, J. L. (1997). *Corporate culture/team culture*. New York: American Management Association.

Sillars, A. (1980). Attributions and communication in roommate conflicts. *Communication Monographs, 47*, 180-200.

Sillars, A. L., & Scott, M. (1983). Interpersonal perception between intimates: An integrative review. *Human Communication Research, 10*, 153-157.

Sillars, M. L., & Parry, D. (1982). Stress, cognition, and communication in interpersonal conflicts. *Communication Research, 9*, 201-226.

Sillars, M. L., Weisberg, J., Burggraf, C. S., & Zietlow, P. H. (1990). Communication and understanding revisited: Married couples' understanding and recall of conversations. *Communication Research, 17*, 500-532.

Singer, L. (1994). *Settling disputes: Conflict resolution in business, families, and the legal system*. Boulder, CO: Westview.

Skopec, E., & Kiely, L. (1994). *Everything's negotiable when you know how to play the game*. New York: American Management Association.

Stafford, L., & Daly, J. A. (1984). Conversational memory: The effects of recall and memory expectations on remembrances of natural conversations. *Human Communication Research, 10*, 379-402.

Stein, J. (1989). Getting to the table: The triggers, functions, and consequences of prenegotiation. *International Journal, 44*, 431-464.

Stern, P. V. D. (1961). *The writings and speeches of Abraham Lincoln*. New York: Crown.

Strauss, A. (1978). *Negotiations*. San Francisco: Jossey-Bass.

Strauss, A. (1993). Facilitated collaborative problem solving and process management. In L. Hall (Ed.), *Negotiation: Strategies for mutual gain* (pp. 28-40). Newbury Park, CA: Sage.

Susskind, L. (1993). *Guide to consensus building and dispute resolution techniques for use in government-industry conflicts*. Unpublished manuscript.

Susskind, L., & Cruikshank, J. (1987). *Breaking the impasse: Consensual approaches to resolving public disputes*. New York: Basic Books.

Thibaut, J., & Kelley, H. (1959). *The social psychology of groups*. New York: Wiley.

Thomas, K. W., & Pondy, L. R. (1977). Toward an "intent" model of conflict management among principle parties. *Human Relations, 30*, 1089-1102.

Tjosvold, D. (1990). The goal interdependence approach to communication in conflict: An organizational study. In M. A. Rohim (Ed.), *Theory and research in conflict management* (pp. 15-28). New York: Praeger.

Toffler, A. (1991, November). Shock wave (anti warrior). *Wired Magazine*, pp. 1-14.

Tracy, K., & Spradlin, A. (1994). Talking like a mediator. In J. Folger & T. Jones (Eds.), *New directions in mediation* (pp. 110-132). Thousand Oaks, CA: Sage.

Tutzauer, F., & Roloff, M. (1988). Communication processes leading to integrative agreements: Three paths to joint benefits. *Communication Research, 5*, 360-380.

Ury, W. (1995). Conflict resolution among the Bushmen: Lesson in dispute systems design. *Negotiation Journal, 11*, 379-390.

Ury, W. L., Brett, J. M., & Goldberg, S. B. (1988). *Getting disputes resolved: Designing systems to cut the costs of conflict*. San Francisco: Jossey-Bass.

von Bertalanffy, L. (1955). General systems theory. *Main Currents in Modern Thought, 11*, 75-83.

Wallenstein, P. (1991). The resolution and transformation of international conflicts: A structural perspective. In R. Vayrynen (Ed.), *New directions in conflict theory* (pp. 129-152). London: Sage.

Walster, E., Walster, G., & Berscheid, E. (1978). *Equity: Theory and research*. Boston: Allyn & Bacon.

Walton, D. (1991, January 15). Getting along can get you ahead. *USA Today*, p. 3D.

Walton, R. (1969). *Interpersonal peacemaking: Confrontations and third-party consultation*. Reading, MA: Addison-Wesley.

Weaver, R. G., & Farrell, J. D. (1997). *Managers as facilitators*. San Francisco: Berrett-Koehler.

Weeks, D. (1992). *The eight essential steps to conflict management*. Los Angeles: Jeremy Tarcher.

Wells, V. D., & Galanes, G. (1986). The Symlog dimensions and small group conflict. *Central States Journal, 37*, 61-70.

Williams, G. (1983). *Legal negotiation and settlement*. St. Paul, MN: West.

Wolff, R., & Ostermeyer, M. (1998). Dispute resolution centers: Citizens' access to justice. *Texas Bar Journal, 51*(1), 51-53.

Yarborough, E., & Wilmot, W. (1995). *Artful mediation: Constructive conflict at work*. Boulder, CO: Cairns.

Zartman, W. I. (1989). Prenegotiation: Phases and functions. *International Journal, 44*, 237-254.

Zinsser, J. W. (1996). Employment dispute resolution systems: Experience grows but some questions persist. *Negotiation Journal, 12*, 149-162.

Name Index

Subject Index

About the Authors

Myra Warren Isenhart, PhD, is president of Organizational Communication, Inc., a firm she founded in 1990 that offers training and consulting services. Typical seminars focus on conflict management, negotiations, team building, personal leadership development, public speaking, and interpersonal and small group communication. Typical interventions involve the development of professional teams in a workplace. A partial client list includes the Colorado Outward Bound School, Computer Technology Associates, Coors, Hewlett-Packard, Honeywell, Kaiser Permanente, The National Council on State Legislatures, and the Western Executive Seminar Center.

Myra has an undergraduate degree from Wellesley College and an MA and PhD from the University of Denver (DU). She has received mediation training from various institutions, including Harvard Law School Mediation Program and the Center for Dispute Resolution. She is an active member of the Society for Professionals in Dispute Resolution and a Guidelines Member of the Colorado Association of Mediators and Mediating Organizations.

Myra also has an extensive background in higher education. She has taught undergraduates at the University of Denver and the University of Colorado at Denver. For 10 years, she was a faculty member at St. Thomas Theological Seminary, teaching graduate courses in communication skills for leadership. In addition, she served as internal consultant to the rector, assisting in establishing a national board of trustees, merging with another seminary, and integrating the student body. Currently, she teaches in the Communications Division of University College, DU. She is the author of many articles on communication and organizational development.

She has served on the boards of a number of nonprofits, including the Colorado Outward Bound School, the Institute of International Education, the Episcopal Diocese of Colorado, and The Conflict Center, where she is immediate past president of that board. She is married and the mother of three grown children and a perpetually adolescent Black Lab named Max.

Michael Spangle, PhD, is Director of Applied Communication, managing the graduate programs in communication and ADR at University College, University of Denver. In addition, he teaches courses in conflict management, negotiation, facilitation, and team communication. He holds an MDiv from Luther Theological Seminary, an MS from Kearney State College, and a PhD from the University of Denver. He has more than 25 years of professional experience as a consultant, counselor, and teacher. Some of the groups with whom he has worked are U.S. West; U.S. Department of Health and Human Services; Colorado Convention and Tourism Bureau; the National Real Estate Association; and many schools, hospitals, and church groups. He has published many articles and co-authored a book titled *Interpersonal Communication in Organizational Settings*.

About the Contributors

Marjorie Corman Aaron, Esq., is a former executive director of the Program on Negotiation at Harvard Law School and taught courses in negotiation there. A graduate of Harvard Law School, she formerly practiced civil litigation with a Boston firm and acted as Assistant District Attorney in Plymouth County, Massachusetts. She has published in several journals, including the *Negotiation Journal*, where her article "The Value of Decision Analysis in Mediation Practice" was awarded a prize for excellence from the Center for Public Resources. In June 1998, she moved to Cincinnati, Ohio, where she practices negotiation, mediation, and dispute resolution.

Jo Anderson is Director of the Illinois Education Association-National Education Association's Center for Educational Innovation. The Center is a catalyst for positive changes in education and provides Illinois schools with the resources, expertise, and motivation to experiment with school restructuring. He has facilitated collaborative negotiations in more than 50 situations in Illinois and other states. A recognized expert in innovative negotiating processes such as win-win and interest-based bargaining, he is also a founder and facilitator of the Consortium for Educational Change, a network of 50 school districts throughout the Chicago suburbs that are working collaboratively to restructure and improve their schools.

Edward A. Dauer, Esq., is Professor of Law and Dean Emeritus at the University of Denver, as well as an active mediator and arbitrator. He holds degrees from Brown and from Yale Law School. From 1986 to 1997, he was president of the National Center for Preventive Law. From 1990 to 1993, he chaired a national group that investigated the application of ADR to health care, an inquiry that resulted in a book published by the Center for Public Resources (CPR). Another book, *The Manual of Dispute Resolution*, was awarded the CPR's book prize for 1994. His present research interests include adapting ADR to medical malpractice cases with the objective of contributing to "patient safety," or improvements in the quality of health care.

William R. Drake is the Executive Director of the Western Justice Institute. Mr. Drake's career began in city planning; he held senior management positions with the National League of Cities and the U.S. Conference of Mayors. He was Deputy Director and Vice President of the National Institute for Dispute Resolution (NIDR) for 9 years. He is a consultant in dispute resolution and strategic planning in the United States and abroad. He has conducted technical assistance work on-site in more than 70 cities, 37 states, and three foreign countries, and has helped eight state governments create state offices of mediation. He is an advisory board member of the *Negotiation Journal* and co-founder of the African Centre for the Constructive Resolution of Disputes in South Africa.

Michael Jenkins, Esq., is Community Development Coordinator for the City of San Diego, with responsibilities that include development-related negotiations with major industries, negotiation and management of contracts, business finance, and policy formulation. Previously, he headed San Diego's Business Expansion and Retention Program, engaging in negotiations with firms such as Sony, Qualcomm, and SGS-Thomson. He has practiced law and continues to teach in law schools. His degrees are a BA from Drake University and a JD from Southern Illinois University. He is admitted to practice law in California, Illinois, and Texas and is a certified mediator. He has published articles on the topic of state and local government law, and co-authored one on mediation.

Joan B. Kelly, PhD, is Executive Director of the Northern California Mediation Center in Corte Madera, California. She is an experienced mediator and trainer in divorce, family, organizational, and business disputes. She is a past president of the Academy of Family Mediators (AFM) and the Northern California Mediation Association, and a founding member of the California Dispute Resolution Council. She received her PhD in clinical psychology from Yale. Her research, clinical, and teaching career has focused on child and family adjustment to divorce, custody, and access issues. She has received many awards, among them the Distinguished Mediator Award from the AFM.

Daniel H. Kruger, PhD, is Professor of Industrial Relations at the School of Labor and Industrial Relations at Michigan State University. He holds a BA from the University of Richmond and a PhD from the University of Wisconsin. He has won a Fulbright grant, published three books and 150 articles, and received many honors for excellence in teaching. He has been director of the Training Center for Employment Security Personnel, U.S. Department of Labor, and was appointed to the Federal Service Impasses Panel by Presidents Reagan and Bush. His ADR service includes being a hearing officer for the Michigan Civil Service Commission, an arbitrator in the public and private sectors, and a fact-finder.

Speed B. Leas, MDiv, is a nationally known consultant to religious organizations and an educator of church leaders, including pastors, laity, and church executives throughout the United States and Canada. Trained at the Yale School of Divinity, he is ordained a minister in the United Church of Christ. He has an extensive background as a management consultant to churches and has earned a special reputation as an authority on conflict. His experience with conflicted congregations, judicatories, and church agencies places him in a preeminent position in the nation. From this work and his research, he has written seven books and numerous articles and monographs.

Jack Lemley is an expert in the management and organization of construction of multibillion-dollar infrastructure projects worldwide, including serving as Chief Executive of the English Channel Tunnel project. He is the CEO of American Ecology Company and resides in Boise, Idaho. He has served as a technical advisory board member, dispute review board chair, claims consultant, and expert witness. As senior vice president of Morrison-Knudson Company, he directed the construction of the Tom Bigbee Waterway. He was a management consultant for the engineering and construction of a new tunnel connecting the City of Boston and Logan airport.

Leonard J. Marcus, PhD, is founding Director of the Program for Health Care Negotiation and Conflict Resolution at the Harvard School of Public Health. He completed his doctoral work at Brandeis University and was selected as a Fellow for the Kellogg National Leadership Program. He has directed a number of projects intended to advance development of the health care negotiation and conflict resolution field. Under a Hewlett Foundation grant, he is developing a curriculum, research agenda, and conceptual and applied framework for the field. He teaches negotiation and conflict resolution courses. He is lead author of *Renegotiating Health Care: Resolving Conflict to Build Collaboration.*

John Marks founded Search for Common Ground in 1982 and serves as its president. He currently oversees projects that include the Search for Common Ground in the Middle East, in Burundi, in Angola, in Macedonia, in Ukraine, Common Ground on Race, and the Common Ground Network for Life and Choice. In 1987, he established Common Ground Productions. He served as a Foreign Service officer in Washington, D.C., and Vietnam, as executive assistant for foreign policy to the late Senator Clifford Case, as a fellow at Harvard's Institute of Politics, and as a visiting scholar at Harvard Law School. He is the author of several books and numerous articles.

Christina Sickles Merchant, PhD, a highly experienced dispute resolution professional, is most widely known for her work in fostering sustainable partnerships between labor and management throughout the private, public, and international arenas. She is an independent dispute resolution consultant after 26 years as a mediator, facilitator, dispute systems designer, and program manager with several federal agencies. She co-authored a popular book titled *Designing Conflict Management Systems: A Guide to Creating Productive and Healthy Organizations.* She is a past president of the International Society of Professionals in Dispute Resolution (SPIDR).

Christopher W. Moore, PhD, is a partner in CRD Associates, an international collaborative decision-making and conflict management firm located in Boulder, Colorado. He has worked in the field of decision making and conflict management for more than 20 years and is an internationally known mediator, facilitator, dispute systems designer, trainer, and author. He was trained by the U.S. Federal Mediation and Conciliation Service and the American Arbitration Association and holds a PhD in political sociology and development from Rutgers University. His extensive experience as an intermediary has focused on facilitating or mediating multiparty public, environmental, organizational, and labor-management issues.

Barbara Ashley Phillips, Esq., is a professional mediator. She introduced mediation into business disputes in the early 1980s as founder of American Intermediation Service in San Francisco. She mediates a wide spectrum of practical and technical issues, ranging from disasters to lawyer malpractice, from construction to sexual harassment, from aviation accidents to complex contract and environmental issues. She teaches negotiation and mediation skills and consults on settlement negotiation strategy and design. She did her undergraduate work at UC Berkeley and took her law degree at Yale. She has practiced law and served as an Assistant United States Attorney.

Nancy H. Rogers, Esq., is the Joseph S. Platt-Porter Wright Morris & Arthur Professor of Law at the Ohio State University College of Law. She teaches courses in dispute resolution and is the co-author of three books, including a textbook on ADR and two treatises that were awarded Book Prizes by the CPR Institute for Dispute Resolution. She served as Chair of the American Bar Association Standing Committee on Dispute Resolution and the Dispute Resolution Section of the Association of American Law Schools. President Clinton appointed her to the Board of Directors of the Legal Services Corporation. A graduate of Yale Law School, she practiced law before teaching.

Rosemary Romero is President and Executive Director of Western Network, a nonprofit firm based in Santa Fe, New Mexico. The firm offers services designed to improve decision making in a variety of arenas. She has designed and facilitated numerous public involvement projects; assessed the potential for neutral conflict resolution services in diverse cases; consulted with public and private organizations on the use of ADR techniques; trained hundreds of people in negotiation, mediation, and public involvement skills; and promoted the use of mediation in the environmental field. Her background in Native American and Hispanic issues brings a heightened awareness of cross-cultural issues.

Mary Rowe, PhD, is Ombudsperson at MIT and Adjunct Professor of Negotiation and Conflict Management at the MIT School of Management. She received her PhD in economics from Columbia University. Her responsibilities include hearing hundreds of concerns a year, consulting to managers, teaching, research, and writing numerous published articles. She was a co-founder and first president of the Corporate Ombudsman Association, now the Ombudsman Association. She has helped to set up ombuds offices in several hundred corporations, government agencies, and academic institutions and has helped to design several major integrated dispute resolution systems.

Frank E. A. Sander, Esq., is Bussey Professor and Associate Dean at Harvard Law School. His AB and LLB are from Harvard. He served as law clerk to Chief Judge Calvert Magruder of the U.S. Court of Appeals for the First Circuit and Justice Felix Frankfurter of the U.S. Supreme Court. After brief stints with the U.S. Justice Department in Washington, D.C., and a private firm in Boston, he began teaching at Harvard Law School, specializing initially in taxation and family law, and, since 1975, in dispute resolution. He has written and lectured on various aspects of ADR both here and abroad and has served as an arbitrator or mediator in several hundred cases. He was a member and chair of the American Bar Association Standing Committee on Dispute Resolution.

Cynthia Savage, Esq., Director of the Office of Dispute Resolution for the Colorado Judicial Branch, is a lawyer, mediator, mediation trainer, and former hearing officer, and has been involved with ADR since 1985. She was Director of the Mediation Arbitration Center and a clinical law professor at the University of Denver College of Law from 1988 to 1996. She has published and given numerous papers and presentations on issues related to ADR. She received her law degree from Harvard Law School and her BA in psychology from the University of Michigan.

John R. Schumaker, PhD, is the Natural Resource Alternative Dispute Resolution Program Leader for the Bureau of Land Management (BLM), U.S. Department of the Interior. He has extensive experience as a mediator and arbitrator in community, consumer, and family issues. His PhD in forestry, wildlife, and range sciences is from the University of Idaho, where the emphasis of his dissertation was on using ADR processes to prevent or resolve natural resource disputes. He led a team of BLM employees that developed a natural resource ADR strategic plan and toolkit that established policy regarding the use of ADR processes in BLM's public land management activities.

Marshall Snider, Esq., is an arbitrator and an administrative law judge with the State of Colorado. He has arbitrated in the areas of education, food, trucking, transportation, service industries, public sector grievances, and petroleum, among others. He is a member of the American Arbitration Association and is on the roster of arbitrators for both the Federal Mediation and Conciliation Service and the National Mediation Board. His law degree is from George Washington University.

Lawrence Susskind, PhD, Ford Professor of Urban and Environmental Planning, has been on the faculty in the Department of Urban Studies and Planning at MIT for 30 years. He is one of the country's most experienced public and environmental dispute mediators and a leading figure in the dispute resolution field. He has served as court-appointed special master, trainer, and mediator for neighborhood, municipal, state, and national agencies and organizations in North America, Europe and the Far East. He is founder and president of the Consensus Building Institute, a not-for-profit that provides mediation and dispute system design services to public and private clients worldwide.

Mark Udall was elected in November 1998 to serve the 2nd Congressional District of Colorado in the U.S. House of Representatives. He won this closely contested race as a two-term Colorado State legislator. His activities there centered on protecting the environment and managing growth. His father, "Mo," served in the U.S. House for 30 years and ran for the Democratic nomination for president in 1976. His uncle, Stewart, was Secretary of the Interior under President Kennedy. Representative Udall, a graduate of Williams College, had a long and successful career with the Colorado Outward Bound School. For 10 years, he was its Executive Director.

Printed in the United States
144556LV00003B/4/A